THE
MAN
WITH THE
REVERSIBLE
FOOT

To order additional copies of *The Man With the Reversible Foot*, by Susan Phelps Harvey, **call 1-800-765-6955.**

Visit us at **www.reviewandherald.com** for information on other Review and Herald® products.

THE
MAN
WITH THE
REVERSIBLE
FOOT

DICK STENBAKKEN:
PREACHER, SOLDIER, INNOVATOR,
ACTOR, AND ADVENTURER

REVIEW AND HERALD® PUBLISHING ASSOCIATION
Since 1861 | www.reviewandherald.com

Review and Herald® titles may be purchased in bulk for educational, business, fund-raising, or sales promotional use. For information, e-mail SpecialMarkets@reviewandherald.com.

The Review and Herald® Publishing Association publishes biblically based materials for spiritual, physical, and mental growth and Christian discipleship.

This book was
Edited by Gerald Wheeler
Copyedited by Megan Mason
Cover designed by Daniel Anez / Review and Herald® Design Center
Interior designed by Emily Ford / Review and Herald® Design Center
Cover photo courtesy Dick Stenbakken
Typeset: 11/13 Minion Pro

PRINTED IN U.S.A.

18 17 16 15 14   5 4 3 2 1

Library of Congress Cataloging-in-Publication Data
Harvey, Susan Phelps.
  Man with the reversible foot : the Dick Stenbakken story / Susan Phelps
Harvey.
    pages cm
  ISBN 978-0-8280-2753-3
  1. Stenbakken, Dick, 1940- 2. Seventh-Day Adventists--United
States--Biography. I. Title.
  BX6193.S74H37 2013
  286.7092--dc23
  [B]
                                    2013028396
ISBN 978-0-8280- 2753-3

Table of Contents

"I Had No Idea
How Serious This Was"

The young chaplain took an inadvertent step backward, feeling the rough wood of the door behind him. Across the small, dimly lit room, the gun wobbled slightly in the first sergeant's shaking hands, but his steely gaze never wavered. The Colt .45 remained aimed directly at Dick's heart.

Chaplain (Captain) Dick Stenbakken sucked in a deep breath, sent a silent prayer heavenward, and took stock of the situation. What was going on here? What had so badly shaken the company's highest-ranking enlisted man, a strong, burly career soldier, a 22-year veteran? What had brought him to this point? And what was Dick going to do about it?

Nothing in his past—not basic training, not the chaplains' course, not his graduate degrees from Andrews University, not his years at Union College or Campion Academy—nothing had prepared him for such a moment. Or had it, all of it, been part of God's plan to equip him to meet this challenge?

Minutes before, a runner had knocked at the door of Dick's quarters at Long Binh, Vietnam's largest American base. It was late on a Saturday night in 1971, and he would be preaching the Protestant service on base the next morning. He had been reviewing his sermon notes. Setting his papers aside, he answered the door. A man from headquarters stood outside.

"Sir, the first sergeant has requested that you come to his hooch," the soldier said.

That's unusual, Dick thought. A slight sense of unease spread through him. Saturday night was not a normal time for a meeting with the sergeant, and Dick knew the man wasn't a regular churchgoer. But he followed the runner out into the warm, humid night, and they quickly walked past his unit's buildings.

The Forty-eighth Transportation Battalion occupied only a small part of the huge Army base. The whole installation was the size of a city. The sandbags stacked around each structure's perimeter were a hardly needed reminder that it was a war zone. They passed the unit headquarters. Out of the corner of his eye Dick saw that the light was still on in the colonel's office. *The brass is working late too,* he thought.

When they reached the door of the first sergeant's quarters, or hooch, as soldiers would call it, the runner disappeared, his errand completed. Dick approached the rough, weathered wooden building, so like all the others on base. As he stepped closer to the closed door, he noticed two small points of light shining through it. *Knotholes?* he wondered to himself as he knocked.

"Who is it?" a gruff voice barked.

"It's Chaplain Stenbakken. You sent for me?"

"Come in!" Somewhere in the back of Dick's mind another small warning bell rang. He outranked this man. A more appropriate response would have been "Come in, sir! Thank you, sir!" Nevertheless, Dick entered the small room, closing the door behind him.

The sergeant sat at a small folding table, not 10 feet away. He was wearing fatigues, his sweat-stained T-shirt stretching across his broad chest. A half-finished bottle of whiskey stood at his elbow. The sour smells of alcohol, sweat, and fear filled the air. Leaning on his left elbow, in his right hand he held a loaded .45-caliber automatic, leveled right at Dick. The man's shoulders were shaking, and Dick wondered if his trigger finger was too.

"Come in, shut the door, and lock it," the sergeant ordered, his red face, bloodshot eyes, and trembling body adding force to his words.

Quickly Dick considered his options. Several wild possibilities chased each other through his head in those first few seconds. Should he be John Wayne, charge the guy, grab his weapon? Or should he make like the road runner and take off like a rocket? Neither seemed wise.

Instead, he went into prayer mode—not the falling-on-your-knees-and-shutting-your-eyes kind, but the kind during which you call out silently but desperately to your heavenly Father, "Tell me what to do!"

Something dawned on him. Those weren't knotholes in the door—they were bullet holes! And the conviction came—when a guy is pointing a loaded gun at you, you do what he says. Or there will be holes in you.

Then, quietly, feeling the support of the Holy Spirit, he took command of the situation. Slowly he turned around, trying not to think of the .45 aimed at his back, and slid the barrel lock shut on the door. *Snick.* For good measure, he turned the lock in the doorknob. Two locks. *Snick, snick.*

Then he faced the sergeant again, stepping to one side so that the armed man could see that the door was indeed locked. "Is there any other way to get into your hooch?" he asked.

"No," the sergeant said, shaking his head distractedly. "No, there isn't."

"No back door, no window, no way for anybody else to get in?"

"No, no, there's no other way," the sergeant replied impatiently.

"OK. So we're alone." Dick spoke calmly. "No one can get in or out. I'm going to stand right here by the door. I won't come any closer. Obviously you're upset. Can you tell me what this is about?"

The soldier hesitated, shifting slightly in his chair while keeping the gun trained on Dick.

"Look," Dick said. "I have a wife and two little kids at home. I want to get back to see them." A vivid memory had burned itself indelibly in his mind—Ardis at the airport only six months before when he left for Vietnam, Baby Rikki in her arms. By her side stood 2½-year-old Erik, little blue jacket, white-blond hair, his face pressed against the glass, hoping for one more glimpse of Daddy. Would he ever see them again?

"So I'm not going to move closer," he repeated, keeping his voice firm and low. "Put the gun down, and let's talk about what's going on."

His training may not have prepared him for this particular circumstance, but Dick's instincts told him he needed to get the sergeant to focus on reality—on the here and now. The man had called for his chaplain. Somewhere in his confused mind he knew the padre was the one person in the unit that he could trust. "I'm here. I'm listening to you." And he said it again, "Put the gun down and let's talk."

Dick's words finally penetrated the sergeant's fear. The man's head turned slightly to focus on the weapon. The look on his face said, "There's a gun in my hand!" It was as though he didn't even know it was there. Somehow that was even more unnerving. Slowly the man laid the .45 on the table next to the whiskey bottle.

"All right." His muscles beginning to unknot themselves a little, Dick sent a silent thank-You prayer upward. "You called me. What's going on? How can I help you?"

"I got a letter from home. From a neighbor. My wife has left the house and taken the kids with her. Nobody knows where they are."

OK, Dick thought. *He's having domestic problems. That's bad. But it doesn't explain the fear in this man's eyes—or the trembling of his body. Something else is going on here.*

"What else? What else is happening?"

The sergeant's fear was palpable. "The druggies," he rasped. "The druggies in the unit are going to frag me. They say I'll never get home alive."

That was easy to believe. Drug use was widespread in Vietnam. Marijuana and even heroin were easy to get, and the men were often idle. That led to boredom. It was a dangerous combination. As first sergeant, the man in front of him was responsible for blowing the whistle on drug users. It was his job to come down hard on them, and obviously he had enforced some strong disciplinary measures on somebody.

His eyes wild, his voice strained, the man grew even more agitated. He admitted that he had become so terrified of the drug users that he had even taken the gun with him to the latrine—locked, loaded, and cocked. Dick shuddered to think how dangerous that could have been. But there was more.

"About a half hour ago," the sergeant said in a voice not much louder than a whisper, his eyes boring directly into Dick's face, "somebody opened the door to my hooch and rolled a hand grenade under my feet. That's when I put those bullet holes in the door." He glanced at the gun again as though he was about to blow some more holes—in something or somebody.

The grenade hadn't exploded. If it had, it would have blown the sergeant to bits. The perpetrators had removed the detonator. So it had been a threat. The message was clear. Back off, or you're dead. A hand grenade was as easy to come by in Vietnam as a can of Coke.

The pressure on the man had become too much. Life in a combat zone, trouble at home, and now this. When he had seen that grenade coming at him, he had known he was going to die. Something had snapped. The sergeant's mental state was precarious, and the situation was deadly. Dick knew he had to take some action. He had to get the man some help. This was what his ministry was about—would always be about. Never before had he felt his commitment more deeply, nor God's assurance more strongly.

"All right," Dick began, "here's what we're going to do. I'm going to get the CO [commanding officer], and either he or I will be back here within 15 minutes. When I leave, lock the door, and don't let anybody but me or the commanding officer in. Don't open this door for anybody. One or both of us will be back in 15 minutes." The man nodded.

Dick turned and unlocked the door. As he opened it and stepped outside, he added, "Don't start blasting more holes through the door if somebody knocks. Remember, I want to see my kids." As he left the sergeant's hooch, he heard the door lock behind him. *Snick. Snick.*

Fifteen minutes, Dick thought. *Why'd I say that?* He had no idea where the commanding officer was, but the company compound wasn't all that large. The first place he looked was the most obvious—the officers' club. The CO was sitting there, eating and talking with other officers. Dick filled him in on what had just happened.

The man shrugged it off. "Yeah, I know he's got some problems, but the sarge is a tough guy, Chaplain," he said, taking another forkful of food. "He's just upset. You're overreacting. He'll be OK. Just let him go."

"No, I won't let him go. I told you he's unstable. He has a loaded gun." Dick looked at his watch. "I told him one or both of us would be back in 15 minutes, and five minutes have already gone by. This man is in serious trouble. He needs some action immediately." The CO continued to eat his meal. Dick waited a few more seconds and then asked point-blank, "Are you going to go to his hooch?"

"No. I'll deal with it in the morning."

Dick wheeled around to leave the room, but not before giving the CO the benefit of his strongest glare. "Where are you going now?" the commanding officer called after him.

"I'm going to the colonel."

"Chaplain, I told you. The guy's going to be OK."

"He will be when the colonel hears of the situation. He'll solve it."

The CO dropped his fork. "Oh, all right! I'll go! Don't go to the colonel with this."

"Thank you. Do you want me to come with you?"

"No, no, I'll handle it." The CO pushed back his chair. "I'll send for you if I need you."

"I'll wait right here."

Dick waited. Another 10 minutes went by. Twenty minutes. Thirty minutes. Then the commanding officer walked into the club, his face as white as a sheet of paper. "Chaplain, you just saved a man's life. That guy would have killed himself—or somebody else." He explained that the first sergeant had had a complete mental breakdown. After posting an all-night guard around his quarters, the CO had begun arrangements to have him transported out of the unit and out of Vietnam the next day.

"I apologize," the commanding officer said, rubbing the back of his neck and shaking his head. "I just had no idea how serious this was."

But Dick knew how serious it had been. As serious as facing down a loaded gun. As serious as feeling the assurance of God's presence in one of the toughest situations of his life so far. As serious as knowing, in the deep fibers of your being, that you're where you need to be, doing what you need to do. Yeah, you could say it was serious.

Chapter 2

"How Could I
Have Been So Blind?"

Frances Ryan stood alone at the open window of her small, plain room on an upper floor of the Salvation Army Hospital and Home for Unwed Mothers, half listening to the voices of the children playing in the street below. The enticing smells of dinner cooking at homes along the avenue wafted up to her window. Soon families would gather around their tables for their evening meal. She sighed.

In her mind's eye she could see beyond the street to the homes, offices, shops, and factories of Denver, Colorado. It was the summer of 1940, and the city would be bustling on this hot, hazy afternoon. Beyond the buildings stretched the cool green of the surrounding countryside, and in the distance, the mountains. Frances felt her heart lift a little. The thought of the mountains always made her feel better.

Her home was somewhere among them, as were her parents, her family—almost all that was dear to her. Raised in the tiny town of Collbran, in ranch country along Plateau Creek, more than 200 miles from Denver on the western slope of the Rockies, she had had a happy childhood. Those mountains, those clear, rushing rivers, those green meadows were all she had known.

Again Frances sighed. But she had left all that behind. It had seemed like the right thing—the only thing—to do at the time. She had come to Denver just out of her teens, seeking an education and a future not available in her small community. It wasn't easy for a young girl from the mountains to make her way alone in the city, but Frances was intelligent, ambitious, and determined. Two years of college and a good job later, she was self-sufficient, and the future looked bright, with even more success within her grasp.

However, things hadn't worked out the way she had planned. Frances dabbed at the tears in her eyes, then twisted the damp handkerchief in her hands. Everything had changed when she met Al. Tall, debonair Alexander

Greenwalt, with his Clark Gable good looks, his money, and his air of sophistication. Al was at least 10 years older than she, and he and his father ran a well-established livestock auction business in Denver.

Maybe it was his Russian background, or his German heritage. Or perhaps it was the brown felt fedora he often wore cocked over one eye, but whatever it was, something about the man mesmerized her. He wined and dined her, opening her eyes to a side of life in the city that she hadn't previously known. *Oh, let's face it,* she thought to herself angrily. She, usually the most careful and levelheaded of young women, had let him sweep her off her feet, like those silly girls in the movies.

And suddenly her plans changed into something else, her ambitions for a career replaced with dreams of marriage, a home, and a family as Mrs. Alexander Greenwalt. At the time it had seemed the most wonderful future in the world. Frances Ryan—petite, dark-haired, blue-eyed, sensible Frances Ryan from Collbran, Colorado—was head over heels in love.

Then all that changed too. The unthinkable happened. She had gotten pregnant, and Al wasn't happy about it. In fact, he was soon gone. Although she wasn't entirely sure, she suspected there might even be a wife, or at least a fiancé, that Al had neglected to mention.

Frances leaned her forehead against the window's cool glass. *How could I have been so blind, so foolish?* she thought. The tears flowed again, the soggy hankie in her hands of little use. Al's abandonment, her sense of loss, her guilt at allowing herself to be so easily duped—all of it had been devastating. But worst of all had been the loneliness that had followed. Determined to tell no one about the baby, she would not subject her family to the embarrassment and shame of a child born out of wedlock. Gossip of that kind in their small town would have been shocking and upsetting for her parents.

Only a short time before, her beloved brother, Larry, had died unexpectedly of a heart attack. He had been so young, so full of promise. Her family was still grieving his loss. She would not add to their pain. No, she would leave her job and have this baby alone. No one in her family would know. In fact, she hoped they would never know.

The Salvation Army home had been a godsend, and she would always be grateful for the loving care she had received there through those long, lonely months of pregnancy and the difficult premature delivery that followed. Dr. Harvey had been kind and helpful, too, in arranging the adoption. The adoption! Her eyes overflowed again.

A loud wail came from across the room. Despite her tears, Frances smiled. The baby was only a month old, but already his personality was becoming apparent. He was definite about what he wanted and when he wanted it. Crossing the room, she picked him up from his bassinet and put him over her shoulder, feeling his fuzzy head bobbing against her neck, patting his little back until he quieted. He was such a tiny scrap of humanity! Born a month early, he had struggled hard for life in those first few weeks, but he was strong and healthy now, thank God.

Frances called him Larry, after her brother. *Maybe I'll put that name on the adoption papers.* Today she would give him up. As she breathed in his sweet baby smell, the tears caught in her throat. How could she possibly let him go? But she had had many months to come to this decision, and she was sure she was doing the right thing. Somehow she had to give her child a chance at a better life. It was the one gift—the only gift—she could give him. She snuggled him closer. Just a few more minutes! But she hadn't known it was going to be this hard.

Her life stretched ahead of her, lonely and empty. But somehow, right now, she had to be strong for her baby. She looked down at the adoption papers on the table by the door. Under "Reason for Allowing Adoption," the compassionate Salvation Army representative had written, "The mother loved her baby, but didn't feel that she could give him a good life." Picking up the pen in her free hand, Frances Ryan signed her name.

Chapter 3

"That's the Boy for Us!"

Oliver Thor Stenbakken locked the front doors of a Safeway grocery store in Denver and pocketed the keys. It had been a good day, but he was glad to be going home to Celia. His wife was the most important person in his life.

Actually, when he thought about it, only a few things mattered to him: his wife, his job managing the Safeway, and sports. Oliver felt a big grin spreading across his face. He did love sports! But tomorrow something even more important than any sports event was going to happen. He and Celia were adopting a baby boy.

As he got into his car and headed toward their home on South Downing Street, the thought of Celia made him smile again. She was so excited! Oliver loved that about her. He knew he was a quiet kind of guy, usually keeping his emotions inside. Tall, slender, dark-haired, he resembled his Norwegian forebears in both appearance and manner. By the time he was 40 he had achieved some moderate success, thanks to hard work and determination. But love and marriage had eluded him. And then, through an acquaintance at work, he met Celia Reed.

Beautiful, brown-eyed, red-haired Celia took his breath away. He couldn't believe she'd accepted when he'd asked her out. But she had, and soon their relationship blossomed into something more than friendship. However, shadows of pain and sadness lurked in her eyes. As he got to know her better, Oliver discovered why.

Celia was divorced. It had been a disastrous marriage, and it had left her with scars. Oh, maybe not visible ones, but scars just the same. She came from Golden, Colorado, a one-time mining community west of Denver in the foothills of the Rocky Mountains. Her dad worked for the Union Pacific Railroad. Raised in the Seventh-day Adventist Church, she had married another Adventist when she was still rather young.

The groom was Bob Kalin, a talented musician. Bob, as it turned out, was also a scoundrel. His promiscuous behavior had devastated and humiliated Celia, who saw her dream of a Christian marriage and family crumble and blow away like the red Colorado dust. A dreadful social disease, contracted from her husband, left her barren.

Oliver Stenbakken had once seen a picture of Celia with Kalin—although his face had been scratched out of the photo. Oliver didn't care one bit about her past. In love with Celia, he determined to erase the bitter shadows that haunted her. So they had been married, and together they had made a comfortable, happy life.

They had a nice little house, with a big front porch, on South Downing Street near the University of Denver. But something was still missing. And tomorrow that something would be absent no longer. Norwegian or not, Oliver had to admit he was pretty excited, too. They planned to name the baby Richard Oliver Stenbakken. His son . . .

Dick Stenbakken had always known he was adopted. From his earliest memories he could recall being told that he was special to his parents. "We wanted you," his mother would say, giving him a squeeze. "We picked you out."

"Yes, indeed," his dad would add. "We could have chosen other baby boys, but we took one look at you, and we thought, *That's the one. That's the boy for us.*" And Dick would grin, secure in the knowledge that he was wanted and loved by his family.

Somehow that sense of being chosen became a pervasive presence in his life. In future years he would see it as a theme—that idea of chosenness and choice. It would make him acutely aware of his own choices and how they affected his life and those of others. And he would realize that being chosen by God, and in turn, choosing to accept God's plan for his life, would be his greatest source of satisfaction and fulfillment.

Chapter 4

"What More Could a Kid Ask?"

Ten-year-old Dick scooted a little farther down in the back seat of the family sedan, the rough wool upholstery scratching the backs of his legs. Another car sped by on the road just a few feet away, its headlights sweeping the interior of the 1949 Nash, filling it briefly with eerie light. The boy looked down at the book on his lap. It had gotten too dark to read some time ago, but he had kept trying until the light had faded entirely away. He attempted to snatch a few more words each time a car went by.

He wasn't exactly frightened sitting alone in a car outside a tavern on a slightly seedy Denver street. He wouldn't let himself be frightened. It was more that he was lonely and bored. Really bored. Idly he scratched at a mosquito bite on his knee and peered once again at the bar's closed door, the garish neon sign above it almost the only light on the street. Would Mom and Dad ever come out?

The last time his parents had left him in the car while they drank and smoked the evening away, a policeman had come along. He had not been happy to see a skinny little boy alone in the back seat of a parked car outside a saloon, and he had gone inside to "have a word" with Mom and Dad. Judging by the expressions on their faces when they came out a few minutes later, the policeman had indeed "had a word," but evidently the message hadn't stuck. Here Dick was again, alone and bored. But not scared.

In a way, he guessed, it was kind of his own fault. Not long ago he had refused to enter a bar with his parents, even though they'd urged him to, promising to buy him a soda. They'd taken him to bars before, and he hadn't liked them one bit. He'd hated the noise, the smell, the smoke— all of it. Having had enough, he never wanted to go back. And he never had. Maybe he was stubborn, or perhaps he had an already well-developed sense of right and wrong. At any rate, his parents respected his wishes, at least to the extent of allowing him to wait for them in the car.

Finally, he heard the door of the bar slam, and saw his parents approaching the car, holding on to each other, both of them grinning foolishly and stumbling a little. At that moment, he made up his mind that he would never, ever touch alcohol or tobacco. Never. Ever. And he never did.

Dad started up the Nash, and Mom turned around and smiled at her son. The big car headed slowly for home through the dark streets. The boy relaxed. Things were good again. And tomorrow would be a big day. His parents had decided he was old enough to move down into a bedroom in the basement, a bigger space with room for all his projects, even the woodworking tools he was beginning to collect.

And best of all, he was going to have his very own radio down there! He couldn't wait to listen to *The Shadow, Henry Aldrich,* and *The Lone Ranger.* Oh, and *Sergeant Preston of the Yukon.* Dick grinned to himself in the dark back seat. Life was good!

And life was indeed good most of the time in the cozy bungalow on South Downing Street. Dick had a caring, stay-at-home mom, a hardworking dad, a neighborhood school close enough to walk to, a big front porch to read on, a bicycle, a dog named Sandy, and some good neighborhood buddies. He didn't know it, but his family was living the post-war American dream. The fact that both his parents were sometimes fighting demons of their own presented itself to him only once in a while.

During his entire childhood Dick and his family lived in the South Downing Street house. His parents taught him to be respectful and accountable. They didn't hover, but rather gave him a great deal of freedom in that safer and more carefree time. The Stenbakkens never adopted another child, most likely because, when they got Dick, his father was 42 years old. Although he loved his parents dearly, he never learned to share his taciturn father's only real passion—sporting events of all kinds.

Instead, as Dick grew, he developed a lively curiosity about the world and everything in it, and an interest in making things with his hands. By the time he reached his teens, his creativity found an outlet in woodworking. For a 13-year-old, he possessed a great deal of ingenuity and an uncanny ability to get his hands on the things he needed. Before his father even knew what had happened, the boy had assembled a complete woodworking shop in the garage.

His dad, no Mr. Fixit, took one look at the table saw, the jigsaw, and the other dangerous-looking equipment his young son had collected, and shuddered. "You're going to cut your fingers off!" he warned, but, fortunately Dick never did any serious harm to himself. Soon he was doing all kinds of carpentry—even making such things as furniture and cabinets.

When Dick wasn't making chairs and tables and birdhouses in the garage, one could often find him polishing his beloved Schwinn Hornet. The bike was painted burgundy with white stripes. With its big fat white-walled balloon tires, a basket on the front, a rack on the back, a horn button on the tank, and chrome fenders, it was the envy of the neighborhood.

Dick was something of a loner, but when he made a friend, it was a good one. Lee was a neighbor kid who lived at the other end of the block. A little older than Dick, he was tall, lean, and square-jawed, with intense dark eyes. Dick thought Lee looked a little like Dick Tracy of the comics, except that his friend was a gentle soul, and, instead of a gun, his hands often held a hammer or a saw.

Like Dick, Lee loved to make things. The two boys would spend hours scouring the alleys in the neighborhood, looking for "valuable" trash. Their creative hands would cobble other people's junk into whatever the boys could think up. The two became inseparable friends.

Lee could neither hear nor talk. He had never heard speech, and the only sounds that came out of his mouth were high-pitched staccato squeaks. But Dick hardly noticed. He and Lee were so intent on their shared projects that they quickly developed a private sign language that allowed them to communicate as well as any two talking and hearing people. Other kids sometimes stared at Lee or even laughed at the sounds he made. But not Dick. His friend was his friend. The disabilities didn't matter at all.

Despite their careful instilling of a moral compass in their only son, church attendance had little or no place within the Stenbakken family. Dick's father claimed no faith at all. His mother's disastrous first marriage to an immoral man who claimed to be a Seventh-day Adventist had left her scarred and bitter about religion in general and Adventists in particular.

The boy didn't miss what he didn't know, although somehow he developed a fondness for listening to Billy Graham on the radio. Something about the great preacher's voice and his passionate pleading with his listeners to accept Jesus Christ as their personal Savior reached into his heart and soul. Every Sunday night in his basement room he listened closely to Graham's program, followed by a half-hour concert by the Mormon Tabernacle Choir. But upstairs it was as though religion didn't exist.

That is, until Aunt Stella came to town.

Chapter 5

"It Fits Like a Glove"

Dick thumped the heavy coal scuttle down beside the cookstove in his grandmother's kitchen. Grandma's house had an old-fashioned stove, and when he dropped in for a visit, he often found himself pressed into service to bring in coal, but he didn't mind.

In the front room Aunt Stella and his grandmother were sitting at the dining table, deep in conversation. From the way his aunt looked up quickly and smiled as he entered the room, he was pretty sure they'd been talking about him. Aunt Stella's words confirmed it. "Dick, honey, would you like to come to church with Grandma and me sometime?"

Stella was Mom's older sister. She had come to Denver to live with Grandma Reed, who had had a slight stroke and needed someone to look after her. Stella moved into Grandma's little bungalow on South Marion Street, just a few blocks from his house.

Dick was in the habit of riding his bike over to visit Grandma occasionally, but now that Aunt Stella was there, he came more frequently. Drawn to his aunt, he liked the way her eyes sparkled behind her wire-rimmed glasses when she smiled at him. And Aunt Stella, in turn, soon became very fond of her creative, quirky young nephew.

Although his parents weren't churchgoers, Dick knew that Grandma attended the Seventh-day Adventist church. Friends would come by and pick her up every Sabbath morning. No one had ever asked him to go, nor had it occurred to him to invite himself. But there was something special about Aunt Stella. She was an ardent Christian, and her goodness showed. The boy didn't think twice about it. If she wanted him to come to church, he'd give it a shot.

"OK, sure," he replied. "Sure, I'll come with you this weekend." So when the friends from church came by to pick up Grandma and Aunt Stella that Sabbath, they were surprised and happy to include an 11-year-old boy in the party.

Denver's South church was small, and the people were friendly. To Dick, it instantly felt like home. The music, the kids' Sabbath school class, the preaching—all of it spoke to his hungry heart. Maybe those Sunday nights alone in his room, listening to Billy Graham, had prepared him. Being in the little church made him feel the same way he did when he listened to the Mormon Tabernacle Choir. What was it that Mom would say when something seemed exactly right? "It fits like a glove." Yes, the little Adventist church fit him like a glove.

Soon Dick discovered an appetite for spiritual learning and Bible study that would stay with him all his life. Whether it was talking with Aunt Stella about spiritual things, attending a Sabbath afternoon Bible study group, riding his bike the few blocks down to Porter Adventist Hospital to go to a branch Sabbath school in the nurses' dorm, he embraced his newfound faith and lifestyle wholeheartedly and without reservation.

Before church one sunny Sabbath morning at Denver South, Dick watched as pastor Alten Bringle and the deacons moved the heavy wooden pulpit away from its central place on the platform, exposing a trapdoor in the floor that opened to the baptistry below. It was the day of the boy's baptism. He had given his heart to God, and he knew he was ready to take the step. Everybody was there—his mom and dad, Aunt Stella and Grandma, aunts and uncles, and all of the new friends he'd made at church.

As he stood in the baptistry with his hand on Pastor Bringle's arm, an overwhelming sense of belonging flooded his young heart. The boy who loved family had a whole new family now. The only child had brothers and sisters! After church there was a big family dinner at Dick's house, and he and his dad played catch in the backyard all afternoon.

The next few years were a time of spiritual learning and growing for him, most of it experienced on his own. Although his parents respected his decision to be an Adventist, they weren't interested in joining him in it. The more he rejoiced in his new life in Christ, the further removed he became from the life his parents were leading. He felt the separation keenly, and he knew his mom did too.

Although a zealous new Christian, Dick was no goodie-goodie. He still spent plenty of time hanging out with Frankie and Lee and the other kids up the street. There were good times with Mom and Dad, too. Dad was fond of Aunt Stella, and delighted in stopping by to see her and Grandma, bringing a hand-packed quart of ice cream from Dolly Madison's on Evans Avenue.

In time Dick discovered the Denver Central Adventist Church, closer to downtown, on the corner of Ninth Avenue and Sherman Street. The much larger congregation had more kids and an active youth program. He enjoyed getting involved with this young people's group. Riding the bus downtown on Sabbath morning, he would enjoy Sabbath school and church and then take in a Tom Mix movie matinee at the Jewell Theater on South Broadway before heading home. Later on, as his understanding of Sabbath deepened, he would spend long Sabbath afternoons on the front porch, reading the Bible and other spiritual books.

Eventually Mom began to accompany him to church, especially to Denver Central. At first he suspected she did it more to spend time with him than because of anything else. But gradually she came to the realization that she wanted to be rebaptized, and Dick attended that ceremony with great joy. His Dad never joined the church, however, excusing himself because of his need to work on Saturday as a grocery store manager. Despite that, the boy knew his dad was supportive. Concerned and caring, both parents always gave him the space to exercise his own choices and individuality.

During the summer before he started fifth grade, Aunt Stella began talking with him and his parents about his transferring to the Adventist school. It was less than a mile away, and the bus stopped right outside their door. Grandma encouraged him to do it, too. Mom and Dad said, "Sure, fine, if that's what you want."

So he made the switch to Denver Junior Academy and, once again, felt as though he had "come home." He loved the classes, the teachers, and the kids. Again something fit like a glove. Realizing that it was a sacrifice for his parents to send him to a tuition-based church school, he loved them all the more for it.

Mable Madsen was his first Adventist teacher. They were to become great friends, but not before Dick tested the limits with her. One day, when he had failed to complete a math assignment, Miss Madsen made him stay in during recess to finish it. He could hear the other kids shouting and playing outside. Hating math, he slouched in his seat, stared at his paper, and stewed.

Miss Madsen had stepped out of the room, and all at once, it occurred to Dick that he was alone. He could just get up and leave! So he did, picking up his stuff and walking out the back door. Fuming all the way, he marched home.

"You're home early," his mother said when he walked through the door. "What's going on?"

Full of righteous anger, Dick told her his sad story. "I'm not going to put up with it!" he declared.

Mom didn't lecture him or chide him for his behavior. Nor did she tell him to turn around and head right back to school. All she said was "You need to work on your math."

Stomping downstairs to his basement room, he threw his books on a chair and flopped onto his bed. He wasn't going to work on anything—he was done!

The next morning while he was eating breakfast, he said to his mother, trying to sound casual, "Mom, I need you to write me an excuse for yesterday afternoon. Say I was sick or something."

"I don't think so," she replied with her sweetest smile. "You know Dad and I want you to have the freedom to make your own choices. But when you do, you have to live with them. You're going to have to go back and explain yourself to Miss Madsen."

His teacher didn't lecture either, having something far more diabolical in mind. She didn't say a word when he came into class that morning. Instead, she just went on as though nothing had happened. Tense, he waited for something to happen. He knew it would. About midmorning, Miss Madsen called him up to her desk.

This is it! he thought. But when he stood beside her desk, she only handed him some papers with a smile, and said, "Dick, please take these to the principal's office." When he looked down at the papers, he saw that they were folded so that he couldn't see what was on them. This was even worse than he had thought. The principal's office! The boy was sure he was holding a full written account of his bad behavior. He was doomed.

But it turned out to be just a delivery run. The principal took the papers, thanked him, and that was it. Shaking his head, Dick returned to class.

The rest of that day Miss Madsen called on him frequently—more than usual, it seemed to him. Each time, he thought, *This is it!* She asked him to do all kinds of things, but never, not even once, did she say a word about his behavior the day before.

Dick died a thousand deaths that day. Nobody yelled at him or told him what a foolish thing he had done. He took care of that himself. You make a decision, you live with it. It was a lesson well learned.

Chapter 6

"Don't Read That One!"

Dick attended Denver Junior Academy through the eleventh grade while living at home on South Downing Street. School was good, but he had discovered a new favorite place—its woodworking shop.

Bill Garrison, the woodworking teacher, was a rather ordinary-looking man of medium height and thinning blond hair. You wouldn't give him a second glance unless you noticed the intensity of his eyes, twinkling behind silver wire-framed glasses.

Admiring Mr. Garrison, Dick worked hard to earn his respect. When the teacher put him in charge of the school's toolroom, Dick was like a kid in a candy store. The shop and toolroom housed an impressive collection of valuable hand tools and power equipment. It was his job to check out the hand tools and check them in again, making sure they were sharpened and cleaned, ready for the next use. Dick loved having that toolroom in his charge. His garage workshop at home was great, but this one was far better.

Although he had already taught himself the basics of woodworking, he learned a lot more from Bill Garrison. Not all of it was in the woodworking shop. Bill also taught Bible and history. His teaching style was precise, but never stuffy and overbearing. He explained things clearly, especially when it came to opening the Scriptures to his students in exciting ways. His greatest characteristic was that he was genuinely interested in kids, and they knew it.

Bill and his wife, Agnes, personified Christian education at its best. They had no children of their own, but volunteered in the youth department at church and often had kids over to their house. Dick and his friends considered themselves Bill's kids.

Dick observed Bill closely. The man conducted his classes, and indeed, his life, with precision, exactitude, and accountability. When Dick sought to emulate him, Bill willingly mentored him, helping to sharpen those very characteristics. "Plan in advance, look ahead, and always be prepared." That was Bill's way. It became Dick's, too.

In class Bill taught facts and data—information that became a part of Dick's background of knowledge. But it was the other lessons he learned from his teacher that helped mold him into the person he was to become. His mentor and friend showed Dick how a Christian man conducts himself—leading with integrity, serving with dedication.

Another Bill—Bill Miller—taught math at DJA. It was never Dick's favorite subject. Mr. Miller had springy jet-black hair and darting black eyes. Energetic and quick-moving, he reminded the boy of water drops dancing on a hot stove. His enthusiasm and verve made math palatable for Dick, even though he continued to dislike it.

DJA's principal, Bill Nelson, also taught some courses in literature. A former Navy officer, he was a true career educator. An impressive-looking individual—lean, handsome, wavy-haired, and well-groomed—he carried himself with a thoroughly professional demeanor. You didn't need to read the sign on his door to know he was the principal. Dick thought Nelson looked as if he had stepped out of a men's fashion magazine. He could have been a model.

The kids in Mr. Nelson's literature classes often urged him to tell stories about his adventures at sea during World War II. It didn't take much to get him going, and once he'd started, he'd regale the students with tales from his war experience, leaving them wide-eyed and slack-jawed.

Mr. Nelson also exposed his students to a wide variety of American literature. When they were studying Edgar Alan Poe—and there were quite a few of Poe's stories in the literature book—he'd say, "I want you to read this one and this one, but don't read that one."

Naturally, the kids asked, "Why shouldn't we read that one?"

"Well, that one is not really an uplifting story," their teacher would reply. Of course, all the kids read that one first. Dick was never sure whether Mr. Nelson had meant that to happen.

By now in his early teens, Dick was still a skinny kid and continued to be something of an introvert. Although a serious student, he liked to have fun but was never the class clown. Mr. Garrison's principle of accountability and Dick's own inner compass guided him. He was always aware that church school was not free—not like public school. Realizing that his parents were sacrificing to keep him there, he felt a sense of responsibility to do well and to make them proud.

The thought of skipping school never once entered Dick's head (after that incident in the fifth grade). In fact, he tended to be overresponsible, always taking everything seriously. While he had lots of friends, he still never minded standing alone if the situation called for it. He wasn't a follow-the-herd kind of person. Nor was he a total nerd, either, although he got better than average grades all the way through school.

It was that accountability thing. If he got a C, he had to know what he had done wrong. He had an innate need to do well and to deliver. It wasn't something anybody ever told him—unless you counted his mother's favorite saying: *Whatever you do, do it well.* Mom didn't pound that into his head, but it was said frequently enough, and it made perfect sense to him.

It was the same way with his hobbies, such as model building. He and Lee and some of the kids in the neighborhood still got together to construct model planes and cars. Dick liked the exactitude that good model building required. Everything had to be perfect—the decals had to be affixed straight with no sloppy glue showing. The finished product had to look exactly as it did on the box, only better. Dick loved throwing himself into a project, focusing on it 120 percent. Even in his teens he was becoming the king of meticulous detail.

Like most schoolboys, he found girls to be pests as a rule, at least early on, though he made a few exceptions for his good friends who happened to be female, such as Phyllis Smoak, who lived not far from his school. They were just about the same height, and with her dark chestnut-colored hair, sparkling brown eyes, and constant smile, she beguiled him. He liked the fact that Phyllis was a good musician who loved to sing. And he also appreciated that she was serious about her studies, just like him.

Sometimes, as did other boys his age, he'd get a terrible crush on some pretty girl, worshipping her from afar, too shy to let her know how he felt. As he began to mature, however, the girls he found the most appealing were always serious-minded students, with qualities that indicated real depth of character. Often they had a creative bent similar to his own.

Joan Swanson lived near his grandmother's house. Often he'd ride his bike over to see her, just to say hi, and they developed a good friendship. She was bright and musical. They goofed off together, had fun, and hung out with other kids.

Ramona Zeigler became another good friend. Smiling and friendly, she liked serious music, including Dick's old favorite, the Mormon Tabernacle Choir. They listened to classical records together—Tchaikovsky sometimes, or Mussorgsky's *Pictures at an Exhibition*. In addition, they enjoyed the Robert Shaw Chorale, Montovani, and Tennessee Ernie Ford.

Although country-western music didn't appeal to Dick, for some reason he liked Ford's storytelling style. He and Ramona listened to one record again and again: "Sixteen Tons." They really liked that one. "Others," a hymn about service, was a special favorite. (Years later, while he was in college, he had the words to "Others" gold-embossed on black paper and mounted in the front of his Bible. It's still there.)

Dick would rather listen to the Norman Luboff Choir than the more popular stuff of the day. Aunt Emma, his dad's sister who lived in Denver, took him shopping in a record store at the mall one day. She offered to buy him a current hit, "Tutti Frutti," by Little Richard. "No, thanks," her nephew said, his head buried in the classical section. Later on in college he discovered folk music, such as Joan Baez's distinctive vibrato and Odetta's powerfully rich and husky voice. Eventually he even learned to appreciate some Benny Goodman.

Dick sang in the choir at Campion Academy, but he never learned to play an instrument. Mom and Dad tried to get him into piano lessons when he was younger, but "it didn't take," as they say. He'd memorize a piece by ear, playing it repeatedly until he could perform it perfectly, but he never learned to read music. Nevertheless, he enjoyed music immensely, and he still does.

Like most kids who attended the church school, Dick usually had a part-time job. He started working at Porter Adventist Hospital when he was in the sixth or seventh grade. One of his summer jobs was trundling huge laundry carts from place to place. He had to push the carts full of soiled linen up a steep ramp to the laundry. For a scrawny teen, that took some effort. But the real issue was coming back down the ramp with a load of clean laundry. Freshly folded sheets made the carts much heavier.

There was no way Dick's skinny arms could keep a loaded cart from hurtling down the ramp. So he would stand at the top of the ramp, give the cart a shove to get it going, then drag both feet and hang on for dear life. Using his shoes for brakes worked most of the time. Mom couldn't understand why her son wore out his shoe leather so rapidly that summer.

Another of his jobs at Porter was working for Call Service. Dressed in a red bellhop-like jacket, he'd run errands, deliver packages, push patients in wheelchairs, or do whatever was asked. The job was good for him. He met a lot of people that way, and it helped him overcome his shyness.

His next job, when he was about 16, was as a full-fledged hospital orderly. The job fit him well, as he enjoyed helping people. Soon he entertained thoughts of becoming a doctor. He liked the idea of being a medical missionary, serving both God and his fellow humanity. And, to tell the truth, the size and horsepower of the sleek conveyances in the doctors' parking lot did not escape his notice.

H'mm, he thought, *I could serve others and help myself at the same time!* He was not adverse to the idea of living well. No, not at all. Being a doctor seemed like a good plan, all around. Dick congratulated himself on having made one of the most important decisions of his life. It was good to have that career thing settled.

Denver Junior Academy would later become a full 12-grade school and would be renamed Mile High Adventist Academy. The transition to a full 12-year program had been under way for some time, with the school adding another grade each year. However, by 1957, when Dick was ready for his senior year, the school still offered only 11 grades of study. So he, along with 20 or so other juniors, transferred to Campion Academy in Loveland, Colorado, less than an hour away. It was his first experience with living away from home.

Living in the dorm offered him some unique opportunities to do one of his favorite things—pull practical jokes on his friends. He and his roommate, Duane Becker, picked Buzz Bell, the guy next door, to be the hapless recipient of one of their finest pranks. Buzz worked in the broom shop. When he returned to the dorm at the end of his shift, he would be covered with straw dust and needed to take a shower before going to supper.

Bell took quick showers, so when he left his room to head into the shower room, Dick and Duane knew they had only five minutes or so to work. The plan was to hide all of Buzz's clothes. Socks, shorts, shirts—everything the guy owned. They realized that they couldn't secret his stuff in their room. Since they were already infamous for their practical jokes, that would be where he'd look first, so they decided to conceal his things in *his* room.

As soon as Buzz was in the shower, they bolted to his room, lifted his mattress off the box springs, and carefully laid all of his clothing evenly across the springs. Then they replaced the mattress and bedspread. The bed was about an inch higher than before, not enough to notice.

When Buzz got out of the shower, he quickly discovered that his clothes were missing. Clad only in a soggy towel, he threw open the door to Duane and Dick's room and demanded to know what they'd done with them.

The boys, deep in study, looked up from their books. "Who, us?" they pleaded in innocent tones. "Look in our closets and drawers. We don't have anything of yours in here—honest!" Buzz slammed open their closets and pulled out their dresser drawers, but found nothing.

Only after Buzz, cold and hungry, clutching his wet towel, searched several more rooms, accusing one boy after another of stealing his garments, did the two culprits relent and tell him where his things were.

Dick and Duane always locked their room after that.

At Campion Dick continued his practice of making friends with girls. It was not serious dating, more like just good friends. Sometimes the girls didn't quite see it that way, as he found out to his chagrin.

He was friends with Elaine Price, for instance. Very pretty, with red hair, blue eyes, and a sparkling, upbeat personality, she was a serious girl who planned to be a nurse. And she was a singer. Dick always liked girls who appreciated music. They became good friends at Campion. She was his steady girl—kinda, sorta.

Although he lived close enough to go home on weekends, Elaine didn't. And in those days, your girlfriend didn't go home with you.

Jeannie Richards, an old classmate from Denver Junior Academy, was also a good friend. "Jeannie with the light-brown hair," friendly, quiet, and studious, she lived near Dick in Denver, so he hung out with her a lot when he went home. It was not a relationship—they were not dating, of course. They were just good friends.

One weekend Denver Junior Academy's basketball team came up to play Campion's team. And Jeannie rode up on the bus with the team, throwing Dick in a panic. *What am I going to do?* he thought to himself. *If I show up with Jeannie, I've cooked my goose with Elaine. But if I show up with Elaine, there will be no more good times with Jeannie when I go home.*

Dick took a typical teenage boy's way out. He hid. "I'm behind in my studies," he told his friends, "so I think I'll stay in the dorm and hit the books."

"Coward," they said. "You need to show your face." Realizing that they were probably right, he waited until the game was nearly over, then sauntered into the gym and stood at the back, hands in his pockets, elbows akimbo, watching the game. Across the gym he thought he spotted Jeannie, but he couldn't be sure she had seen him.

Suddenly he felt a soft arm linking through his. "Hi, I missed you," said the lovely Elaine Price, her voice startling him close to his ear. Across the gym, he could see the equally lovely but not nearly as happy Jeannie Richards. She'd spotted him, all right.

Well, you could say that something went out of both of his romantic relationships that evening. Somehow, to the girls' credit, they remained friends, but at least one of the romances definitely cooled. That experience taught him something about women and the difference between "steady" and "just friends." He was learning that Bill Garrison's lessons in precision and accountability applied to personal relationships, too.

While Dick was growing and developing at academy, changes were also taking place at home on South Downing Street. Campion was close enough so that Dick could go home on the weekends, and he did so as often as he could. Mom and Dad were always glad to see him, and he knew how important he was to his parents, especially to his mother. And, of course, their love and support meant everything to him.

Dad was consumed with the grocery business, and between that and his interest in sports, he was involved and busy. But Mom was another story. As an only child, Dick was used to her focusing most of her thoughts and attention on him, but he was concerned that it was becoming unhealthy. Her mother—Dick's beloved Grandma—had passed away while he was at academy, and perhaps that was part of the problem.

But, for whatever reason, the older that Dick got and the more independent he became, the harder it was for Mom to let go. Sometimes he even had the uncomfortable feeling that she was jealous of his friends. Also, he noticed that his parents were still drinking, occasionally to excess. Such concerns were almost too big a burden for a teenage boy to carry. His response was to redouble his efforts to do well in school and make them proud. He knew he owed them a great deal.

Then it was his last year at the academy. Like all high school seniors, he was thinking about his future and what his career path should be. The idea of being a doctor still made sense to him. Dick had liked working at the hospital, and he didn't mind the thought of making some serious cash.

He assured himself that it wasn't all about the money, since he felt a strong tug to do something that would make a difference in people's lives. A doctor could minister to others both physically and spiritually. Yeah, that was it. By studying medicine he would serve his fellow humanity by being a doctor with a silver Porsche Speedster. Mentally he congratulated himself.

Only 18 years old, he had already confirmed his life's work. It was good to have that behind him.

All the seniors had to take vocational preference tests in their final year of academy. Dick tried to worm his way out of them. After all, he had already decided what he wanted to be. But the school required the tests, so he decided to have some fun with them. Since he was convinced the tests were useless anyway, he devised a plan to "throw the test" by giving answers that would bend the results toward being a park ranger. Liking the outdoors, he thought that would be a cool career, too.

To his surprise, the tests were interesting, and he soon became absorbed in the questions, his plan to trick the results fading away. Quickly he began to answer each query honestly, even though he was pretty sure he already knew what the outcome would be.

Nobody was more astonished than Dick when the test results came back. They indicated that people who scored the way he had would be happiest following one of two career paths: first, "socially focused service, such as a counselor, therapist, educator, or minister," and second, "service in the military, especially as an officer."

Dick had to laugh out loud. Those tests had to be bogus! No one in his family had ever been a therapist, a teacher, or a counselor, and for sure, no one had been an officer in the military. He thought about his gentle homemaker mother, and his mild-mannered, hardworking, sports-loving, grocery store manager dad. What a preposterous idea! It was a good thing he already knew what he wanted to do with his life.

Chapter 7

"Dick, I Want You to Be a Minister"

The second semester of Dick's senior year at Campion Academy began. One weekend he and Elaine attended a concert in Fort Collins. They'd ridden the school bus to town with other students, all of them dressed in their best for the occasion. The music was terrific. It was an excellent symphony orchestra. At the intermission, almost everyone stood up to leave, girls to go to the powder room, guys to hang out in the lobby.

For some reason, Dick remained behind in the nearly empty hall. Leaning back in the velvet-covered seat, he looked around him, his mind drifting idly. Taking in the beautiful concert auditorium, he thought about how satisfying this moment was—being a senior, enjoying the music, being with his girl and his friends. Academy was nearly over, and somewhere out there, his future beckoned brightly, silver Porsche and all. *Ahh,* he thought, *life is good!*

And then he heard a voice. Clear, firm, and gentle. Commanding but not demanding. "Dick, I want you to be a minister."

Ready to laugh, he spun around, sure that his good friend Alden Curtis was playing a prank on him. But there was nobody there. Nobody. Shocked, dumbfounded, he knew he'd heard a voice! Was he losing his mind? Did he imagine those words? But no, that voice had been as clear as a bell. And the message was clear, too.

Elaine and his friends returned to their seats, the intermission over. Silently turning the experience in his mind, Stenbakken said nothing of what had happened. The lights went down and the orchestra began playing, but the memory of that voice echoed in his head more loudly than Mozart. It had been real. The memory was vivid.

Nevertheless, he decided to pay no attention. Disembodied voices didn't fit with his pragmatic, sensible personality. And the ministry certainly didn't match what he had decided to do with his life. So he dismissed it. Sort of. Assignments, class schedules, girls, and dating—all the hustle and bustle of a senior headed for graduation crowded the memory out—nearly.

Then came the Week of Prayer at Campion Academy. Each morning Jack Everett, the pastor of the Seventh-day Adventist Church in Montrose, Colorado, presented a spiritual message tailored especially for young people, emphasizing the importance of doing what God wanted, and explaining how to find real fulfillment in a life of service. Dick could buy into that. He enjoyed listening to Pastor Everett. It was comfortable just to sit back and let the man's well-chosen words wash over him each morning.

Friday night arrived, and with it the usual culmination of the Week of Prayer—a testimonial service. Dick thought he'd rather get his teeth pulled. He disliked such programs. People standing up because they knew they were expected to, saying they were grateful for this or that. So plastic, so predictable, so boring. However, Friday night worships at Campion Academy were mandatory. Since he couldn't dodge it, he trudged over to the chapel, taking his seat with his fellow students, guys on the left side and girls on the right.

As he sat there, listening to his classmates, he began to formulate what he would say when his turn inevitably came: "I'm grateful for a Christian education, for my family's support, for my friends, and for the gospel." That ought to do it. Then he'd sit down. Mission accomplished. He let his mind wander.

Dick sat quietly as others testified, not bored, but somewhat disengaged, knowing what was expected of him. His eyes drifted to a reproduction of a painting that hung on the wall directly in front of him. Warner Sallman's *Head of Christ*. He'd seen it before. It had been hanging there all year. Although he had always appreciated the painting, now he could not take his eyes off the face of Christ. Something riveted him to that picture. With part of his mind, he was aware of the other students saying the kinds of things he had been planning. But in another part, the memory of that voice in the concert hall returned, sharp and razor-focused. "Dick, I want you to be a minister."

With his eyes still on the picture of Christ—that serene face, those eyes lifted heavenward—and the memory of the voice in his head, he heard Pastor Everett say, "We need to dedicate our lives to Christ and make a decision to follow Him." Dick had done that years ago. The question now was how to follow Him in a vocation. He had thought he had it all figured out. But as he kept looking at that picture, the memory of those vocational preference tests suddenly came back. And that voice, "Dick, I want you to be a minister."

You have to be kidding, he groaned inwardly. But the memory of the voice was fresh, insistent, and unrelenting. Soon he began to squirm. This was not what he had intended. His plan at that point, if he had one, was to testify when his turn came, nod his head in pious agreement, and get on with his life. But something had changed. Here was a new decision point, and he knew it.

Serving God wasn't the issue. He had convinced himself that he could do that as a well-paid physician. Either he had to say yes to that voice inside him, or he had to say, *No way. I'm going to go in my own direction.* By now he was near panic. But he felt a conviction that he must make his decision before the service was over. He was looking at his future. The time had come to own it.

Near the close of the meeting he rose to make his testimony. His little rehearsed statement forgotten, he said, "As most of you know, my goal has been to go into medicine, but that has changed. I feel called into the ministry. It is my intent to be a minister." Once the words were out of his mouth, he felt a sense of relief and fulfillment, tempered only slightly by a *What have I done?* feeling.

Then he sat down.

His fellow students and his teachers sat in silence. There was no laughter, no mocking jokes. Instead, he felt their acceptance. Nobody was totally surprised. They knew Dick to be a solid, serious person—a spiritual leader at Campion. (He and Phyllis Smoak would be voted "most dependable" that year.)

As he took his seat, he caught Elaine's eye. She was sitting on the other side of the chapel with the girls. On her face was a look of surprise. His girl, she was planning to be a nurse, and was seriously dating a young man she thought was going to be a doctor. It was a major change of direction for her.

With a sinking feeling Dick realized that he hadn't thought about her reaction. Suddenly, he wondered what his parents would think. More important, what was *he* thinking? As sure as he was of his decision, he still had that slight sense of *What have I done?*

As they left the chapel after the meeting, several of his friends from the dorm clapped him on the shoulder. "That was a surprise," one said.

"A good choice," another commented. "You will do well."

Wow! he thought. *I needed that confirmation!*

At 18 years of age, Dick already understood himself pretty well. He knew that when he made a decision, he threw himself into making it happen. If he chose the ministry, he would be totally committed—but he had to be *sure*.

That night, after his roommate had gone to sleep, Dick, alone in the dark, began to pray. *Lord, if this is what You want me to do, please confirm it so that I will know it is from You and for You, and not just my own thinking.* Perhaps he was secretly wishing to hear nothing, but he was willing to listen, too.

And then a text came to his mind: John 15:27. Dick was no mystic. He had never opened his Bible and pointed a finger at a text, expecting some magic intervention or enlightenment. However, the passage seemed to be more than a mere feeling. For one thing, the impression was just numbers— no words. He had no idea what the passage actually said. Despite his years of Bible classes, it didn't ring a bell at all. His interest and curiosity piqued, he had to look it up. Getting up from his knees, he fumbled for the light switch and opened his Bible.

"And you must also testify, for you have been with me from the beginning" (NIV). That phrase jumped off the page and exploded like Fourth of July fireworks. He sat back in his chair, feeling pushed there by the force of those words. Always he had known he was an adopted child. His parents had never hidden that from him. They had made it clear that they had *chosen* him, picked him out from all the others. "You have been with me from the beginning."

God had chosen him too. And now the Lord was picking him out to be a minister. The message was clear. This was God's summons. He would help Dick accomplish it. All doubts surrendered, he determined to hone and sharpen his focus to meet that call.

It was February 27, 1958. The date is written in ink in the margin of his Bible, next to John 15:27. That text would help shape the rest of his life and ministry.

Chapter 8

"Good Shot, Stenbakken!"

It was June 1958 and all was in readiness for graduation in the Campion Academy gymnasium. The gym was a big place. More than a basketball court wide, three games could go on in it simultaneously. On this graduation day charcoal-gray and green crepe paper streamers, the colors of the class of '58, decorated it.

Wearing a black gown and a mortarboard with charcoal-gray and green tassels, Dick marched with his classmates down the center aisle between the folding chairs, Elgar's *Pomp and Circumstance* ringing in his ears. He glanced down at the wooden floor on which he had recently played basketball and roller-skated, then took his seat.

His feelings were the usual combination of excitement and sadness. Academy graduation effectively marked the end of his carefree youth. Only a couple months before he had made a commitment to prepare himself for the ministry. His life was changing. With his friends going their separate ways, he realized he would probably never see some of his academy buddies again—or at least not for years.

Glancing down the row of solemn black-gowned students, he caught the eye of his girlfriend, Elaine Price. She smiled back. Elaine was lovely and sweet. Without doubt she'd had a civilizing influence on him. They'd been good for each other. Soon she would be leaving for California to attend nursing school at La Sierra College. How would their relationship weather the separation?

Looking down the opposite row, he spotted his friend Alden Curtis. Alden and his girlfriend, Janice Starkebaum, were engaged, planning to be married soon after graduation. Dick didn't know whether to be jealous or worried for his friend, who would soon become half of "an old married couple." He and Alden had been friends for a long time, but soon they would take radically different paths. How long would it be before they saw each other again?

Thinking of Alden reminded him of Spanish class, and he felt himself grinning. The class met here in the gym, in a little classroom in the right-hand corner next to the stage. One day Mr. Thompson, the Spanish teacher, had been late for class. His students hung around outside the locked classroom door for a few minutes, and then gathered up their books to leave, deciding the teacher wasn't coming. Just then Thompson arrived. Key in hand, the students following, he led the way to the classroom door.

To Dick's way of thinking, the only class worse than Spanish was math, and Spanish didn't beat math by much. Not happy because the teacher had shown up, he was horsing around with his friends at the back of the line. Holding his Spanish book by the corner, he pretended to throw it underhand at Mr. Thompson's retreating back. Somehow, as he wound up for a big show-off swing, his arm clipped his pants leg. The Spanish book leaped from his hand, flew through the air, and hit Mr. Thompson squarely between the shoulders of his well-pressed blue suit. The book covers slapped together, making a sound like a gun going off. "Good shot, Stenbakken!" Dick's friend Alden shouted cheerfully.

Mortified, Dick hastened to explain that it had been an accident. "Yeah, yeah, sure, sure," replied the long-suffering Spanish teacher. Actually, the man was pretty nice about it. Dick sighed. While he sure couldn't claim to be perfect, he had to admit that there had been some good times in academy. Now he'd miss them—even miss that rat fink, Alden.

The graduation ceremony began. The speaker was Sydney Allen, a Bible instructor from Union College. Leaning forward in his seat, Dick studied him. The man would be one of his major professors when he started college in the fall. It was time to "put away childish things."

The summer after graduation Dick got his old job back as an orderly at Porter Adventist Hospital in Denver. He worked on the medical and surgical floor, usually taking the 3:00-to-11:00 shift. The job was comfortable. He already knew a lot of the staff, and he enjoyed the work. Being an orderly again got him thinking about his future. Perhaps he'd better keep an open mind about the medical side of things. Of course, he accepted God's call to be a minister. While he was clear about that, it didn't mean he had to shut every other door, did it?

Life was good that summer. His old teacher and friend Bill Garrison gave him the keys to the woodworking shop at Denver Junior Academy, an unprecedented display of trust in a guy Dick's age. In his spare time, using plans he found in a *Popular Mechanics* magazine, Dick built a stereo system with speaker cabinets and a console.

His parents bought him a car right after graduation—a 1952 Dodge sedan, lemon-yellow with a black top. It wasn't fancy, but Dad made sure it was a sound vehicle. As he said, it was a practical car to get his son wherever he needed to go. Dick was glad to have it, although it wasn't exactly a chick magnet.

September came. Packing up his stereo and other belongings, he drove the Dodge about 500 miles due east to Lincoln, Nebraska, the home of Union College, arriving just in time for registration.

The registration process was tedious. Every single faculty and staff member carried a pen or pencil, and it seemed that Dick needed the initials of everyone on the sheaf of papers in his hand. It included papers for where to park, how to register for meals, and on and on. Everything was checked and double-checked, especially class schedules.

The classes were pretty general in the first year, but his schedule included chemistry because he had signed up for a double major. Religion would be his primary field of study—no doubt about that—but premed would be secondary. Call it hedging your bets, or label it stubbornness, he was still hanging on to the silver Porsche by a thread.

His dorm room faced the red-brick administration building. Its seven-story tall clock tower loomed over the campus. The clock chimes bonged every 15 minutes. Dick and his roommate, Wayne Rowe, heard the clock chime every single time, day and night, for the first week. They were sure they'd never get used to it. However, by the second week they began saying "What clock tower?" to newbies, and they never noticed the chime again. They were college students, settling in, adjusting to the rhythm of life as freshmen. Dick liked his classes and his instructors, especially the theology classes. It was going to be a piece of cake!

Then he hit chemistry class—or rather, it hit him. It was like walking into some alternate universe. Chemistry made no sense! The periodic table might as well have been in Swahili. Dick redoubled his efforts, concentrating as hard as he could. After all, he had a good brain and surely he'd get this!

Up to that point in his young life he hadn't experienced much of the bitter taste of failure, and he didn't care for the flavor. However, the harder he tried, the worse it got. He simply couldn't understand it. Each time he went to class, it was like digging himself into a hole, deeper and deeper, with no way out.

When he got his first chemistry grades, they were dismal. The drop date for the class was looming. Should he do it now, it wouldn't appear on his record. Keep going, though, and the grade would be there forever. Dick knew he had to have that class, not to mention many more like it, if he were to maintain his premed major. What to do?

Once again, panic forced him to his knees. "Lord, You know I want to do what You've called me to do," he prayed. He meant every word of his prayer, but the concept of ministry through medicine still exerted a strong pull. Once again he needed a sign. He didn't want to move forward with the wrong attitude and the wrong goals.

Just as it had happened months before, a text popped into his mind. First Corinthians 1:13. Just as before, it was only a reference. He didn't know what the passage said. Turning to his Bible, he read "Is Christ divided?"

The rest of the text was important, but to Dick, that first phrase told him all he needed to know. Christ was not divided. He had one aim and one goal.

Finally, he got the message. One goal. That's what *he* needed too. Now he realized why he'd been uncomfortable. He'd been operating from a divided base, trying to go in two directions. Another person might successfully do it—but not Dick—not with his penchant for committing himself 120 percent. It was time to get out of the way and let God lead *completely*.

That September in 1958 Dick finally surrendered himself totally to God's plan for his life. Dropping chemistry and the premed major, he centered his focus entirely on the ministry. He didn't even hear the *vroom* as the silver Porsche sped away, exiting his imagination for good.

A sense of peace followed. From that point on, ministry and only that became his focus. It was more than a calling, more than a vocation, more than a job or a title—it was his passion. As a result he began to enjoy his theology classes even more. And as he grew in understanding, it dawned on him that "ministry" was a wide umbrella.

The voice he had heard in the concert hall in Fort Collins didn't say "I want you to be a preacher." Nor had it announced "I want you to be an evangelist." Dick realized that ministry was not a narrow lane, but a broad road with many different possibilities. He began to keep files on the various aspects of the ministry, paying special attention to the academic requirements for each one. Whatever avenue or avenues the Lord chose for him, he resolved that he would get the finest preparation for it he possibly could.

One afternoon he rode into town with a group of his friends from the dorm. The guys liked to go into Lincoln for snacks and cheap haircuts at the barber college. Dick had some time to kill, so he strolled down Main Street. Coming across an Army recruiting office, he walked in and looked around. A brochure on military chaplaincy caught his eye.

Not long before, while on a weekend home leave, he had listened to a Seventh-day Adventist Army chaplain speak at a vespers meeting at the Denver Central church. With his new awareness of the many directions a career in ministry could take, he was intrigued to hear the military officer share his experiences.

They were sure "outside the box" for an Adventist minister. Dick had always liked things that were "outside the box." Picking up a leaflet from the stack on the table in the recruiter's office, he took it back to the dorm and start a new folder in his file of possible ministry vocations.

His busy schedule and renewed academic focus didn't leave much time for socializing. Still, he enjoyed the camaraderie of college life, and, somewhat to his surprise, he was elected president of his class. He and Elaine Price were still a couple, even though she was taking prenursing at La Sierra College, nearly 1,500 miles from Union College. Both of them were absolutely committed to their studies. That dedication was one of the important things they had in common. They continued to correspond regularly throughout their first year.

Over time, however, both realized that a long-term relationship wasn't working for either of them, and by the end of their first year they decided to break things off. There was no heart-shredding breakup, but rather a mutual acknowledgment that being separated by half a continent wasn't a good way to build a future together. While they agreed they would always be friends, the time had come for both to date other people.

Chapter 9

"You Owe Me a Malt!"

It was during his sophomore year at Union College that Dick Stenbakken really noticed Ardis Dick. Any red-blooded college guy would have noticed her beautiful blue eyes behind stylish cat's-eye glasses, soft, wavy light-brown hair, and trim figure. But the thing that impressed him most about her was that she was part of a group of straight-A students. While they weren't snobby, everyone knew they were the cream of the crop. They exuded leadership, scholarship, and popularity.

She's an interesting girl, he thought. *But I'm not sure I'm in that league.* Contenting himself with admiring her from afar, he told himself he was so committed to his studies that he had little time for dating anyway.

The fact that her great-uncle Everett Dick was a highly revered professor at Union College further enhanced Ardis' aura of unobtainability. Prof. Dick had been at Union College forever. He was "Mr. Union College" in many people's minds. (When the college built a new administration building in 1975, it named the structure after him.) His reputation was well deserved.

Everett Dick was the first Adventist ever to earn a Ph.D. degree, and the first Adventist with a Ph.D. to teach at an Adventist college. A world-renowned historian, he specialized in mid-American and Plains area history and had authored numerous books. (Scholars still recognize his book *The Sod-House Frontier* as a definitive work on the history of the northern Plains.)

In their sophomore year at Union, Ardis and Dick sat in the same row in Prof. Dick's American history class. Dick enjoyed the class immensely. Expecting his students to learn on their own what was in the textbook, Prof. Dick used the class period to tell pertinent stories, often quoting original letters he had discovered in his research. Occasionally he would burst into an authentic frontier song, singing enthusiastically and quite off-key. History, as Dick grasped for the first time, was more than names and dates. It was about real people, and Prof. Dick made that realization possible.

Well known for springing "nickel quizzes," he would shift gears away from his storytelling and ask five questions, to which all the students had to respond in writing. The quiz scores counted toward the final grade. If you cut a class and missed a quiz, too bad for you.

One day, late in the semester, the teacher distributed a corrected nickel quiz. As Dick passed the sheets down the row, he glanced at Ardis' grade and saw that she had bested his score. Catching her eye and without thinking about it, he said, "I'll bet you a malt that I'll beat you on the next quiz." It just popped out of the blue. Or maybe not entirely. After all, he had been aware of her, impressed by her dynamic personality.

"Oh, I don't think so!" she replied. Although bright, serious, and committed to her studies, those sparkling blue eyes and her warm laughter hinted that she was also a lot of fun.

The next time Prof. Dick threw a nickel quiz, Ardis scored higher than Dick. "You owe me a malt!" she told him teasingly, waving the paper under his nose with a triumphant smile.

Not liking being beat at anything, not even a nickel quiz, he was a little chagrined—maybe even a little intimidated. Add to that his natural frugality—that voice in his head that said "Why buy food at the malt shop when you're already paying for three meals a day in your college fees?" So it took him a while to pay up. But she didn't let him forget it. Finally, he said, "Yeah, OK, a bet's a bet. Let's go get a malt."

They walked across the street to the Chat 'n' Nibble, the local veggie burger and shake hangout. Together they crossed the black-and-white checkerboard-tiled floor to a booth with slick red plastic seats. Dick ordered two chocolate malts, and while they waited for their drinks to arrive, the two leaned their elbows on the white plastic table and began to chat, getting to know each other a little better.

Now he was glad he had lost the bet. This young woman was quite captivating! That day at the Chat 'n' Nibble the two of them began a friendship, but it would be many months before it turned into anything more serious.

Ardis Dick had had an upbringing totally different from Dick Stenbakken's. She was a preacher's kid whose Midwest Adventist roots went back four generations. While he was growing up in one place, hardly ever leaving Denver's South Downing Street, her family moved frequently, never living anywhere more than four years.

Ardis' father, Avery Dick, was a career pastor who had been born on a farm in LaHarpe, Kansas. His parents were Adventists, and so were his grandparents. As a young man, he worked his way through Enterprise Academy and Union College, setting type in the print shop.

His parents had both attended Union College, and it was there that Avery met Arline McTaggart, a Minnesota farm girl. The two soon discovered that they shared similar values and dreams, and she became his wife in June 1938.

Avery started out as a pastoral intern after graduation, working in what was then called the Wyoming Mission. Ardis was born in Rock Springs, Wyoming, during that time. Pastorates in Colorado and Missouri followed. Then her father accepted a call to China. The little family—Mom, Dad, 7-year-old Ardis, and her 6-year-old little brother, Aubrey—left the U.S. on February 14, 1947. They traveled for 28 days in a converted troop ship with a group of 60 missionaries, and were among the first Americans to enter China after the war.

Communism had begun rapidly to gain control in China. With the Communist armies approaching closer and closer, the missionaries had less than two years to work before being evacuated. In November 1948 they fled the Communists, going to Kulangsu Amoy, a little island off the south coast of China. Again the Communists came, and again the missionaries had to leave, this time to the Philippines. There they settled in the beautiful city of Baguio. Avery Dick was president of the Mountain Province Mission, pioneering the denomination among the aboriginal peoples.

The family spent happy years in the Philippines until May 1952 when they returned to the United States, prompted by the poor health of Ardis' younger brother. Aubrey had had a bad case of the measles before the family went to China, with an extremely high fever that resulted in recurrent seizures, now growing progressively worse.

Back in the States, the family settled in Goodrich, North Dakota, where her dad pastored a district of small churches. Ardis' mom taught school, and Ardis attended Sheyenne River Academy in Harvey, North Dakota.

Ardis' dad had always wanted to further his education, but in 1956, when he requested a leave of absence from the North Dakota Conference to attend the seminary, its administration turned him down. Not to be deterred, Avery resigned his pastorate, moved his family to Takoma Park, Maryland, and enrolled in the Seventh-day Adventist Theological

Seminary—then called Potomac University. Ardis' mom enrolled in college, and Ardis attended Takoma Academy.

The family was well settled into their new routines when disaster struck. The year 1957 was a difficult one for the Dick family. Ardis came down with mononucleosis and was hospitalized. The day the hospital allowed her to return home, her brother Aubrey died in a drowning accident, just four days after his sixteenth birthday.

Despite their grief, the family soldiered on with their education, with help and support from family and friends. Ardis' dad graduated from the seminary in 1958 with a Bachelor of Divinity degree in Old Testament studies—what we would now call a Master of Divinity. Her mother, whose college career had been interrupted long before by marriage, completed her teaching degree at Washington Missionary College (now Washington Adventist University) in the same year. Ardis finished Takoma Academy that year, too, making three Dick graduations in one year.

When it came to choosing a college, Ardis never thought of going anywhere but Union College. Her parents were moving to Canada to teach at Oshawa Missionary College (now Kingsway College), but she didn't want to attend there. Besides, Union was the family tradition. Everybody in her family went there. She had a second cousin and an uncle who were currently students. And of course her dad's uncle, Everett Dick, was on the faculty. Uncle Everett and Aunt Opal loved having students around. They would be her family while she was at Union.

As far back as she could remember, Ardis had always wanted to be a nurse. Blame it on those *Cherry Ames* mystery storybooks she had read as a young girl. Designed to encourage girls to be nurses as a way of supporting the war effort, they made a nursing career appear quite glamorous.

But during her senior year of academy she had a job as a nurse's aide at "the san," now known as Washington Adventist Hospital. While on duty one hot day, she fainted. Maybe it was the weather, or perhaps it was because she hadn't eaten breakfast, but for whatever reason, she went out like a light, wrenching her neck as she fell. After that, nursing lost some of its allure.

Nevertheless, lacking an alternate plan, she enrolled in the nursing program at Union. And she hated it. After a few desperate weeks, she had a talk with Uncle Everett. She told him how unhappy she was, expecting him to urge her to stiffen her resolve and give nursing a fair chance. But he surprised her when he said, "Well, then, change your major."

So, heaving a huge sigh of relief, she withdrew from nursing and switched to English. It fit like a glove—then, and ever after. And she was lucky enough to snag a job in the registrar's office, where she worked all four years of college.

Ardis had expected college to be fun, and it was. Right from the beginning, when one of the first guys she met at the first-year "handshake," or mixer, asked her for a date, she was popular. The students who became her close friends were an elite group—upperclass students and leaders in the school. Dating frequently, she made a lot of long-lasting friendships.

Although she carried a full load of class work, she still participated in many extracurricular activities through her college years. During her sophomore year she was associate editor of the college yearbook and then editor during her junior year.

Even though she dated often, she was never one of those girls whose goal was simply to find a husband. She was in college for an education. During her last semester at Union she received straight A's and would graduate with distinction.

Ardis was aware of Stenbakken as early as their first year. No doubt they crossed paths that first day, when he registered and she worked in the registrar's office. Certainly she noticed when he was elected first-year class president. Nice-looking and courteous, Dick's manner was almost courtly. Most of all, she knew he had a reputation as a studious, serious, hardworking young man. She noticed that he tended to make a big deal of being thrifty—but it didn't escape her that he drove one of the coolest cars on campus, a big white Dodge with ridiculously long tail fins. After that malt shop episode, she counted him among her friends, but nothing more than that.

Then, sometime around the end of October of their junior year, Dick finally asked her for a real date. She discovered that she was thrilled. Dick, as it turned out, had become something of a catch. They attended a college-sponsored Saturday-night concert. The guest artist was a countertenor.

Neither Ardis nor Dick knew exactly what a countertenor was, but they soon found out. The singer, while an accomplished musician, had a voice so high it could peel paint right off the wall. The music was, well, excruciating.

Desperate to show her a good time, he demonstrated for her that he could turn his left foot around 180 degrees—something he had always been able to do because of a hyperplastic tendon in his left hip. Despite the accompanying bad joke—"This music really turns me around"—Ardis had a good time anyway, and the two never dated anyone else but each other after that.

Early in their dating history Ardis learned to appreciate his quirky sense of humor and to give back as good as she got. One day when they were out for a walk together, she invited him to be her guest at the Sadie Hawkins banquet, an annual event to which the girls asked the guys. Glancing down at some dandelions along the path, he quipped, "I'm sorry, but I won't be able to afford anything but a dandelion corsage."

"That's OK," she said, playing along with the joke. The evening of the banquet arrived, and there was the usual bustle of activity in the dorm. As the guys arrived to pick up their dates, they first sent corsages up to the girls' dorm rooms. Someone delivered a pristine white box to Ardis. When she opened it and lifted the flowers from their shredded-paper bed, she found a beautiful, beribboned, lace-trimmed corsage of—dandelions.

Minutes later, a second corsage box arrived for her. "Don't open that, I don't want to see it," she told her roommate, and pinning the dandelions to the shoulder of her pale-blue formal, she headed for the door. Head held high, she strolled into the Rees Hall lobby and crossed the floor to meet the waiting Stenbakken, passing by all the other guys waiting for their dates, and displaying his pathetic flowers for all to see. He learned his lesson. Pulling pranks on Ardis had its consequences.

That summer she and her parents went camping in the mountains near Denver, and she invited Dick to join them. He was then working as an assistant pastor and youth director at the Denver Central church. It was a job he was thrilled to have, but he took time off to accompany her and her family. Dick had a great time, with Ardis and her parents in their tent, and he in his own little one nearby. Ardis' dad especially impressed him, sharing his passion for ministry, as well as his commitment to the importance of education.

Afterward, driving back to Denver alone, Dick found himself thinking, *This relationship could get super-serious. I could fall in love with this girl. She's everything I could ever want in a wife.* He slammed the heel of his hand on the steering wheel. It was thrilling—and frightening!

Could God be leading him in this direction? He sensed that Ardis could be ready to commit to a relationship, but Dick himself was cautious. He wanted to spend those three years at the seminary. Still, he could see no negatives to the relationship going further, other than his own hesitation.

By the start of their senior year, he and Ardis were definitely serious. As the year progressed, couples around them began to get engaged. Dick firmed up his plans to attend the seminary that fall, and Ardis began to submit résumés for a teaching job. She had a couple interviews with academy principals about prospective positions. But Dick was still on the horns of his dilemma. What should he do about his relationship with Ardis?

The president of the Colorado Conference of Seventh-day Adventists, R. S. Joyce, made a recruiting trip to campus that fall. He interviewed Dick and offered him a job pastoring in the conference. Pleased and excited, Dick would have loved to start his career in his home conference. But there was a hitch. The conference president didn't see any reason Dick needed to go to the seminary first.

"Why would you want to go to the 'cemetery'?" Joyce joked. At the time, the question wasn't so unusual, even if the manner of asking it was. Few Adventist Church leaders, including conference presidents, had advanced degrees, and almost no pastors did. The denomination considered a bachelor's degree sufficient.

Dick explained how strongly he felt about getting the best possible education he could, to prepare him to be the best minister he could be. But his explanation fell on deaf ears. The Colorado Conference wasn't interested in sponsoring him through three further years of education, or even in holding the offer open while he completed his training. Dick was on his own. And his quandary about marriage only deepened.

By now he knew that he was in love with Ardis. He should have been ready to commit himself to her, but he had a chauvinistic outlook on life. All his hesitation came down to one thing: his stubborn pride wouldn't let him ask a woman to support him through the seminary.

All his young life he had had an "I can do it myself" attitude, and so far, that had served him pretty well. But things were different now. Ardis wasn't going to wait forever. She was proceeding with her own plans, and if he didn't speak up, they weren't going to include him. Still he wavered, unable to reach a decision, unwilling to declare himself.

Constantly he prayed about the situation. The decision was not just about his life and what would make him happy. It was about his calling and what would help him fulfill it to the best of his ability. Always he kept going back to those texts: "You have been with me from the beginning" and "Christ is not divided." Dick knew he felt God's assurance that she was the right person to be his partner in life and in the ministry, but how could he ask such a lovely, bright young woman with a great future ahead of her to support *his* calling? He prayed some more—and dithered some more.

Ardis and Dick had developed the habit of spending their dates at the home of their friends Jim and Roxy Hoehn. The Hoehns were in the same class as Ardis and Dick, but because they had gotten married between their junior and senior years and lived off-campus, the college deemed them suitable chaperones for a young unmarried couple.

One evening Jim Hoehn took Dick aside for a man-to-man talk. "Dick," he said, "You have to fish or cut bait."

Although he knew exactly where the conversation was going, Dick still feigned ignorance. "Listen to me," Jim continued, "I'm serious. We're all about to graduate, and Ardis needs to know where your relationship is going. You're not being fair to her, man. She needs to know."

That little nudge from a good friend was what it took to get him over the hump. He made the decision to risk asking Ardis to marry him. On his next break he told his parents of his intentions and bought a watch—a pretty little gold Bulova with a rectangular face. At the time, watches were the engagement gift of choice for Adventists, most of whom didn't wear engagement or wedding rings.

The next weekend, when he and Ardis arrived for their regular Saturday night date at the Hoehns' house, he had the watch tucked in the pocket of his tan jacket. "Here, Dick, let me take that jacket," Jim said, reaching for it.

"No, no, I think I'll keep my jacket on."

"Come on, Dick, it's warm in here. Let me hang your jacket up for you," Roxy urged.

Still, Dick refused to give up his jacket. Something about the look on his face cued Jim and Roxy. They excused themselves, claiming that they had to finish up some laundry. Left alone with Ardis, he screwed up his courage, pulled the watch out of his pocket, and to the *thunka-thunk* of the washing machine in the next room, proposed. And Ardis immediately said yes.

Going back to the dorm later that night, hand in hand, they felt as though they were walking on air, at least four feet off the ground. Ardis wore the watch into the dorm, where several of her friends immediately spotted it, and congratulations ensued all around.

Ardis called her parents from the dorm lobby phone and got her mom on the line. "Dick asked me to marry him, and I said yes, and he gave me a watch and it's official," she announced, all in one breath. Then she broke into a grin as she listened to her mom's brief reply.

"What did she say?" he queried anxiously.

"She said, 'Well, it's about time!'" Ardis replied. They set the date for the end of the summer, August 20, 1962.

When Dick explained his long period of hesitancy, she understood, although she was a little annoyed that he would think she might have preferred not to work after marriage. Of course she planned to work, whether married or not! What did he think she'd been training herself for?

"Anyway," she said, "none of that matters now." Being a preacher's kid herself, she realized his commitment and knew better than most what was ahead for the two of them. "You're called to the ministry. I know that, and I'm going to support that."

They also discussed his heritage, or lack of it. He had been frank with her about it. "You know I'm adopted. I don't know my biological background, and I've never had any particular interest in finding it out," he reminded her. Ardis was already aware of most of his history, although they hadn't discussed it in detail. But her love and support were unconditional.

For Dick, getting engaged was both a scary and a humbling experience. Once again God had taught him an important life lesson. He had to admit he couldn't achieve his life goals entirely on his own, regardless of his rock-solid commitment to the ministry. Instead, he needed a partner—the right partner—and with God's help, he'd found her. Neither of them knew exactly what the future held. But with their love for each other and their faith in God's plan, they were ready to forge ahead.

Chapter 10

"Hang On for Dear Life!"

Dick got his first real taste of pastoring during the summers following his junior and senior years of college. Pastor Ernie Lutz had invited him to serve as the associate and youth pastor of Denver Central Seventh-day Adventist Church. It was a real learning experience to work closely with him, providing leadership for a large and lively group of young people. The first time the Colorado Conference had ever put an undergraduate on their payroll, Dick was well aware of both the honor and the responsibility.

Taking groups of kids on hiking expeditions was a welcome part of his job description. One warm summer day he was with a group from the church, hiking above Glacier View Ranch (the Colorado Conference campground) in the Indian Peaks wilderness area. Just northwest of the Arapahoe Peaks was a steep snowfield, about a mile long and maybe half a mile wide, the upper end of which went right up over the Continental Divide.

Dick and his buddy Jim Coleman (who would later become an Air Force chaplain) decided to climb the snowfield, although neither had any real experience with ice climbing.

Borrowing a friend's ice ax, Dick then attached a set of crampons to his hiking boots for better traction. He and Jim started up the snowfield, leaving the rest of their group to watch from below. Corn snow—small, pea-sized balls of ice, and hardly the easiest surface for inexperienced hikers—covered the surface. About halfway up, the angle got much steeper. Dick managed to keep climbing by cutting footholds in the snow with the ice ax. Jim hiked up on his left, finding footholds mostly on rock. But melting ice was making Jim's path extremely slippery.

"Why don't you come over onto the snow with me?" Dick called. "We can rope ourselves together like they do in the movies." When Jim did, Dick tied the two of them together with the quarter-inch yellow nylon cord he had brought along, and they continued to make their way up the steep snow.

"Hang on!" Jim yelled suddenly, feeling himself starting to slide. Dick glanced down just as the slack in the rope between them ran out, yanking him off his feet. Now they were both slipping down the slope. Dick tried jamming the ice ax into the snow, but it wouldn't hold. The handle end had a spike on it, so he tried that, and it finally stopped their slide. They came to a stop, spread-eagled facedown across the snow.

As they struggled to their feet, Dick asked, shakily, "You OK?"

"Yeah, I'm OK. How about you?" Once they realized that both of them were still alive, with all limbs present and accounted for, they grinned at each other, and having learned nothing, started back up the snowfield.

Jim had supplied himself with a hunting knife, and by jamming it into the steps as Stenbakken cut them, he followed his friend's lead. Then as Dick took another step, the ice broke out from under his foot, spinning him around.

"Hang on!" he screeched, sliding headfirst down the slope. He felt the rope pull taut as Jim dug in, then stretch, and finally snap in two. Jim had managed to stop himself up above Dick, but Dick went careening down the snow-covered rock face on his belly. Realizing that he was heading straight for a granite outcropping below, he managed to flip himself over onto his back, hoping to use his heels as brakes, but they wouldn't dig into the loose corn snow.

Now he was flying down the slope flat on his back, like a luge rider without a luge. As he gained speed, he was going too fast to pull himself into a sitting position. Then he remembered the ice ax. Jamming it under his right arm, he hoped to use the wide blade as a brake. The ice ax dug in, sending up a huge rooster tail of snow into the air. To his friends, watching anxiously from below, it looked like a giant white feather plume. The ax slowed him slightly, but it also pulled him to the right, closer to the rock outcropping.

Calculating as best as he could where the outcropping was, Dick flipped himself over onto his left side just before he got to it. He missed the rock, but fell off a ledge into soft snow, burying himself completely and vanishing from sight. To his friends it looked as if he had just disappeared. Jim couldn't see him from above, and nobody below could spot him either.

When he came to his senses, Dick couldn't see anything but white. Then he realized his glasses were packed with snow. The stuff also filled his mouth. He heard Jim call, "Where are you?" Slowly he dug himself out, and stood up, shaking like a leaf. Then he climbed up onto the edge of the drop-off.

"I'm here. I'm fine!" he yelled to Jim, who had come down the slope a lot slower than Stenbakken.

His friends down below had seen the whole thing, and were greatly relieved to see that Dick was alive after his spectacular slide. His left elbow hurt a little, and when he looked down at it, he saw that the snow had ground off the entire sleeve of his shirt and most of the skin of his elbow. Other than that, he had no injuries at all.

Pastor Lutz put an arm around him and thumped him on the back. "Wow," he marveled, shaking his head. "We were praying hard down here. You were gathering speed like crazy." As Dick realized how close he had come to total disaster, he admitted to himself that he should probably get more experience before he tried anything like that again.

Still, on the other hand, he congratulated himself silently, with the foolishness of youth, *I made it!*

Despite that hair-raising experience, the summer of 1962 flew by in a flurry of plans—moving plans, plans for enrolling in seminary classes for Dick, for nailing down a teaching job for Ardis, and for finding an apartment. But the first order of business was to get married. So while he worked as a youth pastor in Colorado, she spent her summer in Canada with her parents arranging their wedding. She enlisted a talented friend, Bob Tan, to design the wedding dress of her dreams, and her mother ordered yards and yards of off-white silk peau de soie and brought Bob's design to life.

August 20 dawned sunny and hot in Lincoln, Nebraska—extremely hot. Not a cloud hung in the sky. The wedding took place in the College View church. Aunt Opal Dick was the coordinator. Ardis' father, Avery Dick, officiated.

The wedding party included friends and several small cousins. Ardis carried spider mums, lily of the valley, and yellow roses. Flowers also topped the wedding cake. She thought the typical bride-and-groom figures were "hokey." Another item she and Dick chose to omit was the word "obey" from the wedding vows. Theirs was to be a partnership of equals.

Dick had charge of the honeymoon arrangements. He had been bragging up the honeymoon venue for weeks. His aunt and uncle, Emma and Ray Fahlender, had offered the young couple the use of their cabin in the mountains. Although Ardis hadn't seen the cabin, she knew that the Fahlenders were his "rich relatives," so she was looking forward to luxurious, if rustic, accommodations. He expanded on that theme, praising the clear air, the majestic trees, and the breathtaking mountain views. "The cabin's beautiful," he promised. "There's a huge fireplace with a big leather sofa in front of it." The two envisioned exhilarating mountain hikes followed by romantic evenings in front of the fire.

The newlyweds spent their wedding night in Lincoln, and the next morning packed up the Dodge and drove out of town, heading for the mountains of Colorado. After a long, long drive, they arrived at the Fehlander cabin well after dark.

Unlocking the door, Dick pushed it open. At first, all they saw were ghostly white shapes, glimmering in the pale moonlight. Then he found the light switch, and they quickly realized that bed sheets covered everything in the cabin. Quite dusty bedsheets. Evidently nobody had used the cabin for a long, long time.

After gathering up the sheets, they took a good look around. Just as advertised, one wall of the living room was filled with a handsome fieldstone fireplace with a big green leather couch across from it. The mountain air was chilly and they were eager to relax together in front of a cozy blaze. Dick found some newspaper, kindling, and logs, checked to be sure the damper was open, and soon had a fire going. Almost immediately smoke billowed out into the room.

Belatedly, he realized that he hadn't examined the chimney. Finding a ladder, he climbed to the top, and sure enough, there was a slab of stone across the chimney's opening, put there to keep small creatures out while the owners were away. Of course, the stone was now too hot to touch. Although it took him a while, he managed to nudge the heavy slab aside, but not before the cabin had filled completely with heavy, thick smoke. Bad as it was, though, smoke was only the start of their problems.

Back when Dick had been building up the idea of this rustic but luxurious hideout in Ardis' imagination, he had neglected to mention a thing or two. One rather important oversight was the cabin's lack of indoor plumbing. So when it was time to get ready for bed, he pointed out that there was a "nicely appointed" outhouse, located just a short distance up the path behind the cabin. Gripping a flashlight and gathering her courage, Ardis headed up the path. Soon she returned, reporting that the outhouse, while it might be nicely appointed, was also padlocked.

"No problem!" Dick said cheerfully, grabbing a large ring of keys from a nearby hook in one hand and the flashlight in the other and heading confidently up the path.

But of course, none of the many keys on the ring fit the padlock. *I'll just yank the padlock out,* he thought, feeling a little desperate. *I can fix it in the morning.* So, using the only tool he had at hand, he wedged the flashlight under the padlock, hoping to pull it out by the screws. He gave it a mighty heave. The padlock didn't budge, but the flashlight gave up the ghost.

So, by now completely out of options, Ardis and Dick went to bed. The next morning they discovered the cabin had no running water. That was about all the newlyweds could take of rusticity, so they packed up the car again and drove down to Colorado Springs, where they checked into a motel. That evening, as they settled in to begin their worship together, they discovered that he had left his Bible up at the cabin.

Early the next morning the hotel maid startled them awake as she entered their room. When they had gone to bed the night before, they had left the key in the outside lock of their room! That morning they drove back up to the cabin to retrieve Dick's Bible. They have never been back there since.

Shortly after that memorable honeymoon, he and Ardis loaded their meager belongings into a U-Haul trailer, hitched it to the Dodge, and headed to Berrien Springs, Michigan, arriving just in time for the start of his classes at the seminary, and for Ardis to attend the presessions for her first teaching job at nearby Eau Claire High School.

During the first presession, Ardis, wondering who would be mentoring her and showing her the ropes, asked the school's principal a question: "Who is the head of the English Department?"

"You are! You're the only person on the faculty with a degree in English!" So Ardis, with the ink barely dry on her diploma, invented her own program. It must have been a good one, because, in her third year of teaching, she was voted Teacher of the Year at Eau Claire High.

The couple soon settled in at B2, Garland Apartments, a part of the university's on-campus married student housing. They remained there for the three years Dick was in school. The couple loved life on the campus. A list of their friends from those seminary days reads like a Who's Who of Adventist leadership: Jan Paulsen, Niels-Erik Andreasen, Milt Erhardt, Bob and Anita Folkenberg, Larry and Gillian Geraty, Joe and Stella Greig, Jim and Roxy Hoehn, and Mitch and Patsy Tyner were a few of their many neighbors and friends during those years.

Dick worked as a janitor in the apartment building part of the time. Just as in the old days with his buddies on South Downing Street, he kept his eye out for "finds" in the trash. His wife never knew what he might bring home. Also, he snagged a part-time job doing some public relations writing for the university. And Ardis, when she wasn't teaching or writing lesson plans, took advantage of the area's bounty by freezing and canning all the fruits and vegetables she could.

One of the only worries on Dick's mind as he began his seminary training was what was happening at home in Colorado. During that last summer he'd spent at home his mother's behavior had grown increasingly odd. In addition to the drinking, he was pretty sure she was taking prescription pain pills. Dick noticed that her voice was sometimes slurred on the phone, and he had witnessed her in a falling-down-drunk condition at least once during one of his breaks from college.

He hadn't realized how bad the situation was until he and Ardis were married. Mom's attachment to him was such that she simply couldn't understand that he could love his wife and still love his mother. In her mind she saw Ardis as a competitor for his affection, and no matter how hard he tried, he couldn't persuade her differently. Nothing he could do could change her unhappiness. But being the devoted son he was, he was troubled by it.

Chapter 11

"Brandy and Wine"

Dick's seminary classes lived up to his expectations, and they were high. From the time he had first accepted God's call to the ministry, he had known he wanted to prepare himself to be the best minister he could be. And as he recognized more of the various directions a career in ministry could take, his conviction deepened that a good education was essential.

An experience he had while still in college added another dimension to his understanding. A fellow theology student had received an interesting assignment: "Go to another church—not your own denomination—attend the worship service, observe, and take notes." Dick overhead his friend say that he planned to visit St. Mary's, the largest Catholic church in downtown Lincoln.

"Hey, I'll go with you," he offered, his curiosity piqued. "I'm up for that."

The next Sunday, as Dick looked through the St. Mary's bulletin, he noticed an announcement of a class for "inquirers," or people interested in becoming Catholics. Although well grounded in his own faith, he was curious about what other people believed and why they did so. *If I'm going to be working in a community where there are Catholics,* he said to himself, *I ought to know more about Catholicism, right?*

So he called the St. Mary's church office and explained his interest to the priest, being perfectly honest about who he was and why he wanted to know more about Catholicism. The priest was gracious and cordial. "Well," he said, "we'd be happy to have you join our class, but there is another parish, Holy Family, on Sheridan Boulevard, near your college. I'll give you the priest's name and phone number."

Phoning the church office at Holy Family, Dick talked to their priest. "We don't have an 'inquirers class' at present," the priest said, "but why don't you just drop by my office? I'd be happy to talk with you." So that's how Dick found himself the next Sabbath afternoon at Holy Family Catholic

Church, chatting with two young Catholic priests. Dick kept continuing appointments regularly, often taking a friend or two along, sometimes going alone, for the next year and a half.

Like many young Adventists of the era, he had a sort of arrogant naivety toward Catholicism. He thought their creed was based more on tradition than on the Bible. To say he didn't know much about the religion would be an understatement. "Peter couldn't have been the first pope—he was a married man. Didn't he have a mother-in-law?" That was the sad extent of his logic—at first.

But what he found in that quiet, book-filled study was a free-flowing discussion, an exchange of ideas with men who were Christians and equals. The priests were young—not long out of seminary themselves. He enjoyed their fellowship and appreciated their knowledge. They didn't try to convert him—nor he them. Gracious and friendly, they were no dummies but knew their Bibles, were well versed in church history, and understood their theology.

That's when a light went on for Dick. "This is the high level of understanding and expertise I will be dealing with as a minister. I need to be prepared!" Those sessions with the Catholic priests helped to solidify his goal to get a complete and thorough theological education. Up to that point, he had known he would go to the seminary, but he hadn't thought about the importance of the three-year program. So, far from shaking his own faith, his dialog with ministers of another denomination helped to intensify his resolve to study more deeply and widely.

Dick's open-minded approach to learning about other religions didn't always sit well with his theology professors at Union College. His new insights probably caused him to raise some questions in class that were a little unorthodox. Years later he would learn that at least one of his professors had brought his name to an administrative council with the recommendation that they dismiss him from the theology program.

Far from being a negative influence, however, his fellowship with priests served him well in later life. As an Army chaplain, he would work for a Catholic and share a pulpit with a Baptist. He would supervise and serve people from all religious walks. At a time when many Adventists were somewhat uncomfortable with the idea of interfaith cooperation, he would be completely at home.

So, armed as he was with a hunger for education and a thirst for knowledge, it was only natural that Dick took to the seminary like a duck to water. He was enrolled in the three-year bachelor of divinity degree program (now known as a master of divinity) at the Seventh-day Adventist Theological Seminary. At the same time, he took a two-year master's program at Andrews University, leading to an advanced degree in theology and philosophy. Fortunately for him, the two institutions shared a campus.

Finding all the classes fascinating and energizing, he thrived on the challenge of getting into Scripture more deeply, delving into contexts and background. Studying church history, especially under Kenneth Strand, who knew how to bring history alive, brought him great joy. Just as in Everett Dick's history class at Union, Stenbakken learned how historical settings helped one understand events—and not just biblical but current ones as well. He was discovering a much broader way to study and learn—how to dig for himself. Each day offered new insights and challenges.

Many of his teachers were men of giant intellect. Earl Hilgert, professor of New Testament, inspired him to study things out for himself. Kenneth Strand, who taught church history, dazzled his students with his photographic memory. He could recall not only whole passages from reference works, but also the page and paragraph where they appeared.

Siegfried Horn, who taught archaeology, was a consummate scholar. A formal person—the quintessential Ph.D.—his students felt that he lived in an atmosphere so rare that they almost required oxygen in his classes, but they enjoyed every moment of his lectures.

Charles Wittschiebe was just the opposite of Horn. A colorful and voluble character, he'd show up to class wearing a bright, loud Hawaiian shirt covered with hibiscus blossoms. Dick saw Wittschiebe pass Horn in the hall one day, and say, "Hi, Siggy!" It was hard to think of the proper Professor Horn as "Siggy!"

Dick took every class he could get in counseling and psychology, most taught by Wittschiebe. Dick knew he needed to understand people to be an effective pastor. Theology was important, but he had to know how to put a human face on the gospel so that it would be meaningful to the people in the pew. He has been profoundly grateful for that foundation in clinical pastoring, which led to his later interest in family counseling. "Nobody ever called me at 2:00 in the morning wondering about the third toe on the left foot of Daniel's statue," he has said many times.

Life wasn't all study and no play. He found time to tinker and blow off some steam with friends. Ardis drove their only car to work at Eau Claire High, and he needed transportation to get to his classes, so he bought an old bike for $5. Soon he discovered that his "bargain" had a problem. It didn't pedal well. Taking it apart, he cleaned it and got it ready to paint, then found the problem. The gears had a ball bearing missing. But he had no idea where to find a ball bearing to fit.

Finally he decided to paint the bike anyway. Picking up a can of spray paint, he shook it. When he heard a clacking sound, he suddenly stopped shaking. The can had a ball bearing in it! After painting the bike, he performed surgery on the can, removed the ball bearing, and inserted it into the gear. It worked. He had his transportation.

Jim and Roxy Hoehn and Ardis and Dick liked to get together on Saturday nights. One night they decided to make pizza.

"Dick," an aproned Ardis called from the tiny kitchen of their apartment, "we don't have any mushrooms." Since pizza without mushrooms was unthinkable, the wives dispatched him and Jim to Schraeder's Market and admonished them not to come back without a can of mushrooms.

The market was not notably well stocked, especially by Saturday night, so the two men anxiously scanned the shelves and discovered one can of mushrooms. The problem was, another student had the can in his hand. Jim and Dick sauntered up to him. "Are you going to buy those?" Stenbakken asked.

"Yeah, why?"

"Look at the label. Brandywine Mushrooms."

Immediately Hoehn picked up on the scam. "Yeah," he said. "Brandy. And wine."

"Oh," the student said, frowning. "I didn't notice that." Putting the can back on the shelf, he walked away. As soon as he was out of sight, Dick snatched the mushrooms off the shelf. The Stenbakken house had mushroom pizza that night.

As he started his third year of seminary training, Dick was eager to get both a call and a sponsorship for his last year. The "call," in Adventist lingo, was a job offer—a place to begin his ministry. He had completed his master's degree in theology and philosophy from Andrews University, but he still had another year to go to finish up his three-year bachelor's degree in divinity from the seminary. A sponsorship would help relieve the financial burdens the young couple were experiencing.

Most of his fellow students had already received calls, but then most of them hadn't opted for a three-year program. Now time was running out. Dick and Ardis prayed about it often. They believed a "call" meant just that—an invitation from God to serve in a particular place, but the Lord would use a human agency to place it. Dick trusted that process. But which human would it be? And when?

His name was Lee Carter. He had been the youth director for the Colorado Conference. Dick had known him all through high school and college. Just as Dick was about to begin his third year of seminary training, the Wyoming Conference elected Carter as its president. In that role, he was responsible for hiring pastors. Immediately he wrote Dick a letter: "Don't take a call until I have a chance to talk to you."

Meanwhile, back in Berrien Springs, word had reached Dick that his friend and mentor had just become a conference president. Instantly he sent Carter a letter, requesting an interview for a possible position in the Wyoming Conference. The two letters crossed in the mail. (It's odd to think about letters "crossing in the mail" in today's world of e-mail and texting, but that's what happened.)

Fortunately, the two made contact, and in due time Dick had a call—to be the pastor for Wheatland and Torrington, two small churches located on the plains of southeastern Wyoming. The location was less than 200 miles from Denver—close enough for Dick to visit his parents. While he knew the area lacked natural beauty, that was the least of his concerns. He and Ardis were happy to have the call and the sponsorship that went with it.

The last two semesters of seminary flew by, and shortly before the end of the school year, Carter called them. "I know Wheatland and Torrington are closer to Denver, but I would like to move you two to another district. I'd like to put you in Worland."

Worland! Dick knew that it was located in a verdant valley with Yellowstone National Park to the west and the Bighorn National Forest to the east. It had fishing and hunting and mountain scenery galore. Not only that, but his old friends Alden and Janice Curtis lived in Worland. Even more astonishing was the fact that Ardis' dad had served that same district as a young pastor. "Yes, we'd be delighted to go to Worland," he replied. For Dick a call to Worland was like getting a summons to paradise. *Here am I, send me*, he thought with joy.

Other changes were happening as his last year of seminary wound down. Uncle Ray Frahlender died that year, and only a month later, Aunt Emma passed away. She left Dick a bequest in her will—he would have enough furniture to fill their rented home in Worland, her 1962

Oldsmobile, and the princely sum of $3,000. (In today's money that would be about $30,000!) For weeks he and Ardis debated what to do with their windfall of money.

After their years of careful budgeting, they suddenly felt rich. It was a heady feeling and led to some wild ideas. They toyed briefly with the idea of taking flying lessons and a few other even crazier possibilities. One hot day when they were picking beans they came up with the perfect plan: furthering their education by using the money for an extended trip to Europe and the Middle East. They'd have three months to travel—they weren't expected in Worland until the fall.

"We can enrich our ministry by visiting the important Reformation sites in Europe, and by traveling to the Holy Land," Dick said, getting more and more excited as the idea gathered speed.

"And besides, we may never have a chance to travel again!" she added, little realizing that a great deal of world travel awaited them in both their futures.

Both of them excelled at planning and scheduling, and they had a great time designing their trip. They pinned a big National Geographic map to the wall of their dining room. Then they invited students and faculty from Europe and the Middle East over to supper. They pumped each guest for information on the most important things to see in his or her home country. Soon the map sprouted pins. By connecting the pins with yarn, before long they had mapped out a workable itinerary. Next they stocked up on film, buying 50 rolls of 36-exposure Kodachrome slide film.

Selling the old Dodge, they ordered a brand-new sea-blue Karmann Ghia, to be delivered in Luxembourg. At Sears they bought a two-person tent, then purchased air mattresses and sleeping bags in Luxembourg when they arrived. They spent two wonderful months driving the little blue Karmann Ghia throughout Europe, taking pictures and camping all along the way. The pictures they took they had carefully selected with an eye toward sharing their trip with future parishioners or classes.

Two friends from the seminary, Bob and Marilyn Caskey, joined them for the Middle East part of the trip. Together they traveled through Greece, Jordan, Lebanon, Israel, Egypt, and Syria, absorbing the cultures, visiting important ancient and biblical sites.

Ardis and Dick arrived back in New York with just $5 in their pockets. The Karman Ghia had been shipped ahead from Europe and was waiting for them at the dock when they arrived. Good planners that they were, they had left $100 in the bank so that they would have the money to drive across the country, pick up Aunt Emma's furniture and the Oldsmobile in Denver, and get themselves and their possessions to Wyoming. That money had to last them through their first month in Worland, until his first paycheck from the Wyoming Conference arrived.

The couple was almost flat broke when they finally got to Worland. Pastor Carter was there to help them move into their rented house, recently vacated by the former pastor. They had no food—no staples at all. Going through their coat pockets, wallets, and purses, they put together about $14 and change. When they were totally out of gas, the guy at the local gas station gave them credit. Ardis made a list of basic food items, and Dick went to the grocery store. The bill came to just a few pennies less than the money he had in his pocket.

"Sign your receipt and drop it in the box," the grocery cashier told him. Thinking it must be some new method of keeping track of customers, Dick did as told, and took his miserably inadequate grocery purchases home.

That night Dick's new head elder came over to help them move furniture. "Congratulations, Pastor!" he said. "You won at the store!"

"Won what?" Dick asked in surprise.

"Well, every day they pull two register tapes out of a box and post them on the bulletin board. If you return to the store within five days, you get half of your total purchase on the tape for free the next time you shop! I saw your name on the board."

Returning to the store, he claimed his prize, and he and Ardis had another $7 to spend on groceries. God had provided. That $7, coupled with the church members' dinner invitations and generous housewarming gifts of food, got them through the month.

Chapter 12

"You Have to Tag the Animal"

W e've never had an Adventist pastor join our group!" the president of the ministerial association said to Dick, a look of surprise and maybe even consternation on his weathered face.

"Well," Dick replied, looking up at the taller man with a shrug and an ingratiating grin, "I'd like to be the first." Shortly after arriving in Worland, he had found out where and when the local ministerial association met and had arrived at their meeting uninvited. When he told the ministers who he was, they were a little taken aback. Over time, however, the other pastors began to accept him.

Worland was a great place for the newly minted Pastor and Mrs. Stenbakken to begin their ministry. It was no big city—no megachurch internship where the new guy would spend his time carrying a senior pastor's briefcase. The nearest Adventist pastor was at least a half day's drive away. The two of them were on their own—sink or swim—in a town of less than 5,000 inhabitants. They'd either succeed—and learn a lot in the process—or they'd fall flat on their faces.

With its green lawns and wide, tree-lined streets, Worland sat right in the middle of the fertile Big Horn Basin, surrounded by five mountain ranges. The town was at the center of an area of significant natural beauty, with enough hunting, fishing, camping, skiing, climbing, and hiking to satisfy the most avid outdoors person.

The inhabitants weren't there just for the recreation, however. Most were farmers and cattle ranchers. They were good people—rugged and independent—the kind who would give you the shirt off their backs—if it was their idea. Coming from hardy pioneer stock, many of them were descended from the first Europeans to settle in the state, and some even had Native American ancestors.

One of Dick's parishioners had walked to Wyoming all the way from the Dakota Territory, following a buckboard wagon—while pregnant with her ninth child. She died at the age of 104. Another pair of brothers could remember crawling to the top of a ridge when they were boys to watch the last of the gun battles between sheep herders and cattle herders. Self-sufficient, sturdy, and tough—that described the no-nonsense people of the Big Horn Basin.

Dick's pastoral district also included the church in the town of Ten Sleep, so-called because that was the way the Indians marked distances—10 "sleeps" or nights between camps. The town was located approximately 26 miles of rugged mountain road to the east of Worland. A third congregation, at Thermopolis, less than 36 miles down the valley to the south, formed the third leg of the district. Dick would travel from church to church like an old-fashioned circuit preacher, driving Aunt Emma's trusty Oldsmobile or the little blue Karmann Ghia.

Quickly the couple settled into their rented house on Fifteenth Street and began to familiarize themselves with the community. Dick noticed that the town's dozen or so churches represented a good many denominations. One of the biggest churches was Methodist. Worland also had two Lutheran churches, as well as Presbyterian, Episcopal, Catholic, and Mormon congregations. There was an Assemblies of God, a Church of Christ, and even a Greek Orthodox group—all in all, quite a lot of diversity.

He assumed that some of the established ministers in town would soon invite him to join their ministerial association. But not a single pastor called on him. Dick didn't let it hurt his feelings, but he made up his mind that it wouldn't ever happen to another new minister in town—not as long as he was there.

From that point on, until the day he and Ardis left Worland for their next post, he called on every new pastor who came to town. He would read the notices of their arrival in the Big Horn *Daily News*, "published daily, except for Sundays and Thursdays." The paper printed everything, from who was playing cards with whom, to who had a cousin visiting from Iowa. Often it would even print a new pastor's address. Dick would go knock on his door.

"Hi, I'm the Adventist pastor in town," he'd say with a big smile. "I've been here for a few months" (or a few years—whatever applied). "Is there anything I can do for you—show you around, introduce you to people, whatever?"

It was just a friendly chitchat, conducted on the new pastor's turf. Before Dick left, he would ask for the privilege of praying for the new man's ministry in the community. Sometimes a new pastor's jaw would drop. "*You* would pray for *my* ministry?"

Dick would smile and nod his head. "Why wouldn't I pray for your ministry?" he'd say. "People need to know Christ. Some will come to you, and some to me."

Since none of the other ministers contacted him, crashing the ministerial association's meeting unannounced was his first introduction to the town's other clergy. After their initial surprise, they welcomed him in. Some awkward moments did occur—for instance, when the discussion of Sunday blue laws came up.

Washakie County had blue laws on the books, but the authorities weren't enforcing them. One of the meetings had a lively discussion of the issue. Some of the pastors urged that the ministerial association push the community to close everything up on Sunday. Then they began to hesitate. After looking at each other, they glanced at Dick. He could see their minds working—"Maybe we shouldn't discuss that right now."

Nevertheless, Dick kept attending, smiling, and seeking ways to be helpful, and slowly the group found some things they could collaborate on. All the churches began to work together more closely for the good of the community. And Dick was part of that. People saw him as somebody who cared about the community and was willing to work with other clergy. Not pushy, he was just there, as another clergyperson in the community. During his second year in Worland the ministerial association elected him as its president.

Dick also joined the Kiwanis Club right away. Alden Curtis, his old school buddy and now an optometrist working with his father, Clayton, was a member, and it was a great way to get to know the business leaders of the town. The dues and the cost of the lunch each month weren't expensive, but on Ardis' and Dick's no-frills budget, they added up. Dick was gratified when, after a few months, the Kiwanis Club asked him to be its treasurer. He was even happier when he learned that the treasurer didn't pay dues and got his lunches free.

One of his fellow Kiwanians found out that Dick and his wife had just come back from a trip to Europe and the Middle East, and that they had taken lots of slides. Not many people living in Worland in 1965 had been to Europe, and even fewer had seen the Holy Land. Asked to give a program, he was delighted to do so—and glad that he would get to use all those photographs just as he and Ardis had hoped.

After the first presentation, the Kiwanis club wanted more, and Dick obliged by giving several programs. Pastors heard about the talks from their parishioners, and as a result, he and Ardis received invitations to give slide presentations in almost every congregation in town, further breaking down barriers and creating goodwill.

Occasionally, though, prejudice would still raise its head. The Big Horn *Daily News* ran a short article about the Adventists' Ingathering program (a national fund-raising campaign), describing the good things being done with the money it collected. That was too much for the pastor at Zion Lutheran. He made an announcement from the pulpit, reminding his parishioners to give their money to their own church. That pastor took another post not long after, and the interim pastor sent to take his place got appendicitis and was rushed to Billings, Montana, for surgery, leaving the Zion Lutheran congregation without a pastor.

One of the Lutheran lay leaders approached Dick at a Kiwanis Club meeting. "Dick," he said, "our interim pastor has had an emergency. He'll be out of commission for a few weeks. Would you be willing to take the sermon for us this Sunday?"

To this man, Dick seemed an obvious choice—a respected member of the clergy in town, and the only pastor not busy on Sunday morning. Accepting the invitation, Dick spoke at Zion Lutheran for several Sundays in a row. The next year's Ingathering campaign went a little easier.

The Worland Adventist Church was pretty and picturesque, built of white-painted clapboard with a faintly Gothic front entrance porch. Sitting on a tree-filled corner lot in an old residential area of town, it had only one room—curtained off at one end for the children's Sabbath school class. A small bathroom had been built onto the back of the church, but to get to it, you had to go outside.

The church was tiny. Its 25 members filled it almost completely, leaving no room for visitors or expansion. That had not been a big problem—Dick checked the guest book when he arrived, and saw that the church had had no visitors, other than relatives of members, for many years. As far as he could tell, no one from the community had ever darkened its door. In fact, there seemed to be almost no interaction between the church and the community. It became his mission to change that.

The church in Ten Sleep met in a former two-room schoolhouse. It had an outhouse out back and a coal-burning stove, which sat about four feet from the pulpit. Pappy Jacobs, who served as both the head elder and the head deacon, maintained the stove and most everything else in the church.

Every Sabbath morning in winter he fired up the stove at 6:00 a.m. so that by the time Dick rose to preach, the pulpit itself was almost too hot to touch. Those seated in the back of the room were still cold, however. Neither situation lent itself to long sermons or attentive listeners. With Dick's encouragement, the members found a way to move the stove and use a fan to circulate the air, so that everybody, preacher included, was more comfortable.

Over in the Nowood River Valley, approximately 25 mountainous dirt-road miles south of Ten Sleep, was another little Adventist church at a place called Big Trails. It had been lovingly constructed by several families who had since moved away, leaving it empty and unused. The church was a small, shingled structure—one room with a sort of lean-to attached on the side for Sabbath school classes. Dick conceived the idea to move the little building to Ten Sleep.

"If we cut that side room off," he urged, as Pappy Jacobs and other parishioners stood around and scratched their heads, "we could move the side room on one truck, and the main body on another truck." And so it was done. The church, in two pieces, traveled all the way from Big Trails to Ten Sleep, fording the creek between the two towns. They joined the two halves together again on a new foundation next to the Ten Sleep church, and the former church building became a community center and fellowship hall.

Even a couple of years into his stay in the Big Horn Basin, Dick still found himself getting used to the way the people did things there. When it came time to put a new bathroom in the Ten Sleep building, one of the church members, a plumber named Wayne Larkins, volunteered for the job. After setting the toilet and hooking everything up, he said, "Hey, we have to have a vent for this toilet." He needed to make a hole in the slanted ceiling. Normally, you'd use a plumb bob to be sure the hole was in the right place, but nobody had one handy.

"How are we going to get this thing lined up?" Dick inquired. He didn't want to see a hole drilled in the roof in the wrong place.

Larry Warner, another church member, pushed his hat back on his forehead, looked at Dick for a moment, muttered, "I'll be right back," and headed toward his pickup truck. A few moments later he returned carrying a .22 rifle. Pointing the gun upward to where the hole should be and using a level to make sure it was perpendicular, he then pulled the trigger, shooting a .22 round right through the roof. Then he climbed onto the roof, and, using the bullet hole as a guide, cut the larger hole for the vent. It fit perfectly.

Meanwhile, Ardis was busy setting up some much-needed technology for the churches in the Worland district. None of them had ever had a bulletin. She took the project on. Dick scrounged leftover bulletin blanks from one of the larger churches in the area. Then he rigged up a reel-to-reel tape recorder with a foot switch so that Ardis could type the notes he dictated. They bought a mimeograph machine, and soon all the Adventist churches in the district had regular church bulletins, each one with its own specific announcements.

Ardis and Dick's first child, Erik, was born during their second year in Worland at the Washakie Memorial Hospital, right across the street from where they lived. The doctor, who also happened to be the Mormon bishop, jokingly instructed Ardis on when she should deliver in typical Worland fashion. "Just be sure it's not on the first day of hunting season," he admonished.

"Well, if you're not available," she countered, "should I call the vet?"

"No, because he'll be hunting with me."

Ardis and Dick invited his parents for a visit when the baby was born. Their rented house was roomy, and they knew the parents were eager to see their grandson. Ardis was still in the hospital when they arrived.

At first, things went well, but then, while Dick's parents were visiting with Ardis in her hospital room, she had a surprise visit from an old classmate. Anna Streeter lived a couple hours away in the town of Buffalo. The women were close friends. Streeter had driven almost 100 miles to visit Ardis and could stay only for a short while. She wanted to be sure to get across the mountains again before dark.

Ardis was happy to see her old friend, and the two were soon involved in animated talk, catching up on each other's lives. Dick's mother felt left out of the conversation, and she walked out of the room. Dick stayed with Anna and Ardis until Anna left shortly thereafter. Then he went home to find his parents packing to leave, even though they had intended to stay for several more days. Extremely angry, Mom felt that both he and Ardis had ignored and insulted her, preferring their friend's company to hers.

"Look, Mom," he tried to reason with her, "Anna had a short window of time for her visit. You're here for several days. You must know that we weren't trying to snub you."

But she wouldn't listen to anything he had to say. Her jealousy and rage were irrational and intractable. Dick's father put their suitcases in the car, and they drove off without another word.

It was another example of his mother's growing problems. And it didn't end there. She refused to take their phone calls. Occasionally Dad would write a note or sneak out to the drugstore and call them from there. Ardis and Dick were determined not to break the lines of communication. They kept writing once a week or so, sending pictures of Erik, but it was more than six months before they eventually got a response. Finally there came a slight thaw, but the strain in the family never went away.

The Adventist churches banded together to give Ardis a baby shower. In one of those odd twists of fate that seem to occur often among Adventists, the same churches had given a shower for her mother, Arline, before Ardis' birth. Amazingly, there were even a few people present who had attended it.

Young Erik got his Wyoming pioneer credentials early, when Ardis and Dick got invited to a branding down in Thermopolis when the baby was only 2 weeks old. But it was the Worland church that adopted him as he grew. He and Alden and Janice's son, Barry, who was a little older than Erik, became the favorites of the congregation.

One Wednesday evening during prayer meeting, when Erik was about 2, he was kneeling next to his father during prayer. Archie Harvard, one of the old-timers in the congregation, was praying. The man tended to be a bit long-winded. When the child figured Archie had prayed long enough, he piped up, "Amen!" Pausing only for a moment, Harvard then kept right on praying. Soon they heard the little voice again—"Amen." By the time Erik got to his third amen, the entire prayer group was collapsing with laughter.

As Erik outgrew his shower-gift outfits, the Worland congregation was also outgrowing its little white church. It wasn't that the membership had increased significantly—it hadn't. But without more space, it never would. They couldn't have evangelistic meetings or do community outreach in their tiny building. Even inviting visitors was a problem.

Dick and the church's lay leaders pondered what to do about it. Should they build, buy another building, or was there some other solution? Money was tight, so it wasn't an easy problem. It became a regular subject of conversation—that sometimes erupted into arguments—at board meetings, but nobody had come up with an answer.

About this time Dick received an invitation to go elk hunting with Alden Curtis' dad, Clayton, and a friend. Clayton was an optometrist and the town's mayor, but he was also a rugged outdoorsman. Dick had never been hunting before and had never shot at anything but a Coke bottle, although as a kid he had spent plenty of time doing just that. But in the interest of "building relationships," he acquired a hunting license, oiled up Uncle Ray's old, reconditioned Remington bolt-action rifle, and joined the hunting party. He wanted to be a part of his members' lives, and if hunting was what it took, a-hunting he would go.

It was just about sunup on a cold winter morning, and Dick and his two companions were high in the mountains, wading through snow eight inches deep. The three of them fanned out through the forest. Spotting elk tracks everywhere, Dick focused his attention on following them. All at once he realized he could no longer see or hear the other two men. He'd never felt so alone—he was in the wilderness by himself, with no compass.

Being Dick, however, he was less alarmed that he might be lost in the wilderness—*I can always follow my tracks back,* he thought—and more concerned that he might reveal his total lack of hunting prowess. Soon he found himself in a large open area. It seemed a likely place for elk to congregate, so he hunkered down to watch. Then he thought he saw something moving at the other end of the field, more than 100 yards away. Slowly he brought his binoculars up to his eyes, focused, and there stood a five-point elk! Excited, he dropped the binoculars in the snow.

Pulling himself together, Dick braced his body against a tree, took a bead, and waited for the elk to walk into his sights. Then he pulled the trigger. The huge animal went down. A second shot at close range finished him off.

But Dick didn't have a clue what to do next. Was he supposed to skin the animal? He'd cleaned fish, but an elk was on a whole different scale, and he had no hunting knife. When he searched his pockets, the sharpest thing he could put his hands on was the key to the Karmann Ghia. While he was resourceful, even he wasn't going to skin an elk with a Volkswagen key.

Then he thought to himself, *Tag it—you have to tag the animal.* Yes, he had a tag in his pocket—it came with the hunting license. He felt around for a pen or a pencil. Nothing. *I can't leave this beast here untagged,* he thought. *Somebody else could come along and claim it.* It was *his* elk. So he cranked the bullet out of his gun and, using its soft lead tip, wrote his name and the date on the tag. Then he realized he had no way to tie the tag to the antlers. So he used the VW key to unravel the top of his sock, removed a long thread, and with that attached the tag to the antlers.

The other hunters came into view as Dick was tying his tag. They were suitably impressed. These two experienced hunters didn't get anything at all that day, and this novice, this neophyte, had dropped a five-point bull elk. Later Dick skinned the animal, tanned the hide, and mounted the head, teaching himself taxidermy along the way. Ardis, however, drew the line at having it in her living room, and eventually the elk found a home at the Glacier View Ranch in Colorado, where it still hangs today.

But the elk wasn't the real prize that day. Clayton Curtis was euphoric about Dick bagging an elk. Never had he had a minister go hunting with him before, much less beat him at his own game. On the way back down to Worland, hauling the elk in a trailer behind his vehicle, Clayton pulled up at a beautiful spot on a hill overlooking the town.

"I want to show you something, Dick," he said, getting out of his Jeep and swinging his arm in an arc to indicate the land where they were standing. "Wouldn't this be a good place for a new church?" Opening the door on his side of the Jeep, Dick looked around. "Yeah, it's a fantastic place for a church."

"I own this lot. I'm thinking of giving it to the church." Dick nearly fell out of the Jeep, because the man was serious! The church members began working on plans to build a new church on the lot. The owner of the adjacent property, however, didn't want to have a church next door to him. The congregation elected Clayton to talk to him. "If you don't want us to build, buy the land," he told the neighbor. The man took him up on his offer, and Clayton donated the proceeds of the sale to the church.

Now the members began looking for another piece of land to build on. They narrowed the search down to four lots, but the congregation couldn't agree on any one of them. Some felt strongly that the most expensive option, a nice lot across from the new high school, was the only choice. Others argued that any investment was too much for the little congregation to consider. After all, one man said, "We have only 27 members, counting the preacher and his wife, and besides, the whole project is creating friction where we didn't have any."

Dick refused to weigh in. "You people are going to live with this decision long after I'm gone," he told them. All those tough, hardy, frontier types had strong opinions and weren't afraid to voice them. The debate got more than a little hot. Tensions ran high.

Finally Dick suggested a secret ballot after labeling the lots by number. After he led the congregation in a heartfelt prayer for wisdom, everybody voted, marking their choices on 3" x 5" cards. When all the cards were counted, it was unanimous.

Everybody had voted for the lot across from the high school. Dick felt relieved. In his opinion it was by far the best choice. With the Lord's help this group of independent souls had found a unified vision. When he announced the results of the vote, there wasn't a dry eye in the house, not even his own.

Once the congregation got over that hump, there was zero friction as they built the church. It became a true labor of love. Dick drew up the basic plan himself, and when church members had trouble visualizing the finished product, he went home, cut up some file folders, and constructed a scale model.

They hired a general contractor, but there was no building committee—the whole church served as that. Every man, woman, and child contributed somehow. Besides raising money, they carried rocks, dug footings, mixed mortar, and laid block. They worked long hours, shoulder to shoulder. Ardis and Dick pitched in, spending every spare moment at the job site, with baby Erik in his stroller, happily looking on.

The whole community became aware of the little congregation that was building a big church with their own hands. On Sunday afternoons, after the other churches in town let out, the Adventists would look up from their labors to see a parade of cars driving by to check on their progress. That congregation of 27 constructed a structure that would seat about 90 people, with a kitchen, a multipurpose room, two bathrooms, a furnace room, and a plan for future expansion. And when the church was dedicated in 1968, it was completely paid for, with some leftover money in the bank.

The finished edifice was a thing to be proud of, built of rosy-hued block and accented with beautifully laid-up travertine stone, inside and out. It even had a small steeple on top and was a testament to the spirit of the Wyoming people who created it—to their marvelous, giving, generous hearts. It was also a testament to a God-wrought miracle of unity, a beacon of light right in the middle of Worland, Wyoming, across from the high school. And it still is, nearly 50 years later. And best of all, the congregation has continued to grow.

Chapter 13

"I Could Have Helped This Kid"

One hot day in the summer of 1968 Dick was working at Mills Spring Ranch, a church-owned camp in the mountains above Casper, Wyoming. Although he had never once gone away to camp as a kid, he now found himself pulling summer duty as a boys' director at one for preteen kids.

He had spent the previous few weeks wrangling the boys, managing counselors, and directing camp programs. But he enjoyed the chance to work with kids, although it meant being away from Ardis and Erik.

That's why he had been looking forward to today. His wife was driving up from Worland, a long hot road trip of approximately 200 miles. She'd be bringing a vanload of kids for next week's camp and taking home a group of campers who'd spent the previous week at the ranch. Dick had bought a secondhand Volkswagen bus just for such errands.

Dick was standing in an open grassy field at the top of a hill encircled by tall pines when the blue camper van came into view. All the windows were down, and kids' faces and arms hung out of every one. The van raised a cloud of dust as Ardis pulled into the unpaved parking area.

As the children poured out of the bus, he gave her a quick hug before she left to manage her young charges and turn them over to their counselors. The changeover day was always a bit chaotic, but, if all went well, they would be able to grab a few moments together before Ardis loaded up the bus and headed home again.

He chose a shady spot under a pine tree to meet his wife. When she walked across the field toward him, she had an envelope in her hand and a serious look on her face. She held the letter out. "I know this is addressed to you, honey, but I opened it. You need to read it right away."

Taking the long, official-looking white envelope, he read the return address. It was from the General Conference of Seventh-day Adventists. His heart rate increased slightly. District pastors in Wyoming didn't usually get correspondence from the world headquarters office of the church. It had to be serious. Feigning a calm he didn't feel, he said, "You mean, read it right now?" even as he removed the letter from the envelope.

His eyes went first to the signature. The letter was from Clark Smith, the director of the National Service Organization. Dick knew the NSO was the office of the Adventist Church that dealt with military affairs. He had met Smith at Andrews University when the official had visited the campus and given a lecture on military issues and chaplaincy.

Dick remembered being among a group of students that had talked with Smith afterward. Dick's attitude then, as it was now, was to keep an open mind about all the various avenues of ministry in which God might lead him. His impression then had been that while Smith spoke enthusiastically about a career in chaplaincy in general terms, when it came to specifics, his attitude was definitely "Don't call us, we'll call you."

Well, Smith was calling. "We have been asked to fill an opening in the Army for a chaplain, and you meet all of the criteria to fill that slot," the letter read. Then Smith had added, "We don't have any other candidates who meet all the criteria. If you don't accept this call, the church will lose the opportunity to put a chaplain in the Army." (*OK*, Dick thought wryly to himself, *so no pressure.*)

The National Service Organization served as the endorser for the Seventh-day Adventist Church. Only 12 Adventist chaplains served in the various branches of the armed services at the time. The military required that any candidate for a chaplaincy position be vetted by that candidate's denomination—a process the Army calls endorsement. The NSO and Clark Smith were acting in that capacity for the Adventist Church.

How was it that 28-year-old Dick Stenbakken, serving in his first pastorate, not yet ordained, could be the only possible chaplaincy candidate among all Adventist ministers? The answer was pretty simple. The Army's requirements for a chaplain, in addition to the usual health and security clearances, were a college degree, at least two years of pastoral experience, and a Bachelor or Master of Divinity degree.

Dick's 1965 seminary graduating class had only a dozen students who had taken a full three years of study and received such a degree. Most of those graduates had gone into teaching or research. Thus he possessed what was a rare thing at the time—a combination of both the required training and experience.

Now he had received an invitation to go on active duty in the Army.

Could this be what God had prepared him to do? The last paragraph leaped out at him: "If you accept this call, there's no doubt that you will end up in Vietnam within the first year." Well, that was straightforward—and not unexpected. The United States had nearly a half million American troops on duty in Vietnam in the summer of 1968. A need for ministry certainly existed in the combat zone.

Ardis stood quietly, Erik in her arms, waiting for his reaction. Glancing up, he smiled his usual enigmatic smile. "Well, this sounds interesting." Ardis nodded, having been pretty sure how he would respond. She knew his commitment, and they were a team.

The letter may have come from the General Conference, but they believed their call to ministry arrived from God. They would consider the opportunity carefully and prayerfully. Ardis joined him in the shady spot under the pine tree, and they talked quietly, their minds crowded with possibilities, questions, and memories.

Dick thought of Sammy Lee Dellos, a young man from Ten Sleep. He remembered him often, never without a sense of frustration and pain. Sammy was a typical Wyoming kid who had joined the Army to see the world beyond his home town. Finishing his basic training at Fort Riley, Kansas, he had received orders to go to Vietnam with Alpha Company, First Battalion, Sixteenth Infantry Regiment.

Before shipping out, he came home on leave. Some of his family attended the Ten Sleep Adventist Church. The young man accompanied them to a series of evangelistic meetings. There was little else to do in a town with fewer than 300 inhabitants.

But as the meetings progressed, Sammy realized that he needed to recommit his life to the Lord, and on the last Friday night of the series, he asked to be rebaptized. Because he was about to be deployed, the baptism took place the next morning. Dick wasn't even there—it was his first week in Wyoming. He and Ardis had attended the Worland church that Sabbath.

On Sunday morning Sammy left for Vietnam. Dick met him at the Worland Municipal Airport, along with his family and friends. He and Sammy had only a few moments to get to know each other before the plane took off. A stocky young man with an open, round face, Sammy was 23 years old, his blue eyes clear and steady, his blond hair cut in the usual Army buzz.

In their few moments together Dick sensed that Sammy was sincere about deepening his religious awakening. He knew that the young man needed spiritual guidance and support. They had prayer together, and in those few short moments the two young men, only a few years apart in age, established a connection. "I hope you'll let me hear from you from time to time," Dick told him, putting an arm around his shoulder and shaking his hand. "I'd love to stay in touch with you as your pastor."

Dick knew that every unit in the Army had a chaplain. He suggested that Sammy get in touch with his when he got to Vietnam. The chaplain could be of help to Sammy. He'd be right there—not thousands of miles away.

Soon after he arrived in Vietnam, Sammy wrote to Dick. "I went to see the chaplain," his first letter said, "but I just didn't feel comfortable. When I walked into his office, he was sitting with a bunch of guys. They were drinking beer, smoking cigars, and telling jokes."

Dick was sure that couldn't be typical of all the chaplains in Vietnam, and perhaps Sammy had misinterpreted what he had seen. But that unfortunate first impression meant that the young man's chaplain wasn't going to be much help to him when it came to spiritual guidance.

Dick wrote back to Sammy, and the two corresponded regularly, starting a long-distance friendship and mentorship. The soldier asked perceptive spiritual questions and was happily digging into deeper Bible study. Then one terrible day Sammy's family was notified that their son had died in action—the victim of a land mine.

Once more Dick was at the airport to meet Sammy, but this time it was to receive his flag-draped coffin. He felt a crushing sense of failure and loss. *If I'd been that chaplain in Vietnam, I could have helped this kid,* he thought. The image of that flag-covered coffin still haunted him.

Shaking his head, he returned to the present. Folding Clark Smith's letter, he replaced it in its envelope. *By God's grace I could meet the needs of guys like Sammy,* he thought. But was he the best person for this assignment? Was it the right time in his life to make such a drastic change? And what about his family? He had a wife and a small son. The Army would be a far cry from their quiet life in Wyoming. Was it fair to subject Ardis to the strain of having a husband in a combat zone?

He needed some advice. Not just any kind—he must talk to somebody with the knowledge and experience to help him make sense of the offer. Of all the people in the world, he could think of only one such person—Jim Harris. Harris was the youth director for what was then the Central Union of Seventh-day Adventists. The man had experience, all right. Shot down during World War II, he had spent time in a prisoner of war camp. Dick knew his advice would be invaluable. A straight shooter, he had tons of leadership know-how.

As Dick glanced up from the letter, his eyes focused on a square-jawed man sitting in a folding chair, writing on a pad in his lap, less than 35 feet away. When he looked more closely, he realized that it was Jim Harris. Dick realized that this was a God-appointed moment. So he and Ardis walked over to Jim, and Dick asked, "Could we interrupt you for a moment?"

Jim looked up from under a shock of sandy hair and grinned. "Sure, Dick." Dick didn't say another word—just handed him the letter and waited while he read it.

Jim scanned the page, and then glanced up at Dick, a big grin on his face. "Do it," he said, almost shouting. "Do it!" Then, lowering his voice, he added, "I'll deny this if you tell anybody else, but I've thought many, many times that I would have liked to have been a chaplain. I think it would be a marvelous ministry."

The campers waiting for their ride back to town were getting restless, so Ardis and Dick said their goodbyes. Loading up the VW bus, she drove away.

When he returned to Worland, he and Ardis spent many hours talking and praying about the opportunity. Finally, they made up their minds— they'd go. Dick wrote back to Clark Smith saying that he would be interested in an Army chaplaincy.

The way the protocol worked, once he had confirmed that he would accept it, the official "call" would be sent down from the church's General Conference to the union conference level, and then on to the Wyoming Conference. His response to Clark set that process in motion late in the summer of 1968. The wheels, while they may turn slowly, do turn once you get them started.

But there was one hitch. Dick was not yet ordained. The unwritten rule was that a pastor should have at least four years of experience before being ordained. For him, that would mean waiting until the end of the year. So the plan was that he would be ordained in January of 1969. After that, the church could officially endorse him to the Army, and the Army's medical, paperwork, and security checking processes could begin.

Life went on in the Big Horn Basin. The couple kept busy with their usual round of duties. In his spare time he worked on a pulpit and Communion table he was building as a gift to the Ten Sleep church. They didn't tell anyone in their congregations about their plans. Nothing was certain yet. They hadn't signed on any dotted line.

And just to be absolutely sure that it was God's will, they did something that many Christians do when confronted with a life-changing decision. Like Gideon, the Old Testament leader of Israel, they "laid out the fleece." They asked the Lord for a sign.

It was time to tell their parents about the possibility of his becoming a chaplain, and the certainty that, if he did, he would go to Vietnam. If both sets of parents accepted the idea, they'd consider it evidence that God was behind the plan.

They talked to Ardis' parents first. Avery and Arline Dick had recently returned to the U.S. from a second mission assignment in the Philippines. Wyoming wasn't so far away from Canada where they now lived, and they made the trip down to visit their grandson—and his parents—as often as they could. On their next visit, after they had cleared the dinner dishes away and tucked Erik into bed, the four of them relaxed in the living room.

"We have something important to discuss with you," Dick began. And he laid out the possibilities, both positive and negative. He emphasized that they hadn't given their final word yet. Avery and Arline understood some of what the church was asking of their son-in-law and their daughter— they had spent their entire lives in ministry. But they had concerns and questions.

The Stenbakkens and the Dicks stayed up late that night. They discussed all aspects of the situation, including the moral principle involved in ministering to men whose job it was to kill. Of course, Dick Stenbakken would not carry a weapon or be directly involved in combat. The Geneva Convention and United States law specified that all chaplains were noncombatants. But still, they knew that some might feel that Dick's presence in a combat zone could in some way endorse the actions of combatants.

On the other hand, who would require the ministry of a chaplain more than those involved in combat? Dick's philosophy was that if a person was in need of ministry, it didn't matter who or where they were. Ardis' parents agreed, and concluded that the chaplaincy could be a good field of service for him. They would be supportive. Not pleased, of course, that the family would be moving farther away from them, but still supportive.

Well, that was half of the "fleece." Actually, he had expected his in-laws to be encouraging, once they understood the nature of this opportunity.

His parents, however, were another story. He didn't look forward to telling them he was thinking of joining the Army and going to Vietnam. Oliver and Celia Stenbakken's level of commitment and involvement in his life was still extremely high. He was an only child—an adopted only child—and Celia had had difficulty accepting his marriage. There was a good chance one or both of his parents might go ballistic when they heard the news.

Dick, Ardis, and Erik made a trip to Denver. As they sat in the living room of the house he had grown up in, chatting, he said, "Well, there's something we need to discuss. I have received an interesting opportunity. It's not a done deal, but it's likely to become one very shortly." Once again, he laid out all the positives and negatives. Then he added, quietly, "What do you think?" Waiting for their response, he held his breath.

"You'd have a chance to work with people from all different denominations!" his father commented.

"What a marvelous opportunity for you to do ministry!" his mom added.

Dick was stunned. There had been no hysterics, no hand-wringing. Nobody had come unglued. Both his parents, while not eager to send their only son halfway around the world to a combat zone, were excited about the opportunity for the service that it would afford. They were totally supportive.

Ardis and Dick had no doubt that they had just witnessed a miracle. The elder Stenbakkens' reaction was an answer to prayer, plain and simple. It was an incredible spiritual affirmation of his call to the ministry of chaplaincy. Now it was time to put the fleece away. Their decision was final. They announced their plans to their church members in their Christmas newsletter.

His ordination took place in the Worland church in January of 1969. At the time it was unusual to have an ordination in a pastor's own church—most occurred at camp meeting in the summer—but this one couldn't wait. The Army would not start its processing until the ordination was a done deal.

On that sunny but cold Sabbath afternoon the church was filled. Adventist Church leaders officiated, with Ardis' dad conducting a part of the service. The congregation contained more from the local community than church members, including many of Dick's friends from the Kiwanis Club and colleagues from the ministerial association.

From his seat on the platform Dick recognized Cyril Hymlovski, the Catholic priest; Peter Sethre, the Lutheran pastor; and Don Cooper, the

Presbyterian pastor. He noticed the Mormon bishop's wife seated about halfway down from the front. Later he would learn that the bishop, who had intended to be there, had been called out to deliver a baby. (He was also the town's obstetrician.)

Also, Dick spotted the electrician who had worked on the church building, as well as the plumbers and the lumber supplier. So many members of the community had had a part in building the church, and they had turned out in force. *I'm so glad we're holding this service here,* he thought. *This is where I've earned the privilege of ordination.* And he recognized that the ordination service itself was yet another opportunity to reach out to the community.

More months passed. The wheels did indeed turn slowly. It had been nearly a year since Dick had received that initial letter from the NSO. Now it was June 1969, and he was finally making plans to go to New York for chaplain school.

Ardis would be traveling to Canada to stay with her parents until he knew where the Army would assign him. Once he completed his initial chaplain's training, they would be together again. It would be difficult to say goodbye, especially because Ardis was pregnant with their second child, but they knew that such partings were part of the commitment they had made.

They were busy those last few weeks, tying up loose ends and saying goodbye to the many good friends they had made in the district. Dick planned to preach at the Ten Sleep church on his last Sabbath, using the pulpit and Communion table he had crafted.

When the Big Horn *Daily News* ran a story about his leaving for the chaplain's course at the end of the week, he got a call from the Methodist church. "We know you're preaching your farewell sermon on Sabbath, but would you be willing to stay over and take our worship service on Sunday?"

"I'd be honored," he replied, even though it meant getting a later start than he would have liked on the long drive to New York. So he preached two sermons that weekend, and both the Adventist and the Methodist congregations gave him warmhearted sendoffs.

To Dick, it seemed especially fitting that his last sermon in his first pastoral district was preached in a Methodist church. It fit his philosophy, his rock-solid conviction that his ministry should expand beyond his own church members—that it should be to all people, regardless of denomination or location.

Chapter 14

"Yes, Sir! Right Away, Sir!"

Dick was sworn into the Army at the local armory, a squat, mud-colored block building located on a side street in Worland. Inside, the color scheme changed to bile green, accented by steel-gray desks and filing cabinets. Portraits of men in uniform decorated the walls. There was no ceremony.

Dick wore street clothes, and the process was low-key and informal, dominated by paperwork. One day he was a civilian pastor in a small Wyoming town, and the next day he was Captain Richard Stenbakken, a chaplain in the United States Army, headed for Vietnam.

Soon he discovered that officers received a clothing allowance to purchase all the items they required. The list was long and included shirts, ties, belts, shoes, and caps. In addition, he must have formal dress blues, a green dress uniform, and everyday khakis, fatigues, and boots. Beyond that he needed an overcoat, a raincoat, and a windbreaker. And more. The only things the Army gave officers before going to Vietnam were two sets of jungle fatigues and two pairs of combat boots.

He purchased his first dress uniform from his old friend Alden Curtis. Drafted into the Army as an optometrist, Alden was finishing his two-year tour of duty about the time Dick was sworn in. Curtis had been a captain. All Alden's old uniform required was a little alteration and a chaplain insignia.

Dick and the blue Karmann Ghia arrived in New York for Army Chaplain School in early summer. Classes convened at Fort Hamilton in lower Brooklyn, which was located right on the water. From their classroom windows, the students had a view of Staten Island and the Verrazano-Narrows Bridge. The traffic on the bridge, and the boats moving through the Narrows, provided constant distraction. It was a long, long way from Worland, Wyoming.

The class was large—about 70 students. Roughly half were like Dick, preparing for active duty. The remaining members were seminary students or reserve chaplains who would be going back to their units.

The basic chaplain's course did not teach you how to be a minister. The assumption was that you already knew theology and pastoral care. The focus was on applying your clergy skills in a military setting. Dick studied military regulations, rules, customs, and rank structure. He learned how to work within the command; how to coordinate with other people in the military. The idea was to take the knowledge and skills you already had and learn to use them in a totally new environment. And of course, there were hours and hours of running and push-ups, as well as classes in map reading and navigation.

Once more Dick had found something he could take to like a duck to water. The military was structured and well organized. Nothing was unplanned or done off-the-cuff. That sort of precision fit him like a glove. He had found his niche. And even more, he enjoyed the interaction with his fellow students.

As an Army chaplain, he would be responsible for the spiritual welfare of soldiers of all faiths. He appreciated the opportunity to learn more about other religions and the various kinds of chapel services he might be called on to perform. His roommate was a Christian Scientist, and they enjoyed long conversations and built a good sense of camaraderie.

Since Dick's weekends were free, he often spent them with old friends in the area. Evangelist Ron Halverson was conducting a series of meetings in Brooklyn. Dick heard about them, showed up, and offered to do whatever he could to help. In his spare time he visited New York City with some of his fellow chaplaincy students. They rode the subway and saw the sights. He was not in Wyoming anymore.

Dick adjusted happily to the Army routine. He enjoyed shining his boots and keeping his uniform in order. His belt's brass buckle was the bane of every soldier. It had to gleam at all times, and soldiers spent hours cleaning it nightly, only to have the shine spoiled by even one fingerprint. Retrieving some car wax from the Karmann Ghia's front-facing trunk, he coated the clean belt buckle with it, buffed it out, and discovered that the shine lasted all week. When he shared his secret with his buddies, his room became a popular place. While it was his first experience as an Army wheeler-dealer, it wouldn't be his last.

While he was learning the ins and outs of chaplaincy, Ardis was 2,000 miles away, getting on-the-job training in what it meant to be a chaplain's wife. She had always been a strong, self-sufficient woman, and she wasn't about to whine or cry about missing her husband, even as her pregnancy progressed. But as the time for the birth of their second child neared, Dick considered taking a weekend liberty to fly to Western Canada to be with his wife.

Even if he picked the right weekend, he knew he would have to be back early Monday morning, no matter what. The Army accepted no excuses. He and Ardis discussed it on the phone, agonizing over whether he should take the chance. Finally they decided he wouldn't fly out. "If I do come," he reasoned, "about the time I have to leave for the airport, you could go into labor—and I couldn't stay." They agreed that that would be worse than not being there at all.

Baby Rikki was born early on a Sabbath morning in August. As it turned out, Dick could have been there. As difficult as it was to be away when his daughter was born, however, it was a positive aspect. He would be ministering to many young men who couldn't be present when their children were born. Missing his own daughter's birth was another link to the people he would serve. And the same was true for Ardis. She would later work with other chaplains' wives who were facing a similar situation.

The chaplaincy class went to Fort Dix, New Jersey, for field exercises. One afternoon Dick and his fellow student chaplains were introduced to the infiltration course. Crawling through sand and dirt, they slithered on their bellies under barbed wire and between eight-foot round pits surrounded by sandbags. But that was only the beginning. They returned to the course that night. Sitting on bleachers with bright floodlights illuminating the field, they received their instructions. This time, the instructors told them, they would traverse the course in the dark.

"But not total darkness," the course instructor said, with a sardonic smile. "Sometimes there will be other lights." Then they shut off the floodlights. The darkness was intense. When Dick held his hand up a few inches from his face, he couldn't see it. *This must be what it feels like to be blind,* he thought. Then the instructor blew his whistle, and four machine guns with tracer rounds opened up across the field they were about to crawl through. The instructor was right. That provided a little light.

The whistle blew again, and the trainees realized what those round pits were for. Blocks of TNT set off from the pits created massive explosions. "Uh, don't crawl into the pits," the instructor said wryly.

Dick was sitting next to a Catholic seminarian, an individual with a droopy, beagle-like face. The man turned to him, sounding even more hangdog than usual. "I think I'm going to be sick," he moaned.

But they did it. With live ammunition overhead and explosions that bounced them off the ground, they climbed up ladders and over logs, down into sand, and squirmed under barbed wire.

They could feel the change in air pressure as the bullets whizzed over their heads. Everybody made it—even the seminarian. And Dick would do it again—and again. When serving as a chaplain to new recruits he often did the infiltration course with them. A chaplain goes where the troops do. It's called a "ministry of presence." You can't minister to soldiers if you don't crawl where they crawl.

Next the chaplaincy trainees went through a gas chamber. First they learned what to do with a gas mask—how to put it on and clear it. Wearing their gas masks, instructors marched them, about a dozen at a time, into a ramshackle wooden building filled with what looked like a white fog. It was tear gas, a nonlethal chemical weapon that nonetheless causes severe pain on contact with mucus membranes or any sweaty area of the human body. The trainees did well while wearing their masks—a good lesson in the mask's efficacy—but not good enough to satisfy the drill sergeant in charge.

Wearing his own mask, of course, the sergeant tapped each trainee on the shoulder, one by one. "Take off your mask," he said, speaking slowly and calmly, "and say and spell your first, middle, and last name, your home of record, and your service number. If you do this too quickly and I can't understand you, you will have to repeat the whole thing."

It was a hot day at Fort Dix, and the trainees were sweating in the confined space. Any place where they perspired felt as if it was on fire—a clear indication that tear gas attacks the skin. "Keep your eyes open and look straight at me," the sergeant warned. "If you don't, I'll stand here till you do."

When Dick's turn came, he took his mask off and stared at the sergeant. Instantly he felt as if somebody had poked their fingers in his eyes—big, ugly fingers gouging with dirty, ragged fingernails. He felt the burning and tearing as the tear gas began to interact with mucus membranes in his nose, eyes, and throat, but he stood at attention and did what the sergeant had directed him to do. Then, when the noncom felt that he had been sufficiently tortured, the man dismissed him.

The idea now was to walk, not run, to the door. Two more big sergeants waited at the exit to make sure you complied. If you bolted for the door before being dismissed, they would grab you and haul you back, and you'd start all over again. By this time you would have breathed a few breaths. Your lungs would be on fire and your eyeballs melting—or so it would seem. Now the lesson was complete. A gas mask is your friend. Exposed to tear gas, you became a believer.

Going through such experiences with fellow ministers, many of whom had by this time become friends, had, surprisingly, its funny moments. They were a mixed group—some older, some younger, some overweight and out of shape. The physical training pared you down if you needed it, or if you were a runt, it built you up. Freddie Winger, a wiry, slender, curly-haired rabbi, kept them all laughing. Getting his instructions before going into the tear gas hut, he quipped, "Haven't my people suffered enough?"

Then, on September 4, 1969, chaplain school concluded and Dick immediately began his first assignment at Fort Benning, Georgia, where he would be a chaplain for a basic training unit. The Army assigned him a chaplain sponsor—a seasoned officer who would help him get settled into his new post and show him around. Once again, Dick admired military structure and organization. Thinking back to his old life, he mused on how useful it would have been as a new pastor to have had such a "sponsor."

Now that he had his first post, Ardis and the children could join him, and the first order of business was to find a house to rent. No on-post housing was available, so Dick checked the newspaper, asked around, and found a possible house not too far from the base. He contacted the realtor, who couldn't meet him right away. Too eager to get Ardis and the children moved to wait, he decided to have a look at the place himself. The house was locked up, but he walked around outside, peering in the windows, hoping to find that it would meet their needs. As he looked in the front window he heard a woman's voice behind him. "Can I help you?"

When he turned around, the woman's polite smile disappeared, replaced by an expression of horror. Her eyes opened wide, and she gasped, bringing her hand to her throat. She staggered slightly, and he reached out to steady her, fearing that she was about to faint.

Immediately, by God's grace, he realized what had happened. She was a serviceman's wife with a husband in Vietnam. When she saw Dick's chaplain's uniform, she assumed he was there to notify her of her husband's death. In a split second he figured it out. "I'm looking for a house to rent," he said quickly.

Dick did rent the house, on a quiet side street at 334 Henson Avenue in Columbus, Georgia. A low brick ranch, it had a spacious front yard and big trees, perfect for a growing family. It was time to bring his home. Dick caught a flight to Denver, and Ardis flew down to meet him, with 2-year-old Erik and 10-day-old Rikki in tow. Finally, he got to meet his little daughter and get reacquainted with Erik.

The family's ministry began right next door with a young widow with a little boy about Erik's age. Her husband had died several months before in Vietnam. A lieutenant, he had just arrived in Vietnam and was being driven to his post, a fire support base out in the boonies. As he'd climbed out of the jeep, a sniper shot had killed him.

It was a sobering thing for Ardis and Dick to live among families whose loved ones were in Vietnam or who had died there, all the while knowing that he would soon be leaving for the combat zone. The reality was quickly sinking in.

Shortly after Dick took up his assignment at Fort Benning, he began to collect information on all the Seventh-day Adventist personnel on the post. He went to the reception station and talked to the guys who made the dog tags. When he turned up one that said SDA, he'd contact the recruit and ask him if he wanted to go to church. Dick discovered that for the first time ever, a lot of noncombatant medics had begun going through the base. The post was the home of the Airborne School. The Army needed qualified airborne medics in Vietnam, so they were taking Adventist guys coming out of Fort Sam Houston with medical training and giving them parachute training at Fort Benning.

Dick made it his immediate mission to round up Adventist recruits who wanted to attend church. He would pile them into his VW van, take them to Sabbath services, and then he and Ardis would bring them home to Henson Avenue for a home-cooked meal.

They had barely moved in when they invited the first vanload of soldiers home after church. Ardis shared what food they had. Since they hadn't had time to go to the grocery store yet, the food was mostly what they had carried in the van for their journey. Those young soldiers ate everything they had on hand until no food remained in the house. Erik loved having all the "big brothers" around, and they treated him as a special pet.

After lunch the soldiers visited a while, and then, one by one, they stretched out on the floor and went to sleep. It was bliss for these recruits to relax in the Stenbakken home after a week of running everywhere they went.

By about 2:00 in the afternoon the house looked as if a major disaster had occurred there, with young men collapsed on every available flat surface. Such Sabbaths were a great opportunity for ministry for Dick and Ardis. Many of the young recruits had been only peripheral members of their home churches, but now, facing Vietnam, life had become more serious.

Ken Shade was one of the names Dick turned up while searching through dog tags. Ken was in one of the basic training units. Dick drove over to the unit and walked into the training area. All the sergeants snapped to attention when Captain Stenbakken approached. "May I help you, sir?"

"I'm looking for Private Ken Shade."

"Yes, sir, right away, sir!" and they summoned Private Shade straight out of training. Dick saw him approaching—a skinny, very young and frightened-looking African American guy with eyes the size of saucers.

The sergeants were showing Dick all kinds of respect, and that only scared the young man more. "Private Shade reporting, sir!" the kid saluted, his arm shaking slightly.

"Are you a Seventh-day Adventist, private?" The young man's eyes got even wider. Was persecution about to start, right here?

"Relax, private. I'm an Adventist chaplain." Shade was so happy he nearly hugged Dick. They chatted for a while, and Dick learned that Ken was only 17 and that his grandmother had raised him. He had talked her into letting him go into the military because he wanted to be on his own. Now he was in his first week of infantry basic training—and he was scared.

"Chaplain, I've made a huge mistake," he confessed. "I'm willing to serve as a medic, but I have realized that my faith won't allow me to train with a weapon. I can't do it, and I don't know what to do."

Recognizing a sincere conviction when he saw one, Dick worked with Ken and with his commander. He helped the young man to apply to be a noncombatant. While they waited for his noncombatant status to be recognized, the Army respected Ken's decision. Although he did all the infantry basic training, he never had to train with a weapon. His superiors saw to it that he got extra courses in first aid and other things when weapon training was going on until his application for noncombatant status came through.

So Ken became part of the Stenbakken family, going to church each week in the van, helping to eat Dick and Ardis out of house and home, and sleeping on the carpet after Sabbath dinner. Erik loved all the soldiers, but he loved Ken the most. The best of buddies, they made a striking pair—tiny Erik so fair and white-haired, and Ken so dark.

Georgia in the late 1960s was not quite as color-blind as little Erik. Dick's vanload of Adventist soldiers included Caucasians, Hispanics, and Blacks. Sometimes they stayed for the potluck dinner after church. At one of them a church member came up to Dick.

"You know they have their own church on the other side of town," he said, inclining his head toward the Black soldiers.

Dick stood there for a moment, gripping a full plate of food with both hands. Then he took a breath. "The troops go with me wherever I go," he replied quietly. That wasn't the end of it, however. Next the pastor talked to him. Some of his members had shared their concerns about Dick bringing non-Whites to their church. He repeated his position. "As long as I go here, the troops go here," he said again. After that the issue faded.

Ken Shade got his orders to go to Fort Sam Houston for medical training. His bus left just before midnight on a Saturday night. He went to church with Dick and the family as usual, and late that night they drove him down to the bus station in Columbus. Erik knew Ken was leaving, and he wanted his buddy to carry him into the bus station. So Ken did, with the boy's parents walking behind, Dick carrying Ken's duffel bag. You could sense the hatred in the faces of the people around them, but it didn't matter. Ken was part of the family.

Dick's typical day at Fort Benning was busy. He'd be in his office by 7:30 in the morning. Some days he'd train with the troops. A fresh group of recruits arrived about every six weeks, and he tried to be wherever they'd be. At night he'd go through the infiltration course with them. He did it so many times that he kept a pair of boots and a set of fatigues just for the purpose.

Such training was a tough time for new recruits. You'd go over a wall and descend into a pit, then in pitch darkness, amid deafening explosions, with tracer bullets arcing fiery red streaks over your head, you'd eat dirt as you crawled under barbed wire. No, it wasn't for the faint of heart. But you had to complete the infiltration course correctly before you could advance to the next week's training. Mess up, and you were "recycled"—sent back to another unit. Nobody wanted that.

One night Dick had gone through the course with the latest recruits and, covered with mud and sand, was talking with some of the men, when one of the drill sergeants called, "Chaplain, we got a problem down here.

Kid won't go over the wall. We've coaxed him, threatened him, but he just refuses to go."

"OK, I'll come down." He found a young man, probably not yet out of his teens, apparently frozen with fear, unable to move.

"How're you doing, soldier?" Dick asked, putting his hand on the lad's shoulder. Looking at Dick in the dim light from the tracers, he noticed the cross on his helmet. "Are you a medic, sir?" he asked, looking even more frightened. Was he about to be taken away on a stretcher?

"No, son, I'm a chaplain. How may I help?"

"I'm not going over the wall," the kid said, shaking his head and backing away from Dick.

"Hey, I've already been over it. You can do it—follow me. We'll do it together—just stay right behind me."

Without waiting for a response, Dick just turned on his heel and headed toward the wall. A quick glance told him the recruit was right behind him. The two of them slithered and slid through the infiltration course, never more than two or three feet apart. When they got to the end, a huge cheer went up. Guys were whistling and clapping. "We made it!" Dick said with a grin, clapping the kid on the back. The drill sergeant was happy too. Nobody wanted the kid to recycle. And nobody had expected the chaplain—an officer—to get down in the dirt and lead him through.

Well, that wasn't a Bible study, Dick thought to himself, *but I'm thinking that trainee will never forget that there was a chaplain there to help him when he needed it.* Ministry was about loving people the way Jesus did—loving them enough to get down in an infiltration pit with them.

Ministry even extended to the shooting range. Recruits had to learn to fire an M14—a semiautomatic rifle. One day Dick watched as some of the soldiers took a firing test. "You ever fired a gun, Chaplain?" the company commander inquired.

"Yeah," Dick replied, thinking of his Coke bottle target practice as a kid, and his hunting experience in Wyoming with Uncle Ray's refurbished World War II rifle. "Yeah, I've done a little shooting."

"Want to try your hand?" It was a little unusual, but Dick had never seen another chaplain at the firing range, so there was no precedent.

The commander gave him a quick lesson in how the M14 worked and put him down in a standing foxhole. Dick braced the big gun against his right shoulder and rested it on the sandbags in front of him. Then he leaned forward in the firing position and clicked off the safety.

"When a target comes up, see if you can hit it," the officer instructed. Some of the drill sergeants had gathered around to watch. Dick could hear them snickering behind him. He had no doubt they were saying, "Betcha the chaplain doesn't even know where to point the thing."

It took Dick a couple shots to figure out the trajectory of the bullets, but then he hit 18 out of 20 targets, including those in his own lane and the lanes on both sides.

Well, that won him some spurs with the command. The soft-spoken, bespectacled chaplain could do things they weren't sure they could do. Dick wasn't surprised. He knew he had a good eye and a steady hand, and his reflexes were quick. It was all in a day's work for a chaplain headed for Vietnam.

Dick also taught the character guidance classes that all chaplains gave their basic training units—advising on military living, cooperation, and morality. He spent a good part of his time doing individual counseling. Then there was planning for the chapel service every Sunday, preparing bulletins, writing sermons, and conducting hospital visits.

The counseling part of his job was most interesting. One of the things he noticed was how forthright the young soldiers were. During his first week at Fort Benning a young man made an appointment to talk to him. Walking into Dick's office, he shut the door, sat down, and in about two minutes laid out his whole life—problems and all—holding nothing back.

To him, the chaplain was an officer—an authority figure. The soldier needed help. There was no dancing around the issues, no chatting for six weeks before they got down to business. Instead, he had instant acceptance of the role of a chaplain. The guy was direct and respectful. Neither he nor the chaplain had time for games. Dick saw the pattern repeated again and again.

It struck him how different it was from pastoral counseling. As a pastor, you were never sure how much a parishioner might reveal to you. They often required time to size you up. You needed time to build a rapport. Sometimes it took two months just to learn their middle name.

The military was different. These kids were drafted at 18 or 19 years of age. Some had never been away from home. Others were newly married and even new fathers. Counseling them was like working in an emergency room, raw and immediate. "Here's my problem. Help me." Constantly Dick prayed for divine guidance as he plunged ahead, reveling in the many opportunities to minister.

Dick was also learning more about the inner workings of the Army. Early on in his tour at Fort Benning, the infantry commander, a Lieutenant Colonel Johnson, had a talk with Dick that was to influence his entire military career. One day he invited him into his office. "Sit down, Chaplain," he said.

Wondering what the man had on his mind, Dick took a seat. "How much do you know about efficiency reports?" the commander asked. Dick knew the basics. Efficiency reports were an essential part of Army life. Your superiors evaluated you on a regular basis, and their written reports became a significant part of your Army record. Excellent reports meant promotions, and promotions meant pay raises. Get too many mediocre— or even just average—reports, and you were out.

"Let me share some reality with you, Chaplain," the officer continued. "I've been watching you, and I think you have potential. I'd like to help you."

By now Dick was listening with both ears. "It's your career, not mine," the man went on. "Here's how to help me write your report. Bring me a summary of your own at least once a quarter. Outline what you have done, what you plan to do, and what you need me to do to help you. Then, the next quarter, outline your progress. Show me statistics, numbers, and facts. Write your information in clear, short sentences."

Dick was beginning to see the light, and the commander could tell that he got it by the expression on his face. "That's right," Johnson nodded. "Give me sentences that I can put in my efficiency report on you. You, in essence, can write your own reports if you're willing to make the effort."

From that point on, throughout his entire Army career, Dick would follow that advice to the letter. Each time he met with a new superior officer, he'd ask, "What are the things you want me to accomplish?" He'd come prepared with a clipboard, and he'd write everything down. Then he'd prepare regular written summaries, detailing how he had responded to each item. It wasn't long before he noticed his own sentences showing up in his efficiency reports.

It made perfect sense. Officers were busy people—they had to write up a whole stack of reports every quarter. Why not give the people who held control over his ministry the information that would make their job easier—and help his career? As time went on, he observed that at least 90 percent of what was in his efficiency reports was stuff he had composed himself. He would never forget that hour Lieutenant Colonel Johnson had spent advising a very green chaplain.

Dick received his verbal orders for Vietnam in February of 1970. He and Ardis still hadn't unpacked all the boxes from their last move. The orders weren't a shock—they knew it was coming. Dick had understood that he would be going to the combat zone. That's where you go—where you're most needed.

Chapter 15

"I'm Not Even Going to Ask
You How You Did That!"

"Fill it up and clean the windshield, please," Dick said to the smiling filling station attendant somewhere in Arkansas. (This was back in the day when such services still existed.) Dick had just pulled his rig up to the pumps. He was driving his family to Canada in the two-toned-blue VW bus and towing the matching two-toned-blue Karmann Ghia behind. They were on their way from Fort Benning, Georgia, to Lacombe, Alberta.

The bus was packed to the roof with their possessions, and in the front seat of the Ghia, he had belted in two additional passengers—the mounted heads of a mule deer and an antelope, souvenirs of his hunting adventures in Wyoming and his taxidermy hobby.

"And could you check the windshield of the car in back," he asked the station attendant, unable to help himself. "The guys back there claim it's covered with bugs." Neither the ministry nor the Army had managed to dampen his offbeat sense of humor. He enjoyed the consternation on the station attendant's face and the way other cars passed them on the road, and then drifted back for a second look.

Dick and the long-suffering Ardis made good time on the long road trip, despite braving some wintry weather and traveling with a 2-year-old and a young baby. Dick had a 30-day leave before going to Vietnam—plenty of time to visit his parents in Denver on the way, and get Ardis and the children settled in with her parents in Canada.

Too soon, though, it was time for him to board the plane at the Calgary Airport. He was taking a commercial flight to San Francisco, where he'd hop a military transport for Vietnam. Walking across the tarmac, he looked back toward the terminal.

Ardis waited at the plate-glass window, baby Rikki in her arms. Erik stood beside her, his pale face and his hands in their red mittens pressed up against the glass. That picture imprinted itself indelibly on Dick's mind. The thought, unwelcome but real, went through his mind. *This could be the last time I ever see my family.* He knew that image would stay with him until the day he died.

Swallowing hard, he waved one last time and boarded the plane. He and Ardis had anticipated this moment. They'd prayed about it and knew how it was going to be. Their commitment to ministry was mutual. It always had been, and it always would be. But leaving was still hard, so hard.

Dick thought about the tradition of the flowers as he settled himself into his seat, and he felt a little better. This custom had started back when he was a pastor in the Big Horn Basin in Wyoming. Every Wednesday afternoon he'd make the trip from Worland down to a nursing home in Thermopolis to visit Rose Palmer, an elderly church member. Rose was 102 years old and well known in the area as the person who walked all the way from the Dakota Territory as a young woman.

Dick made a habit of stopping by the local florist to pick up a single flower for Rose. Sometimes it was a rose, sometimes a carnation or a daisy. No matter what the flower, she was delighted with the gift, and it soon dawned on him that there was someone else who would be just as pleased. He began picking up two flowers, one for Rose and one to take home to his wife, and a family ritual started.

Before he left for Vietnam, he had arranged with a florist to deliver a flower to Ardis every Friday afternoon. Although he knew he would be gone for a year, he had written a check for only six months, thinking what a terrible reminder that flower would be if anything happened to him. Happily, he was able to send another check in six months, and Ardis received a flower every week for the entire year he was away. It was a tradition they both treasured, and they still do.

Dick arrived for his military flight to Vietnam too late to change into fatigues, and was forced to travel in his Class A green uniform, jacket, tie, and all. He got off the plane in Vietnam, after a long, uncomfortable flight, and stepped immediately into the combat zone and the blazing humid weather of Saigon.

The last bus to the Replacement Station, his first destination, had already left, and he was given directions for catching another couple buses, which would eventually get him there. So, hoisting his duffel bag onto his shoulder and juggling his briefcase and chaplain's kit, he searched around until he found the right buses.

The chaplain's kit was a pretty interesting deal. It contained a Communion chalice and small individual cups, Communion bread, candles, candlesticks, a stand for the Bible, a small cross, hymnbooks, containers for grape juice, and the linens needed to set up Communion anywhere, all fitted into a nylon canvas bag about 16 inches long and 8 inches square. It was well-designed and compact, but added to his other gear and made quite a load to carry. Nevertheless, he shouldered it all and rode a succession of buses through Saigon to the Army post.

Hungry, thirsty, hot, and tired, he finally arrived at the front gate of the reception station when he heard a loud voice, "Hey, Dick Stenbakken!" It was Dick Poulin, a Catholic priest and a fellow student from the chaplain's course. Never had Dick been so glad to see anybody in his life. Poulin galloped over, bear-hugged him, and shouldered his duffel bag. Together they walked into the reception station. Finally he was able to get jungle fatigues and boots and shed his hot, sweaty Class A uniform.

Dick didn't know exactly where he would be stationed in Vietnam. It might be Saigon, or it could just as well be some far-off post out in the boonies. Chaplains went everywhere the troops did. The next morning he presented himself at the U.S. Army Vietnam's (USARV) chaplain's office for an interview and an assignment. The command chaplain, Colonel Porter Brooks, was a friendly guy, and Dick enjoyed the exchange.

"Well, it's time to figure out your assignment," the chief said after they had talked a while. "The way we do it, I hand you a dart, and you throw it at the board," he grinned, indicating the huge map behind his desk.

Immediately Dick picked up on the joke. "If I miss the board, will you send me home?"

The chief laughed. "Nice try, Stenbakken. I like your sense of humor. Actually, I'm going to put you right here in Saigon, on Long Binh Post. You'll be assigned to the fourth transportation command." Long Binh was a sprawling logistics facility and the largest U.S. Army post in Vietnam, housing more than 50,000 people. It was enormous.

"The reason we're assigning you here," the officer continued, "is that there are not many Seventh-day Adventist chaplains in the country." Dick nodded. He knew of only one other: Ralph Workman. Workman was with the First Cavalry, stationed at Bien Hoa, about 20 miles from Saigon.

"If there are specific Adventist needs," Colonel Brooks went on, "you'll be able get out to where they are, rather than our having to pull you in from some remote part of the country. And I know the Adventists have a servicemen's center in Saigon, and you'll be near enough to help out with that."

The assignment demonstrated the military's commitment to providing reasonable religious coverage for all denominations. The Army could have sent him out into the countryside somewhere, but then he might not be available if a situation needed his intervention.

He could see clearly that his assignment was twofold: to provide general spiritual coverage for his unit and to be a country-wide resource in the Army for specific Adventist needs. Once again, the Army impressed him with the planning that had gone into this decision. And once again, he felt the Lord's leading. *I am in absolutely the right place,* he thought.

Ardis was greatly relieved when she learned of his posting at Long Binh. As a child, she had been afraid that her family would be taken prisoner before they were evacuated from China. Her greatest fear was that he would be captured and held as a prisoner of war. It scared her even more than the thought of his losing his life. Because of its size and the firepower surrounding it, Long Binh seemed safer to her than a jungle outpost.

But Dick didn't feel especially safe there. During his first week in Vietnam he wrote long farewell letters to Ardis and his children. Then he sealed them in an envelope with instructions no one was to open it except in the event of his death. Then, on his last day in Vietnam, he destroyed them.

The wisdom of his placement became apparent very quickly. A short time after he arrived, for example, he was able to assist Jim Mellish, a noncombatant Adventist medic. Jim had gotten into some difficulty with his superiors because of the Sabbath and other issues, and his unit was about to drop the hammer on him.

The USARV chaplain sent Dick to investigate. Coming from headquarters gave Dick the high-level visibility and clout needed to sort out the situation and get the charges dropped. Dick talked to Jim about his experiences in Vietnam. The kid had some hair-raising stories to tell.

One night he was out on patrol with his unit. As a medic, he went wherever the troops did, even though he didn't carry a weapon. They were sleeping on the ground, and Jim suddenly sensed someone looking at him. Opening his eyes, he saw a Vietcong soldier standing over him with an AK-47 pointed straight at his chest. The two men stared at each other for a few seconds, and then the Vietcong soldier melted into the darkness as silently as he had come, leaving Mellish shaking and praying.

On another patrol Jim was walking point—first man in the line. As he rounded a bend he came face to face with a Vietcong soldier, his pistol drawn. The man fired a seven-millimeter bullet directly at Jim, hitting him in the sternum. The medic went down in the ditch.

I know I'm hit, he thought. When he reached inside his jacket, his hand came away covered with blood. Still flat on his back, he ripped open his shirt and ran his hand over his chest, and his fingers found the back end of the bullet sticking out of his breastbone. Managing to get his forceps out of his medical kit, he pulled the bullet out of his chest and put it in his pocket. Then he picked himself up and, when the firefight was over, went back to work, patching up other soldiers. *Wow!* Dick thought, developing a new respect for the term "noncombatant."

Dick settled into his quarters and located his unit's chapel, a weather-beaten wooden building that seated about 100 people. It was called TC Hill—the transportation command chapel—and was positioned at the crossroads of Highway One into Saigon and the road to Bien Hoa. Dick shared the chapel with Harry Bearce, the chaplain (major) for the fourth transportation's sister unit—the next unit over on the post. Harry was a gentle, quiet man with a ready smile. Rawboned and gangly, he had a head of unruly dark hair. Privately Dick thought he looked a little like Abraham Lincoln. The two became good friends.

The base assigned Dick two assistants. One of them would always be available to serve as his bodyguard, driver, head elder, and general all-around assistant.

The fourth transportation was one of those responsible for getting supplies to posts all over Vietnam. They'd head out in a wheeled convoy, taking food, equipment, and ammunition to other bases on big five-ton flatbed trucks. The rough-and-ready guys would get up about 3:00 in the morning, load their trucks in the dark, form up in convoys, then sleep in the cabs or on the canvas tops of the trucks for a couple hours until daylight. By 7:00, or as soon as it was light enough to be on the road, they'd head out—20 or 30 trucks to a convoy.

Early on in his Vietnam tour Dick decided that he would go out on the convoys with the men as often as possible. As a pastor, he had made it his business to get to know his congregation. And as a chaplain, he wanted to do the same thing. He'd go where the men went. In a way, he found it refreshing. After all, a pastor can't go into the workplace with his parishioners, but a chaplain is expected to do just that.

The convoys stopped occasionally to check their vehicles. When they did, Dick left his jeep and walked up and down the line, talking to the guys.

He carried small New Testaments and the Psalms with him. Sometimes he'd take a Coleman cooler along in the jeep and hand out ice-cold sodas. The guys appreciated that on a hot day.

That was down the road, however. First, Dick had to prepare for his initial convoy. He had read the convoy reports for the previous year—not a particularly reassuring thing to do. About once a week, according to the records, the Vietcong hit a convoy. They were like ducks in a shooting gallery—lined up in single file, rumbling slowly along, with brush, tall grass, and trees on both sides. The enemy could hide in that jungle and attack at will.

Dick had heard about "command detonation," or land mines the Vietcong set off by remote control. He had sandbags put on the floor of his jeep to improve his chances of survival if he ran over a mine.

The day of his first convoy trip arrived. He informed its commander that he planned to accompany them. Then he told that day's assistant, Dave Olson, a fresh-faced kid from Minnesota. Dave checked out the jeep and made sure his M16 was loaded and ready. The unit commander offered Dick a .45 pistol to carry with him. "Chaplain, other guys do it. You can keep it in your briefcase or under your shirt," he suggested.

"Thank you for that," Dick replied, "but the Geneva Convention and U.S. law, as well as my personal convictions, won't allow me to do it."

"OK, Chaplain, your call, but if you change your mind, we have one reserved for you."

Dick never carried a weapon in Vietnam. Some chaplains did, but they were going against the direction of the chief of chaplains. Chaplains, like doctors, were noncombatants. According to the Geneva Convention chaplains or doctors taken prisoner of war were to be allowed to practice their craft or be repatriated. While that often didn't hold true in reality, Dick would not compromise his fellow chaplains by risking carrying a weapon.

That day's convoy headed to Quan Loi, a former French rubber plantation in the jungle near the Cambodian border, now a fire support base. The convoy formed up in the dark as usual, and shortly after dawn it started off and soon entered the jungle. Dick and his driver were in an open jeep, the next-to-last vehicle in the line. Right behind them was an APC—an armored personnel carrier, with twin .50-caliber machine guns mounted on the front.

Turning around in his seat, Dick studied the guns. *Those things could make a hole about the size of a quarter,* he thought. *That could flat ruin your day.* He had to admit that it felt good having those guns right behind his jeep. Noncombatant or not, knowing there was a guy on that APC manning a gun big enough to take down anything was pretty comforting.

As they neared Quan Loi, the road got worse, until they were driving through shoulder-high elephant grass. The road—if you could call it that—was mostly mud. It deteriorated further into two deep ruts. The 10-ton trucks were much wider than the jeep, which was now plowing along at an angle, with the driver-side wheels in a rut, and the passenger-side wheels up on the hump. Dave was doing all he could to stay in at least one of the tracks of the vehicles ahead of them.

Then they came to a place where a truck had swerved. The jeep dropped down into the two ruts—and stuck there. The trucks ahead lumbered on, disappearing from sight. The APC behind them stopped and some of the men jumped out and tried to get the chaplain's jeep out of the mud.

Then Dick heard the APC moving again. Their job was to guard the convoy—not rescue the chaplain's jeep. The APC disappeared, leaving Dick and his driver behind, sitting by themselves in tall grass out in the middle of nowhere in the Vietnamese jungle—one scared young private with an M16 and one unarmed chaplain. Dave looked at him. "What do I do, sir?"

"Put it in four-wheel drive, rev it up, and drop the clutch! And hurry up!" His assistant complied, and the wheels spun wildly, throwing mud and dirt all over Southeast Asia. But then they grabbed hold, and they were able to get the jeep out of the hole and catch up with the APC. All in all, Dick's first convoy had proved to be rather exciting—and from that point on he chose to drive the jeep himself when he went on convoy, even though it was against conventional practice. He figured Olson couldn't drive and shoot at the same time.

Once a day, in the evening when the trucks rolled back in, he would set up a short chapel service before supper. He'd rotate it around to the different motor pool areas in his unit. He and his assistant would stack up crates or spare tires, put some boards over them, and then he'd unpack his chaplain kit, spread the linens over the boards, and offer Communion to anyone who wished to take part. Guys would show up, take Communion if they chose to, sing a couple of songs, and listen to a short devotional message. Then they'd sit around and talk with the chaplain until it was time to go to supper. The services were always well attended.

Then once a week he'd show 30-minute religious films, such as the ones

from the Moody Bible Institute. Whenever a feature film was shown, he'd
have an opportunity to present one of his spiritual films before the feature.
As it worked out, Dick conducted a worship service of some sort almost
every day of the week. In addition, he had staff responsibilities—the usual
reports and paperwork, as well as hospital visits to the wounded.

After he had been in Vietnam a couple months he decided it was time
to do something about the chapel, the outside of which was looking pretty
shabby. He went to see the unit commander. Lieutenant Colonel Larry
Floro was a loud, blustery guy. You could hear his voice for miles—and
that was when he wasn't even yelling.

"How about getting some white paint for the chapel, sir?" Dick asked.
"I'd like to make it stand out—make it look a little more attractive."

"Chaplain, I can't help you," the commander said, loudly and cordially.
"There is no white paint to be had on the post," he continued, waving
his arm to indicate the acres of unpainted buildings all around them. "I
wouldn't even know where to get any. That's a good idea, but I can't do
anything about it." And the next week the officer went on leave, assuming
the matter was closed.

Meanwhile, Dick put out the word that he was looking for four gallons
of white paint for the chapel. He went to see the unit supply clerk, with
whom he'd developed a good relationship. "Chaplain, I haven't seen white
paint since I've been here," the man said, shrugging his shoulders. Still, the
word was filtering out—the chaplain wanted white paint.

One night a kid from another unit knocked on the door of Dick's
hooch. "Sir, you still looking for white paint?"

"Yeah!"

"We're having a barbeque for our unit. If you can come up with two
cases of steak, I can come up with some white paint," the soldier said, then
disappeared into the night.

Dick went to visit their sister unit, the one where his friend Harry was
chaplain, and nosed around. "I'm looking for a couple cases of steak," he
said. "I want to trade them for paint for our chapel. Anybody know where
I can get two cases of steak?"

The sister unit had refrigerator trucks. Part of their job was to deliver
food to the Generals' Mess. The generals were doing well food-wise—steak
was no problem. Two nights later another kid showed up at Dick's door
with two cases of steaks. Then Dick traded the steaks for paint and painted
the whole outside of the chapel, trim and all. It looked good.

When the commander returned from his R&R, he called Dick into the office. "I see you found white paint. I'm not even going to ask how you did that," he bellowed.

"I'm not even going to tell you how I did that," Dick replied, chuckling. That was the way things worked in the military. The pieces went together like clockworks. You had to know how to wind the clock. When you did, it worked well for everybody.

And Dick had proved to himself, once again, that people were his most valuable resource. Even the wheeling-dealing was part of "the ministry of presence." *Build good relationships with people, and the world is yours, white paint and all,* he thought. *Christ did it, too. He came to us. He came where we were. He did what we did.* That's what being a chaplain was all about.

Chapter 16

"What Happened to Marty?"

L ate one Saturday night Dick needed some materials from his office for the next morning's worship service. After walking from his hooch to the headquarters building where his office was located, he saw that the door to his office was open, but that wasn't unusual. He never closed it, except when he was conducting counseling sessions. The office was dark—but Dick knew his way around, so he started into the room, moving toward his desk. Suddenly the hairs on the back of his neck stood up. Somebody was in the room!

In a combat zone you stay vigilant. You pay attention to such sensations. Quickly he flipped on the lights. There, huddled in a corner, cowering as though being attacked by a wild beast, was a young trooper—shaking like a leaf, every muscle in his body indicating his terror. Suddenly Dick wasn't all too comfortable himself, but the kid spoke first. "Hi, Chaplain!"

"What can I do for you? Why are you here?" he asked, keeping his voice calm.

"I just saw the devil!" the soldier replied, his voice trembling with fear. Dick helped him up from the floor, put him in a chair, and sat down next to him.

"Let's talk about it," Dick said.

The trooper, whose name was Marty, began to spill out his fears. They were irrational, but totally real to him. It was obvious that he had been drinking heavily, and possibly there were drugs involved as well. Marijuana and cocaine were as easy to get in Vietnam as 7-Up.

Dick's heart went out to Marty. He knew that many of the troops, out of boredom or loneliness, turned to alcohol and drugs. They spent a lot of their waking hours waiting—waiting to load up, waiting to get in line, waiting to head out with the convoys. The soldiers, many still in their teens, had too much time on their hands. Drugs and alcohol use resulted, and sometimes it got way out of hand, as with Marty, whose hallucinations had convinced him that he had come eyeball to eyeball with the devil.

Dick didn't probe the soldier about his use of chemical substances. He just listened as the kid poured out the horror he believed he had seen. "Marty, God is stronger than the devil," Dick assured him.

"Yeah, Chaplain, that's why I came to your office." The trooper had begun to relax a little. "I knew I'd be safe here."

After reading some scriptures, Dick had prayer with him. The young man had calmed down considerably by now, and he stumbled to his feet to leave. At the door, he paused. "Pastor, do you have a Bible I could have?" Dick always carried New Testament/Psalms combinations to give away. Taking a copy from his pocket, he handed it to Marty.

"Sure, here, take this one," Dick said, and pointed out some passages he thought would help the kid. That was the last he saw of him that night.

A few days later he was walking toward the mess hall when he met the soldier again. He barely recognized the exuberant young man. "Hi, Chaplain, how ya doin'?" Marty was all smiles, slapping him on the shoulder. Then he asked, "Hey, Chaplain, do you have a Bible I could have?"

He's forgotten I gave him a New Testament/Psalms the other night, Dick thought. That wasn't surprising, considering his inebriated state. "Sure, Marty!" he said, taking another New Testament/Psalms from his pocket.

Later that week he ran into Marty again. Running up to him, he said, "Chaplain, I need a Bible. Do you have one I could have?" By now Dick was getting curious about this, but he willingly gave the soldier another New Testament/Psalms. *I don't know what he's doing with them—but it's a good thing I get them by the case.*

The next day another guy in the unit approached Dick. "Chaplain, what happened to Marty?"

What happened to Marty? Dick thought with alarm. That could mean a whole lot of things. The soldier was a perimeter guard—a dangerous assignment. "What do you mean?"

"Well, some of us were hanging around, getting ready to go on guard duty, and here comes Marty walking down to take his position in the guard tower, and he's got his M16 in one hand and this Bible in his other hand.

"One of the guys called out, 'Hey, Marty, so now you're a preacher?' Marty made a right turn, marched up to this guy, grabbed him by the shirt, and lifted him off the ground. Then he stuck his Bible right in front of the guy's nose. 'Take this Bible and read it, or I'll rearrange your face,' says Marty. The other guy took the Bible.

"Marty used to be one of the roughest, loudest, most foulmouthed guys in the unit," the soldier continued. "And now he's into reading the Bible. So I'm asking, What happened to Marty?"

"Looks like Marty found something that suits him better than what he's been doing," Dick replied. Privately he chuckled to himself. The soldier's forceful tactics weren't exactly what he would recommend for one-on-one witnessing—but they were effective when it came to distributing Bibles. He was happy to see the young man's smiling face in worship services. And, as far as Dick knew, Marty never saw the devil again.

About halfway through his tour in Vietnam Dick noticed that something was happening to the left side of his jaw. There seemed to be a growth or a lump forming under the skin. He went to the camp medics to have it checked out.

"We're pretty sure it's benign, but we're not sure what it is," they told him. "It's growing on your parotid gland, and we definitely think it needs to come out. We can't do it here. The tumor is close to major nerves that control your speech, so we're going to send you to a specialist in Tokyo to have the surgery." Dick couldn't argue with that. For a preacher to lose the ability to speak was unthinkable.

Flown to an American military hospital in Tokyo, he had the surgery performed. All went well, and he was recovering in the hospital when Billy Graham came to the city to conduct an evangelistic series. The American ambassador to Japan invited two busloads of ambulatory hospital patients to have dinner with Graham. Dick was one of the lucky ones included in the event.

For Dick, who as a boy had spent his Sunday nights alone in his basement room listening to Billy Graham on the radio, it was a momentous occasion. It was actually the second time he had met Graham. While he was at Fort Benning on his first Army assignment, he had been invited to give the invocation at a Billy Graham meeting, and had been on the platform with him and George Beverly Shea. He had even heard Shea sing "How Great Thou Art." That had been an awe-inspiring experience, but this was even more so.

Graham exuded a sense of peace and power—you could feel it when he walked into the room. Dick would remember that evening in vivid detail long after he had returned to duty in the battle zone. Before he left Japan, he and a buddy climbed Mount Fuji one night, in time to see the sunrise from the mountain's peak. So you could say that Dick had two mountaintop experiences during his brief stay in Japan.

Back in Vietnam and fully healed from his surgery, he took another look at the TC Hill chapel. Now that it was painted a sparkling white, it stood out like a beacon in the sea of weathered-gray, unpainted buildings on the post. Dick thought it could use some additional upgrading, however, especially on the inside.

One Sunday morning he was rolling some ideas around in the back of his mind as he headed toward the chapel for services. As he passed through the officer's quarters' common area he noticed that the remnants of a big party from the night before still on the tables, including lots of wine bottles. The bottles glowed with color as the early-morning sun shone through them.

Hey, he thought, *that's kind of pretty.* Not much about a war zone was pretty, and the image lingered in his mind. Back in his office after the service, he noticed a small ornament sitting on his desk—something left behind by the previous chaplain. A Nativity scene, the background was made of clear plastic, with colored plastic inside, melted and fused together to look like stained glass. It had been on his desk since day one, but now he saw it in a new light. *I could do that with glass,* he mused. His creative juices began flowing.

Heading back to the common area, he gathered up the wine bottles. For the next few weeks he scrounged all the wine and whiskey bottles he could get his hands on—despite the jokes from his fellow officers. "Some of us are worried about your drinking, Chaplain," they razzed.

Dick discovered that if he heated the bottles in an oven, then plunged them into ice water, the quick contraction would fracture the glass. Each shard contained multiple fractures, which scattered and reflected the light, creating beautiful patterns. He had his "stained glass."

Next he turned his thoughts to the design. It would need to be universal and ecumenical, representing all Christian religions. He sketched something out on a big piece of paper. The cross of Christ would be in the center, surrounded by other symbols of faith, such as the Bible, a dove, and a Communion chalice. Then he transferred the finished design to a large sheet of clear Plexiglas and went to work on the project in his office, right on top of his desk.

The "leading" between the sections of the design was black telephone wire, glued to the Plexiglas with contact cement. The post had a craft shop, and from there he obtained plastic casting resin, which he tinted in the colors he needed. After pouring the casting resin into a section, he would carefully arrange the glass pieces in it and pour more resin on top.

Wine and whiskey bottles provided good greens and browns, but his design required some additional colors. For blue, he foraged for Maalox bottles in the hospital, and for red, he appropriated a couple of broken truck taillights from the motor pool. For gold, he scored an especially nice glass ashtray from the officers' recreation area. The only thing he lacked was frosted white glass for the image of the dove. That stumped him until he noticed a gin bottle on the bar in the officers' club. Perfect!

The project took him about 100 late-night hours, and when the window was finished and the resin had cured, Stenbakken hauled it over to the chapel. He cut a hole in the wall behind the pulpit and mounted the window in the opening. The pulpit had a storage space behind it, and Dick wrangled a couple of work lights from the motor pool, mounted them on the ceiling of the storage room, and plugged them in. Voilà! That window lit up the chapel.

The "booze bottle window" became a tourist attraction at Long Binh, always included on the list of things to show post visitors. Dick put a plaque on one corner of the window, dedicating it to the soldiers of the Fourth Transportation Command. On the opposite corner he added another small plaque, asking that the window be donated either to the transportation or the chaplain museum when the current building no longer served as a chapel. After the Vietnam War ended, somehow that window found its way back to the United States, and it is now a part of the collection of the U.S. Army Chaplains' Museum at Fort Jackson, South Carolina.

The Combat Development Group of the Chaplaincy was always looking for ways to improve how chaplains served, and Stenbakken had recently received a shipment of one of their latest brainstorms: freeze-dried grape juice in foil packets. Adventists weren't the only denomination using grape juice rather than wine for Communion. Baptists and others employed it. The canned grape juice the Army supplied was pretty disgusting stuff, and it was hard to carry into the field.

It was standard military procedure that the first Sunday of every month was a Communion Sunday. One Sunday morning Dick thought of a great way to have a little fun. He emptied two of the grape juice packets into white paper cups and headed for the headquarters building next door. The building was empty on a Sunday morning, except for one young sergeant serving as CQ—charge of quarters. Carrying the apparently empty paper cups, one in each hand, he walked up to the CQ.

"We're having a Communion service today, soldier. Where's your drinking fountain?"

"Right over there, sir," the man answered, pointing to a fountain with a five-gallon clear-glass container mounted on top. Putting a cup under the spout, Dick pushed the lever, standing so that the CQ could see the clear water going in. He filled both cups full. Then he lightly swirled them both, instantly turning the contents to purple grape juice.

Finally he took the two cups back to the sergeant's desk and held them so the soldier could see the contents. "Looks like it worked," he remarked nonchalantly.

The kid's eyes got huge. "What time is that Communion service, sir?"

"Nine o'clock."

"I'll be there." And he was, right on the front row. Dick would have loved to have read that kid's next letter home—about the chaplain who turned water into wine.

Early in his Army career Dick had learned that if the supply sergeant is your friend, the world is essentially yours. It was to prove true, time and time again. The coffeehouse was a good example.

Dick wanted to do something to help combat the boredom and homesickness that often got soldiers into trouble. An empty building stood not far from the chapel. It wasn't big, but it had a nice large open area in the middle, with offices at each end. Dick went to command and asked for the building. "Our guys have to go all the way across the post for entertainment," he explained. "We could give them something to do within easy walking distance."

Command granted his request, and he and his assistants took over the building. They moved into the offices and discussed what the other possibilities for its use might be. "What if we started a coffeehouse?" one of the assistants suggested.

"Great idea!" Dick responded. "And we could turn one of these offices into a music room. Guys could hang out there, play guitars, or do whatever they want."

"A music room?" one of his assistants replied incredulously. "We don't have any equipment for that, and no musical instruments!"

"That's OK. We can get some stuff." Nosing around, he found out that the USO had all kinds of equipment, including musical instruments. (The United Service Organizations is a private, nonprofit organization that provides programs, services, and live entertainment for the troops.) He talked to the chief of the USO.

"I'm starting a coffeehouse. What do I need to do to get some musical instruments?"

"Can't help you there, Chaplain. We just supply stuff to the nightclubs," the USO guy said, scratching his head. "We don't usually have anything to do with the chapel."

"Well, this will be an opportunity for you to do it for the first time!" Dick showed his letter of authorization from the command, and that did the trick.

"OK, Chaplain," the USO chief said, taking Dick back into a well-stocked storage area. "Pick out whatever you want."

Not needing to be told twice, Dick selected electric guitars, acoustic guitars, a small drum set, and several other instruments. Then he went to the mess hall and scrounged a pile of foot-square egg cartons. From somewhere else he found some plastic foam. He and his assistants lined the walls of the music room with those materials. Now the men could come in and play drums or wail away on an electric guitar—jam all they wanted—and their music wouldn't blow other people out of the building.

Soon Dick had all sorts of enthusiastic help with the project. The idea was catching on with the troops. One soldier did some perspective painting on the walls. Others made banners and hung posters. Dick nosed around some more and found plastic couches and some tables and chairs. The USO contributed table games. Then he found a popcorn maker and a small refrigerator. They sold cold sodas for five cents apiece—but did not allow alcohol.

Dick made sure that Bibles and other religious materials were always available in the coffeehouse, and while he didn't push them, he noticed that they needed regular replenishing. The coffeehouse became a friendly, welcoming place for the men to hang out. Dick and his assistants had found a way to help alleviate the soldiers' boredom—and another means to do ministry.

Like any soldier in a foreign land, Dick found it difficult to be so far away from his family. He wrote to his parents at least once a week, but their responses were few and far between. Strangely, though, he had heard from friends and family back in Colorado that his mother bragged about him to everybody she knew. He knew she was concerned about his safety and proud of what he was doing, but somehow she could never say those things to him.

His dad had never been demonstrative or open with his feelings. Dick realized they both cared—but somehow they had a hard time letting him know. It was an ache that he carried in his heart, but he accepted it as a fact of life. He wouldn't let it affect his own appreciation for his parents. In fact, he loved them dearly—so much so that he had never once wondered about his birth parents. Dick was a Stenbakken, and that was all there was to it.

He and Ardis wrote to each other regularly. Before leaving for Vietnam, he had supplied them both with small tape recorders—state-of-the-art equipment at the time—and he had taken several children's Bible story books with him. Ardis had the same books back home. Once a week he would send her a tape recording. One side was just for Ardis. At the end of that side, he'd tell her which stories he was going to read, giving her the book and the page numbers. On the second side of the tape he would read the stories to Rikki and Erik.

Dick could picture Ardis and the children gathered around the tape recorder. "OK, kids," his voice would say, "today we're going to read about Chad and his dog. See the little boy there? See that little puppy peeping around the corner?" The children would sit on Ardis' lap and listen to their daddy, entranced, as their mommy turned the pages.

When it was their turn to talk into the recorder, however, Erik and Rikki got shy and tongue-tied. Still, Ardis sent him a tape every week. Letters and tape recordings kept the family as close as possible.

Two or three times during the year Dick spoke directly to his wife, using the ham radio system. He'd sign up in advance for a 19-minute slot. Because of the difference in time zones, his slot would usually come at 2:00 or 3:00 in the morning. He'd speak into the microphone of a ham radio in Vietnam. The radio operator would connect to another ham radio enthusiast in the U.S., who would try to patch him through to Ardis.

Their conversations were not private—they were being broadcast to the whole world. On one occasion he was speaking to Ardis when a deep male voice interrupted. "Your time is about up, sir."

Quickly Dick said, "I love you, honey. Over." All he got back was crackle and static. "I didn't get that last transmission; please repeat." More static and an unintelligible voice. "I still didn't get it." Then the gruff voice came over the line again. "She said she loves you, too, sir!" Dick sighed.

Chapter 17

"Get Away From the Window, Gil!"

Thirty-three of the individuals Dick had met in the chaplain's course ended up on active duty, 28 of them in Vietnam. Though scattered all over the country, they got together occasionally, often at the officers' club on the Long Binh post.

Dick looked forward to such times. It was good to meet with his fellow ministers and swap experiences. Some of their stories were poignant, some hair-raising, and some were just plain hilarious. Ron Diegal, an unassuming, serious man, told a story one night that had his fellow chaplains rolling on the floor, even if he himself failed to see the humor in it.

Diegal was stationed out in the bush on a remote fire support base, where all the lights were turned off after dark. One moonless night he got up to use the latrine. He had no trouble finding the outhouse in the dark, but inside it was pitch-black. Feeling around in his pockets, he found some matches and lit one so that he could see where to sit down. Then he blew out the match and threw it down the hole.

Vietnam latrines were pretty primitive, consisting of 50-gallon barrels cut in half with a blowtorch and shoved in the appropriate locations under a wooden outhouse. The military hired local Vietnamese workers to manage the waste. They'd periodically empty the drums, then pour in diesel fuel and light it to clean the drums. Evidently Ron's match found some residual diesel fuel, and within 10 seconds it ignited. Now mild-mannered Chaplain Diegal was literally sitting on an inferno.

Scorched but not seriously wounded, he jumped up and ran around to the back of the outhouse to put the fire out. But the flames were already out of hand, and now, totally panicked, Ron yelled, "Fire! Fire!"

Naturally, on a Vietnam outpost, when troops hear "Fire!" in the middle of the night, they assume it means incoming. People barreled out of their beds and jumped into bunkers. Then an officer yelled, "Stand down. There's no incoming fire. The chaplain is burning down the outhouse!"

Ron's fellow chaplains had a good laugh at their buddy's expense. "It's not funny, guys! That fire was hot!" he protested. Then he added that when he wrote to his wife and told her his story, she sent him a little pocket flashlight with the warning, "Don't ever do that again!" She didn't think it was funny, either.

The camaraderie and laughter were important to Dick and, indeed, all the chaplains serving in Vietnam's war zone. They each carried heavy responsibilities. All were surrounded by danger, and always, as they enjoyed the companionship, in the back of their minds was the thought *I may never see this person again.* As for Dick, his philosophy had always been to wring the positive out of every situation, to enjoy life to the fullest—and that included exercising his weird sense of humor—and to give God the glory. Nothing about Vietnam had changed any of that.

The danger in Vietnam didn't always come from the enemy. One Saturday night a commotion outside his hooch awakened Dick. Men were screaming, shouting, and cursing. He heard the sound of heavy boots running past. Stepping out to investigate, wearing what he slept in—his fatigue pants and a T-shirt—he stopped a soldier running by.

"What's going on?" he asked.

"There's a rumble," the kid replied without slowing down.

Dick took in the scene. It wasn't hard to figure out what had happened. The enlisted men's club was nearby. Heavy drinking had been going on in it that night, and racial insults had gotten thrown back and forth. Apparently the thing had escalated into a drunken Black-versus-White free-for-all before turning into an all-out riot.

Another trooper came racing past, heading toward the club. Dick couldn't believe his eyes. The man was carrying an M16 rifle! Military rules did not permit weapons inside the post perimeter. Stopping him, Dick pointed a finger. "Turn that weapon in immediately and go to your quarters, soldier."

The kid glanced at him. Although nothing about Dick's appearance identified him as an officer, his voice conveyed enough authority to halt the soldier in his tracks.

"OK, Sarge," he replied with a sheepish look, and reversed his course. Dick just shook his head. An angry, drunk, belligerent soldier was bad enough, but one carrying an M16 could cause a real disaster. The riot was quelled soon enough, and the night returned to relative quiet. *Just another day in the life of a Vietnam chaplain,* Dick thought, going back to bed.

Dick looked forward to Saturdays, most of which he spent at the

Seventh-day Adventist servicemen's center in Saigon. The center was an island of calm in the stormy sea of military life for him, as it was for the Adventist troops who called it their home away from home. It was in the city, not far from the Saigon Adventist Hospital. The 38-bed hospital was located in an old mansion and operated by the Loma Linda University School of Medicine. Its physicians were mostly volunteers, including Alvin Dahl. Alvin had been a member of the Denver Central Seventh-day Adventist Church, where Dick had grown up.

The church itself was inside a nearby walled compound, which also enclosed the homes of the hospital's physicians and Adventist mission personnel. A Vietnamese-style building—more like a house than a typical American church—it had a big open living area with a tiled floor, and a kitchen off to one side.

Worship services met there every Sabbath, followed by a potluck dinner. Participants would set up chairs in the open area for Sabbath school and church, then bring tables in afterward for the meal. Dick shared the preaching responsibilities with Ralph Workman, an Adventist chaplain stationed at Bien Hoa, not far away.

The servicemen's center was also in the compound. It was spartan but comfortable, and provided a place for soldiers on leave to relax and even to stay overnight. Several times during Dick's year in Vietnam he and Ralph held a servicemen's retreat, inviting Adventist soldiers from all the surrounding areas to attend. At a retreat one weekend the 30 or 40 soldiers overflowed the center's dormitory and were sleeping everywhere—on the floor or wherever they could find a space.

Dick was asleep in a room on the second floor. Gil Bertochini, a civilian Adventist pastor and the youth director for Southeast Asia, shared the room with him. Bertochini was to be the next morning's guest speaker.

A loud explosion about 1:00 in the morning jerked Dick awake. By this time he had had enough experience with such things to know that this blast had been very close. In one lightning-quick motion he leaped out of the bed and rolled under it, prepared to shield himself if a second explosion came. Had somebody thrown a hand grenade into the building? A house full of sleeping medics would be a good target. Then he realized that his friend Gil was looking out the window. "Get away from the window, Gil!" he screamed. "A second blast would cut you to shreds!"

Fortunately, no second explosion happened. But right across the alleyway between their compound and the next compound, somebody or something had blown a hole in the wall big enough to drive a car through. Nobody was injured, but it shook everybody up. They suddenly felt extremely vulnerable—in a house full of noncombatant medics, nobody had a weapon. Was the explosion a threat? They would never know, but many prayers of thanksgiving for protection went up that night.

It was one more reminder—as if they needed any—that death was never far away in Vietnam. Dick remembered something that had happened at Quan Loi a few months before. He was idly watching as a forklift loaded a pallet into a helicopter when he realized that the pallet contained 16 body bags stacked like cordwood. Sixteen dead American soldiers—sons, fathers, brothers, husbands, and friends—being shipped to a mortuary, where they would begin their final journey home.

Not for the first time, Dick thought, *There is only a millimeter between a body bag and me.* As he had done many times before, he thanked God for his life and for giving him a passion for ministry and the means to do it.

His tour in Vietnam had now come to an end, but he had one special thing he planned to do before he left, even if it delayed his departure a day or two. It had all started months before with a call for help for a soldier in a sister unit—a combat engineer group. (Combat engineers built such things as roads, airports, and buildings.)

Steve Kastner had an Adventist background, but he wasn't a member of the church—or of any other. But for some reason, when other soldiers resorted to drugs or alcohol, Steve had used his downtime to study his Bible. It wasn't long before he came to the conclusion that he could no longer in good conscience carry a weapon.

He approached his commanding officer with a request for noncombatant status on religious grounds. While soldiers don't change their theological or moral points of view very often, the Army did have protocols in place to deal with such a situation. Steve took the first step by applying to serve as a noncombatant. Steve knew his request wasn't going to get him out of the Army—he just wanted to serve without carrying a weapon.

Steve filed his paperwork. According to Army protocol, his superiors could not order him to carry a weapon while administration considered his case. Until the request was denied, it had to be treated as though approved. But it didn't work out that way for him.

His commander had issued two different orders. The first stated: "From this day on, every member of this unit who goes into the field will carry a weapon." Such a decree was not out of the ordinary. Most of the time engineers had to carry a weapon when working "outside the wire," or off the post.

The second order specified that everyone in the unit would be deployed outside the installation on a specific job on an upcoming date. The commander's intentions were clear. He meant to force the issue with Steve and make an example of him.

Steve's unit chaplain contacted Dick for help because of the soldier's Seventh-day Adventist background. Dick met with Steve, a quiet, thoughtful young man who kept to himself. Having studied the Bible carefully, he was convinced that what he had been taught earlier in his life was right.

The young man wanted to return to the faith of his childhood. He could no longer carry a weapon. Dick came away assured that Steve's conviction was genuine. Then he visited the soldier's commander. The captain had no sympathy for Steve's plight—in fact, he seemed determined to back the kid into a corner.

"This isn't going to fly!" Dick informed the commander. "This soldier has filed the proper paperwork, and according to Army regulations, he cannot be forced to carry a weapon until the matter has been decided." The officer ignored Dick.

The time the unit was to deploy arrived. Steve went out with his unit, but he did not carry a weapon. The commander immediately put the wheels in motion to court-martial him for disobeying an order.

Dick went into action again. Part of his job was to provide appropriate advice to the command, and he intended to do just that. "This will not fly," he told the officer again. "If you pursue a court-martial against this kid on the basis of these two orders, you're going to embarrass yourself and the unit. I'd like to spare you that," he urged.

The captain turned his back on Dick again. "Chaplain, you run your church stuff, and I'll run my unit."

"I'm not trying to tell you how to run your unit! What I *am* telling you is that you have a very high likelihood of being greatly embarrassed."

"Well, that's the way it is," the commander replied, dismissing any further argument.

The time came for the pre-court-martial hearing. Called an Article 32 inquiry, it was like a grand jury investigation prior to a trial. A female Air Force JAG (Judge Advocate General) Corps major had been assigned, under the Uniform Code of Military Justice, to review the case and decide whether to pursue a full court-martial. The hearing convened in Steve's unit's headquarters building. The room was hot and crowded. Steve's commander was there, of course, along with the unit's lieutenants and sergeants. Steve's chaplain and Dick were also present.

Private Steve Kastner stood at attention when the JAG officer walked into the room and took her seat. "Let me examine the charges," she said, opening the large binder in front of her. Complete silence filled the room while she reviewed the paperwork. Less than five minutes had passed when she stood up and, with her left hand, slammed the big binder closed.

"I won't even hear this case, because there is no case" she announced, and walked out of the room, leaving its occupants sitting in shocked silence. The commander looked as though someone had hit him with a baseball bat. He had been made to look foolish in front of all his staff. Dick sighed. After all, he had tried to save the man this humiliation.

The military eventually granted Steve Kastner's request for non-combatant status, and he received noncombatant duty. He and Dick continued to study the Bible together. Steve asked for baptism, and Dick believed he was ready. Baptizing him was one of the last acts Dick performed as a chaplain in Vietnam. It took place at the Adventist church in Saigon on his final Sabbath in the country.

Now Dick could focus on getting out of Vietnam. He needed to hitch a ride on a "freedom bird." That's what soldiers called the chartered aircraft that flew troops home at the end of their tours of duty. Going to the replacement station on the post, he inquired about the next flight headed stateside. "Can't say when something might open up, Chaplain," the person there told him. "Saigon Airport is jammed up right now, with all the troop movement into Cambodia. Could be another three or four days."

Three or four extra days in Vietnam seemed like a lifetime. Dick called a chaplain buddy up at Cam Rahn Bay, on the Gulf of Tonkin. "Oh, yeah," the friend said. "We have freedom birds coming and going all the time. You could process through the replacement station here if you can get yourself to Cam Rhan Bay."

Dick hitched a ride to the Saigon Airport military terminal, hoping to hop a plane to Cam Rhan Bay. "No way, Chaplain. Not a chance for at least four days."

Not ready to give up, he shouldered his duffel bag and walked out to the control tower. "Any birds going to Cam Rhan Bay?" he asked, after introducing himself.

The air traffic controller pointed to a plane sitting on the tarmac below.

"There's one about to taxi out right now." Trotting down to the tarmac, Dick found the pilot and warrant officer. The plane was an old Canadian-built Caribou, designed to haul freight.

"Hey, I hear you're going to Cam Rhan Bay," he said, after introducing himself. "I'm trying to get to the replacement station there. Could I hitch a ride with you?"

"Sure, why not?" the pilot said. "If you're crazy enough to ride with us, we're crazy enough to take you. Throw your duffel bag in the back and strap yourself into the sling seat." So Dick got his ride to Cam Rhan Bay.

A couple of his chaplain friends met him there and put him up for the night. The next morning, well before daylight, he boarded a plane for home, headed for San Francisco. A chartered airliner, it bore the name Evergreen Airways—nothing about it was military. When the aircraft got airborne, everybody cheered. It felt good to be on a plane full of sleepy soldiers, all buzzed about getting out of Vietnam.

The sun came up, and the flight attendants began to serve breakfast. They were all lovely—at least to a plane full of returning soldiers. As one walked by Dick's seat a gentle wafting of real perfume followed her. Dick closed his eyes and took a deep breath, and no doubt so did all the soldiers as she passed down the aisle. The soft, flowery fragrance was so achingly out of the ordinary after Vietnam, where diesel fuel had been by far the best thing they'd smelled for months. It was a delicious reminder of the pleasant reality of where they were headed for—they were going home.

Dick phoned Ardis in Canada as soon as he landed in San Francisco. She knew he was coming home, but not exactly when. The family was eating breakfast when he called. "I thought you weren't coming until tomorrow!" his excited wife said.

"Well, I'm here, and I'll be landing in Calgary in about three hours."

Ardis and her parents lived about two hours away from the airport, but somehow they got the kids ready, climbed into the car on that cold February morning, and were there to meet him when he landed.

Dick didn't expect his children to recognize him. After all, they were very young. And he was deeply tanned after his year in Vietnam and hardly resembled the father his kids had known. Looking around him, he could see how bronzed he actually looked compared to the sea of pale-faced, sun-deprived Canadians.

Then he heard a little voice. "Daddy, Daddy!" little Rikki, who was only 18 months old, began to shout. Dick was astounded and thrilled that she recognized him, until he learned that she called every male in uniform "Daddy"—even the mail carrier.

Three-and-a-half-year-old Erik crawled right up onto his father's lap and told him a story about hunting for his socks that morning. Dick had thought that it might take awhile for the boy to get to know him again, but he didn't seem to realize that his daddy had been away. Dick could only guess that the nightly sessions with his tape-recorded stories had helped.

The next morning was a little different. He was just waking up when he heard the *thump, thump, thump* of little running feet. *What a wonderful sound,* he thought. *It's Rikki.* Ardis had told him that each morning the little girl climbed out of her crib and raced into her mommy's room to jump into bed with her. But this morning she skidded to a stop and stared at Dick in horror. *Who is that man in bed with my mommy?* Then she turned around and raced out as fast as she had run into the room. It took her another three or four days to get to know him.

After a few weeks of leave, Dick and Ardis left for his next assignment at Fort Lewis in the state of Washington. The Army had assigned him as a chaplain to a basic trainee unit. It was the same situation as he had had at Fort Benning—with one big difference. Now when he talked to those kids about what they were facing, he would do it from experience.

After a few months the military transferred him to Division Support Command, the unit responsible for logistics for the Ninth Infantry Division at Fort Lewis. He and Ardis were assigned a house on the post. "You'll love it here," he had assured her. "They tell me we'll have a spectacular view of Mount Rainier from our backyard."

When they moved in, it was still winter. Fort Lewis, just a little south of the Seattle-Tacoma area, shares those cities' rainy winter weather. For the first two weeks all they saw from their back windows was an airfield and gray sky. Then, one day, the sun came out, and there it was—beautiful, cone-shaped, snow-covered Mount Rainier, looking so close that it seemed you could reach out and touch it. It had been there all the time.

Soon Dick met a local resident, a civilian named Norman Becker. Norm was a bear of a guy, with dark unruly hair, big shoulders, bushy eyebrows, and a warm, engaging smile. Having a master's degree in counseling, he had done a lot of corporate-level training. In fact, he had his own private counseling business.

Norm conducted a daylong training event for the chaplains at Fort Lewis. What Norm had to say energized Dick, whose formal training in counseling was limited to the classes he'd had at Andrews University, and he wanted to learn more. After all, counseling was a big part of being a chaplain. Much of what he was doing at Fort Lewis involved it in one way or another.

So the question wasn't whether he'd be doing counseling, but how well. To Dick, Norm made so much sense. His approach combined spiritual values and sound counseling principles, a combination that fit Dick's style like a glove. Then Dick learned of an opportunity for a few chaplains to do extended training with Becker.

I'm on that like stink on a skunk, Dick thought to himself. He put his application in and talked to the installation chaplain. Dick was one of only three or four chaplains selected for the program. For several months he spent half a day, twice a week, learning about counseling from Norm.

About this time the Vietnam War was drawing down, and most of the chaplains he knew were returning home, their tours of duty over. For many, their Army service ended as well. Even those who wanted to remain in the military were usually not allowed to stay. It was "Thank you for your service, but we don't need you anymore." Dick intended Army chaplaincy as his lifetime ministry, and he researched how to make sure that would happen.

The Army has what is called regular Army—the permanent force that is always maintained during peacetime. Congress mandates its size and makeup. If you were part of the regular Army, you wouldn't get cut, even when reduced to its absolute lowest numbers. Unless you did something exceptionally stupid, you had tenure that others didn't have.

But the thing was you had to be selected to be regular Army. It didn't just happen. The military had to review your records, and there had to be an opening. Each corps such as chaplaincy, for example, had only so many regular Army slots. Dick did some more research and discovered that at that time there was only one Seventh-day Adventist chaplain regular Army. He knew that other religious groups of similar size had more than one regular Army chaplain. But Adventists had only one—who happened to be his friend from Vietnam, Ralph Workman.

Dick put in a phone call to the church's National Service Organization and talked to Clark Smith—the same man who had signed the letter asking him to consider becoming an Army chaplain in the first place.

"I think," he told Clark, "that we Adventists ought to have another regular Army slot."

"Oh, no, we've looked into that," Smith responded. "We have only the one slot."

"Yeah, but I've done some checking, and I think we should have two."

"Well, we'll look into it again. Are you interested?"

"You bet. That's why I called you."

About two weeks later Clark called him back. "You know what, Dick? You're right. We contacted the chief of chaplains' office. Adventists do have a second regular Army slot that has never been filled. Are you still interested?"

"Absolutely." So the church nominated Chaplain (Captain) Stenbakken for a slot in the regular Army through the chief of chaplains' office, and, in due time, he was selected.

While researching the process, Dick learned that the Army had a yearlong master's-level training program for chaplains in family therapy. He was already running premarriage seminars at Fort Lewis, conducting character guidance classes, and doing many other things in the course of his working day that touched on family therapy.

Additional training would be most helpful. He decided it was time to make a trip to Washington, D.C. So he hitched a ride on a military transport going from McChord Air Force Base, went to the Pentagon, and presented himself at the chief of chaplains' office.

There he talked to Chaplain Dick Tupy in the Personnel Department. "I'd like to review my records," he said. "I intend to apply for a master's program in family therapy. Could you take the time to go through my records with me?" Although Dick didn't know it, he was talking to the chair of the very board responsible for deciding who got into that particular training program.

Chaplain Tupy graciously reviewed his records with him. Afterward, they were sitting at Tupy's desk, with Dick's files spread out on the desktop between them, when Dick took a deep breath and asked the question point-blank. "What are my chances of getting into this master's program?"

Tupy smiled. "Your chances are pretty good, I'd say." Dick relaxed. That wasn't exactly a commitment, but he'd sure take it as a positive indicator.

The Army accepted him for the master's program. It chose only four to six people a year out of the approximately 1,600 chaplains in the Army. So, at a time when the Vietnam War was ending and the military was drawing down, Dick had received tenure as a regular Army officer and had been selected for a yearlong master's program in family life ministries. The next phase of his ministry as an Army chaplain had begun.

Oliver and Celia Stenbakken, about a year after adopting Dick

1. The house at 1981 South Downing Street in Denver where Dick spent his boyhood

2. Dick at age 4

3. Dick in "uniform" at age 3

4. A 9-year-old cowboy

Characters from Dick's *Miracles of the Master* DVD Series:

↖ The Man Born Blind

5. Twelve-year-old Dick's school photo from Denver Junior Academy, 1952

6. Dick's school photo from Denver Junior Academy, 1955

7. Dick in January of 1955, age 15 going on, say, 35?

8. Dick's basement "home office" when he was the assistant pastor at Denver Central, during the summer of 1960

9. Celia Stenbakken in 1960

1. Ardis and Dick at their graduation from Uni College, with Celia and Oliver Stenbakken

2. Ardis and Dick on their wedding day, August 20, 1962

3. The happy couple leaving the church, headed for their "luxurious" honeymoon cabin

4. Pastor Stenbakken during his first year at the Worland, Wyoming, church

Characters from Dick's *Miracles of the Master* DVD Series:
↖ Malchus

Dick's ordination to the ministry, January 4, 1969, in the new Worland church. Left: R. H. Nightingale, Central Union Conference president. Right: Bill Hatch, president of the Wyoming Conference.

Chaplain School at Fort Hamilton in Lower Brooklyn, New York, in 1969. Dick is in the top row, second from left.

Ardis, Dick, Erik, and baby Rikki just before Dick boarded the plane to fly to Vietnam

Two-year-old Erik watching Daddy's plane leave. Dick carried this image in his heart for the whole year he was away from his family.

Chaplain (Captain) Stenbakken, just returned from a day traveling in a convoy with the troops

1. Dick with Marty, the kid who hid out in the chaplain's office to escape the devil

2. Dick with the U.S. ambassador to Japan and Billy Graham

3. The "booze bottle window" that Dick made out of discarded wine bottles for the TC Hill Chapel

4. The chaplain with the reversible foot gives a demonstration.

5. Dick found time for this studio portrait while serving in Vietnam.

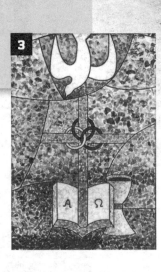

Characters from Dick's *Miracles of the Master* DVD Series:

↖ The Leper

6. A Communion service in Vietnam

7. Dave Olson, Dick's driver,
posing with a convoy

8. Dick baptizing Steve Kastner, his last
official act before leaving Vietnam

9. A very tanned and happy daddy
with Erik and Rikki, just after
he returned from Vietnam

10. Rikki, Erik, Dick and Ardis—while Dick
was in family life training in California

1. Chaplain Stenbakken about the time he returned to the States

2. The two photos that helped convince Dick that he had found his birth mother

3. Dick in character as Matthew in the play Matthew's Miracle, performed at the General Conference

4. Alexander Greenwalt, Dick's birth father, about the time Dick was born

5. The photo of "Sally" that so disturbed Francine Jones

Characters from Dick's *Miracles of the Master* DVD Series:

↖ Luke

6. Frances Ryan Huff, Dick's birth mother

7. Dick and Rikki with Judy Dyer

8. Dick meets his sister Barb for the first time

9. Aubrey and Finn, Erik's and Gelerie's children

10. Erik meets Aunt Barb

11. Elise and Elliot, Jason's and Rikki's children

SECTION D FAITH

JUNE 25, 2010

Friday
Reporter-Herald

NICE TO KNOW
In ancient Rome, a
responsible for dril
and clothing, and

Reporter-Herald/PHIL MCMIC
Loveland resident Dick Stenbakken poses as a Roman centurion in his home. Stenbakken is a retired military chaplain who specializes in f
person re-enactments of historical biblical figures.

Timeless
words of faith

1. An article in the Loveland *Reporter Herald*,
   Dick's hometown newspaper, dated June 25, 2010,
   featuring his first-person presentations

**Characters from Dick's *Miracles of
the Master* DVD Series:**

◤ Jairus

2. Three generations of Stenbakkens
    Front Row: Finn Stenbakken, Elliot Welch, Elise Welch
    Middle Row: Rikki Stenbakken Welch, Aubrey Stenbakken,
        Dick Stenbakken, Ardis Stenbakken, Gelerie Arafiles Stenbakken
    Back Row: Jason Welch, Erik Stenbakken

3. Dick as a Roman centurion

4.   Dick as a Roman centurion

Characters from Dick's *Miracles of the Master* DVD Series:

↖ Simon

Chapter 18

"You Can't Eat
Those Hot Dogs!"

Dick was a student again. He loved learning, particularly when the goal was to improve his skills, and he wasn't averse to adding another degree to his résumé, courtesy of Uncle Sam.

The school was the American Institute of Family Relations in Hollywood, California—the first one in the country to train family therapists and founded by Paul Popenoe, a man often called the dean of marriage and family therapy in the United States. Dick would remain on active duty while attending classes, receiving full pay from the Army. The school would send regular reports of his progress to the chief of chaplains' office at the Pentagon.

The Army paid all expenses, but it was up to Dick and Ardis to find a place to live. Moving to Hollywood didn't appeal to them. It was too urban and too smoggy a place for their two small children, so they looked at other towns farther away from the city. They liked Thousand Oaks, about 30 miles to the west, but at first the houses they saw for rent there seemed pretty bleak. They weren't used to "yards" without a blade of grass. Then Ardis spotted an ad in a local newspaper for a three-bedroom house that looked promising.

They drove out to take a look at it. It was perfect—a pretty brick ranch-style house with a grassy fenced-in yard that had a palm tree in it. Hoping that it was still available, Dick drove as fast as he could to a nearby shopping center, where they found a pay phone, called, and arranged to walk through the house.

It was just as nice inside. The family room had a fireplace, and another little room would make a perfect study for Dick. The location was good, too. California Lutheran University was nearby, and they had an excellent library, which would be helpful. And, perhaps best of all, a school was within walking distance for Erik, who was ready for kindergarten.

So they promptly signed the lease. It would mean a lengthy commute down the freeway to Hollywood for Dick, but he didn't mind. His classes met only two days a week. The rest of the time he had assignments and studies that didn't require him to go into the city.

It didn't take long to move and settle in. Army families soon get such a thing down to a science, and the Stenbakkens were no exception. He discovered that several of his fellow students lived nearby, and they started to carpool together.

His carpoolers were interesting people. Joan Conahey, a social worker completing her master's degree, was a Christian with some limited connections with her church. Joe Speral was a typical California surfer hippie who had served in the Navy. He was bright, very much counter-culture, and an avowed atheist.

It would be hard to imagine three more different people, but the social worker, the atheist, and the Adventist Army chaplain came to appreciate and enjoy each other's company. They would use their commuting time to compare notes, debriefing each other and reviewing what they had learned that day. Once again, Dick reveled in the opportunity to rub shoulders with people from backgrounds so different from his own.

His own quirks provided some learning experiences for his friends, as well. One day he was having lunch with his fellow students in the break room. Dick was eating a vegetarian "meat" sandwich. He and Joan and Joe got to talking about food.

Dick mentioned that Ardis had grown up a vegetarian and had never cooked or eaten meat. Joe found this fascinating. The next day Dick brought another vegetarian sandwich, one containing Wham, a soy-based meat substitute meant to resemble luncheon meat. Joe sniffed it. "That doesn't smell too bad."

"Have a taste," Dick offered. "It's pretty good stuff." Breaking off a corner of his sandwich, he handed it to Joe, who liked the Wham. Soon other students gathered around, eager for a taste of the strange concoction that looked like meat but wasn't. Dick felt as though he was feeding the 5,000. From that day on, people kept an eye on his lunch, always curious to see what oddity he would produce next.

One day, as Dick was cooking a couple of veggie Leenies over a Bunsen burner in one of the labs in the building, Joe happened by. "Dick, you can't eat those hot dogs!" he shouted. "You're a vegetarian!" Dick hastened to explain that he was heating a vegetarian wiener.

"Here, have a bite," he said to his friend. "They're good!" After that, he made sure he brought generous lunches to school with him.

The coursework at the American Institute of Family Relations was an eye-opener for Dick. He was learning about things he had never been exposed to before—including abnormal psychology, diagnostics, and psychological testing. The school offered a variety of classes and lectures, supervision, and workshops.

He especially enjoyed the classes on childhood development, because he had his own live laboratory at home. With Erik in kindergarten and Rikki two years behind him, he could study a theory and then watch it unfold right before his eyes.

His classes on therapy and intervention were fascinating, too. Required to do a certain number of hours of practicum, he had to rustle up his own patients. He and Ardis attended the Simi Valley Seventh-day Adventist Church, and the pastor there was happy to refer families in need of counseling to Dick. The Adventist hospital in the same town also provided some counseling opportunities.

One of his first experiences in Simi Valley taught him a great deal about how—and how not—to deal with a couple having marital problems. The pastor called him one night and asked him to see a couple in trouble. "This situation is beyond my training," he said. "The husband swears he isn't chasing other women, but the wife doesn't believe him or trust him to be faithful. On top of that, they're financially stressed. They're at their breaking point. Will you see them?"

"I'd be happy to." Dick phoned the couple and made an appointment to talk with them in their home—which was his first mistake. He would learn that things went a lot better when he was on his own turf, not a guest in the home of those he was counseling.

When he knocked on the door at the appointed time, the wife opened it. He wasn't sure what he had expected, but it wasn't a tiny, fragile-looking woman who looked as though she couldn't have weighed 90 pounds. She had both of her skinny arms wrapped around a large trash can. "Oh, I'm so glad you've come to see us! Please come in," she said, and then immediately began to wretch and gag, her head bent over the trash can. The horrible sound took him by surprise. *What in the world have I walked into?*

Feeling as though he had entered an alternate universe, Dick followed the woman's petite figure, trash can and all, into the dining room, where she introduced her husband, a worried-looking young man, who rose from the table to shake his hand. The three of them settled into their seats, the wife holding the trash can on her lap.

Things went fairly well at first, as Dick tried to get some background on them and their problems, but as soon as he touched on any sensitive topic such as the reasons they had requested counseling, up came the trash can, and the horrible dry heaves began again. The husband, obviously distressed by his wife's apparent suffering, would lose his train of thought, and the discussion would come to a halt. Dick was at a loss. A year in Vietnam, and nothing had prepared him for such a situation. Counseling of any sort appeared impossible.

When he described the encounter to his supervisor at school, the man suppressed a chuckle. "Well, Dick, what do you think was going on there?"

"I haven't a clue," he admitted, shaking his head. "And I had no idea what to do."

"Well, that's why we're doing this supervision. Who do you think was in control of that session?"

"Not me, that's for sure. And not the husband. He was as helpless as I was."

"Right. The wife was in absolute control of the situation. Anytime something came up that she didn't want to talk about, she'd seize control by heaving into the trash can."

Dick had been so involved in coping with the immediate situation that he had missed the clear diagnostic clues. The issue with the couple was control. The wife didn't trust her husband to be faithful, even though he swore he was not chasing other women. Their finances were in a mess, and they couldn't agree on how to deal with their problems. Rather than working together, they were vying for control. The husband would cope by running away to work, and the wife would seize control by being the underdog, smaller and suffering, proving her husband didn't care. Her behavior may have been unconscious, but it was nonetheless working for her.

With that insight Dick was able to counsel the young couple, helping them to see how they were avoiding the real issues between them. The lesson was an important one for Dick. *When people come to you for help, the immediate problem you see is often not the real one.*

The training brought other breakthroughs. One day, for example, in a small group, a supervisor was sharing some personal issues. As he revealed his private struggle, the man broke down and began to weep. Dick's first reaction was to get up from his seat and try to comfort the supervisor. Then he realized that the man had given no signal that he wanted comforting.

Dick had been about to rush in to help before he received any indication that it would be welcome. *If I rush over there right now, uninvited, I'm meeting my need, not his.* It was another "aha" experience.

Ardis and Dick enjoyed living in Thousand Oaks. They started a youth program in the Simi Valley church, cleaning out and painting an unfinished kitchen and turning it into an attractive space for the youth to meet. Ardis signed up for a class in oil painting at the local community college. She had always wanted to learn to paint, and both her mother and grandmother had done some. Doing remarkably well at it, Ardis even sold a couple of her paintings.

One afternoon Dick arrived home hot and tired after the long commute. It was the end of a quarter, and he had just finished some rigorous testing. He was looking forward to a nice long, relaxing soak in the tub. But when he opened the door, the smell of turpentine immediately clued him in that something wasn't right. Then Ardis met him at the door, and the source of the problem was apparent. In her arms was their poodle, Kandi, her fluffy white fur a mottled red and pink.

Ardis had been doing some painting, using a new technique she'd learned in class. She had covered a canvas completely with alizarin red pigment—a burgundy color. Then, using a wide brush loaded with white paint, she had painted a beautiful pink rose, the red and white paints blending to create the various shades and tones. Setting the finished painting on top of a cedar chest in front of the window in the dining area and taking the kids with her, she had gone to the store.

While she was gone, Kandi had leaped up on the cedar chest, walked across the wet painting, then jumped down, trotted across the tiled kitchen floor, and continued into the living room with its pale-green wall-to-wall carpet. Everywhere she went, she left little red paw prints.

Ardis had come home shortly before Dick to find a little dog at the door who knew she had done something terribly wrong. Ardis had used some turpentine to tackle the mess, but the more she cleaned, the worse it got. He pitched in to help. Nothing they had in the house seemed to be working, so he went to the hardware store and found some French cleaning fluid that was mostly benzene. That, and a lot of elbow grease, did the trick. It took them most of the night, but the carpet was nearly as good as new. That weekend they rented a carpet shampooer and finished the job.

That was probably the worst catastrophe in what was a very good year. The children were thriving, and the family enjoyed the little house in Thousand Oaks, Erik's school, and the fellowship at the Simi Valley church.

All too soon the year ended. Dick knew that his next assignment would be a family life ministry on an Army post somewhere. It was what the Army called a utilization tour—following training, you'd be posted to a place where you could make immediate use of the education you'd just completed. As usual, the Army way made a lot of sense.

Dick wondered where it might send him. He knew Army posts had very few family life centers at the time. Then his orders came. He'd be going to Fort Leonard Wood, Missouri, to start a family life center. The chaplains on the post were doing counseling but with no organized plan or facility. That would be his job.

Getting out an atlas, he looked up Missouri. There, in Pulaski County, right in the center of the state, was Fort Leonard Wood, on the northern edge of the Ozark Mountains. It was the home of the Army's engineering school.

The installation was huge—it was the largest population center in that part of the state and covered nearly 100 square miles. It was also isolated. (Dick would learn later that when a McDonald's restaurant opened up in the town of Rolla, about 40 miles east of the post, whole convoys would form up and drive there for hamburgers and shakes.) Still, it had its own utility railway, and its own hospital (housing the only elevator in the county), and soon it would have its own family life center.

It was just the sort of challenge Dick relished—the chance to start something from scratch and to put into practice all the theory he had learned in the past year. So once again the family did what Army families do—packed up the house and the kids and the dog, and moved the 1,750 miles to Fort Leonard Wood, Missouri.

The fort had a number of cantonment chapels on the post. (*Cantonment* is an old Army term for a permanent military residential installation.) The chapels were little white clapboard buildings, built in the late thirties and forties, scattered throughout the residential neighborhoods on the post. Most were small, with little more than a single large space for conducting services, but one, in the area known as Lieber Heights, was larger. Because it had been built on a hillside, it had a full basement. Dick got the idea that with a little remodeling and fixing up he could use the Lieber Heights building as both a chapel and as a family life center.

He started making plans. The first order of business was to improve the chapel itself. It had had little care for years. Army personnel kept it painted on the outside, but inside it needed a lot of work.

It was time for some good old Army wheeling and dealing—and scrounging. The walls in the chaplain's office were covered with some sort of pinkish-colored pressed Celotex—ugly and totally unpaintable. What could they do to cover it up?

Dick had noticed that the firing range used huge rolls of white muslin cloth, which they stretched over frames on which targets were mounted. The cloth was about six feet wide. *That stuff would be perfect for covering those stupid walls!* he thought. He called the firing range. "I'd like to get some target cloth for a project I'm working on."

"Well, we're not sure how much we can give you, Chaplain, but send your assistant over and we'll see what we can do," was the less-than-enthusiastic reply.

His current assistant was a delightfully perky young private named Vickie Mabry. A petite woman, she made up for her diminutive size with an excess of sparkling personality. He sent Vickie out to the firing range with instructions to get as much cloth as she could get, and then he went to lunch. Dick returned to the chapel just as she came in the door, followed by an extremely large sergeant carrying an even bigger roll of cloth, more than two feet in diameter.

"How'd you do that?" he asked her after the sergeant had dropped his burden on the floor and left.

Vickie smiled her most engaging smile. "I just asked. And the officer in charge said, 'Why don't you take the whole roll?' And then he supplied a sergeant to carry it." They cut the cloth to size and thumbtacked it neatly to the walls, creating a smooth, clean surface.

The family life center was soon up and operating, and with programs, classes, chapel services, and counseling, things began to warm up. Dick decided it was time to redo the basement. It just wasn't in very good shape. The post engineers weren't going to do it—it was up to the chaplain to get the job done.

He set out to scrounge the paint and brushes and rollers he needed. At first, he met resistance from the engineers, but when he let it be known that he had invited the two-star general chief of chaplains from the Pentagon to do a dedication service for the newly opened family life center, the question became, "What color paint would you like, Chaplain?"

Dick and his assistant started painting the entire basement interior.

It was a big job, and several of the other chaplains' assistants on the post volunteered to help. Vickie and Dick and the volunteers painted all day. About 6:00 p.m. he said, "Let's call it a day. We'll wrap the brushes in plastic, and we'll pick up where we left off in the morning."

Early the next morning he walked into the chapel. *That paint smells pretty strong*, he thought. *We should have left some windows open*. He went downstairs. His two volunteers from the day before were just finishing cleaning up the brushes and rollers. They had gone to get something to eat the night before and, having nothing else to do, said, "Let's go back and paint." So they had painted all night long. The job was nearly finished.

Dick was shocked. "You guys didn't have to do that!"

"Yeah, we know. We just decided to stay and do it." Once again, the experience reinforced an earlier lesson he had learned. Treat people well, and they'll do the same for you.

Before long the family life center was completely decorated, with classrooms, a new nursery, and a kitchen—all repainted and cleaned. Everything sparkled. People saw that something was happening in their neighborhood. Soon the little Lieber Heights cantonment chapel had larger congregations than the main post chapel.

With the family life center going full speed all week, with classes on marriage, parenting, budgeting, and many other subjects, plus counseling and all kinds of activities, it was a busy time. Dick would often do the unexpected, such as bringing in someone from a beauty shop to talk to the wives about how to save money on cosmetics. In addition, he conducted a full nondenominational worship service in the chapel every Sunday, plus all the usual congregational activities.

The various units at Fort Leonard Wood had approximately 25 chaplains assigned to them. But Dick was not attached to any unit. His assignment was to be the family life center director for the whole post. He served a diverse population, mostly noncommissioned officers and enlisted people and their families.

Once a month all the chaplains on the post got together for training. Shortly after Dick arrived, the installation chaplain, Colonel Howard Cross, called him into his office. "Dick, you are in charge of the Christmas program for chaplains and assistants this year."

"Yes, sir, it would be an honor." *Piece of cake*, he thought to himself. *We'll do the usual—sing some carols, maybe have some Christmas poetry. This'll be easy.*

Just as he had his hand on the doorknob the colonel spoke again. "One more thing, Dick. I don't want a bunch of Christmas poetry and some carols. We do that all the time."

Maybe this won't be such a simple assignment, Dick thought, his heart sinking a little. "What did you have in mind, sir?"

The colonel thought for a minute. "Well, it has to be spiritual, of course, and it has to have something to do with the Nativity. But most of all, I want something that's entertaining."

"Yes, sir!" Dick walked out, thinking, *What in the world am I going to do? I can certainly do something spiritual, and something that has to do with the Nativity is no problem—but entertaining?* What exactly did that mean?

The colonel's request was not optional—in fact, it would be a misnomer to call it a request. So Dick started looking through every Christmas anthology he could get his hands on. In one of the books he came across a first-person sermon by Frederick Speakman, a well-known preacher and writer. He had written the sermon as though Jesse of Bethlehem, an innkeeper, was talking with Luke, telling him about the night of the Nativity.

This is great! It's about the Nativity, it's certainly spiritual, and I think I can make it entertaining. He decided he'd do it as a dramatic reading. That's when mission creep set in. (*Mission creep,* a term originating in the military, applied to any project that expanded beyond its original goals.) *Why don't I do it in costume?* he thought, growing excited about the possibilities. *I can dress up like the innkeeper—I'll borrow Ardis' red-and-white-striped caftan, wear a burnoose on my head, and get myself a glue-on beard.*

Then getting even more caught up in the idea, he thought, *I could do it sitting at a table, as if I'm talking to Luke in my counting den—just as an innkeeper would do. I could have a stack of coins on the table, and a scroll in front of me—that would be perfect for my notes!*

Dick scrounged and borrowed until he had his costume and props. He rehearsed a few times, asking Ardis to critique him. Quickly he discovered that it wasn't the same as preaching—it was acting, and required a different mind-set. Maybe it even used different muscles. But he finally got it down pat, and on the evening of the chaplains' Christmas service, he was ready. The house lights dimmed, a spotlight turned on him, and suddenly he *was* Jesse, a humble innkeeper of Bethlehem, telling his story.

And it worked. The crowd of chaplains and assistants and their families was spellbound. At the end of the program a Lutheran chaplain, Major

Chuck Saveley, came up to him. The two men knew each other fairly well, since Chuck had been his sponsor when he first arrived at Fort Leonard Wood.

"Dick, you gotta come and do this at my worship services for basic trainees tomorrow morning at 9:00 and 11:00."

"Chuck, this wasn't worship—this was entertainment."

"No, no, Dick, it was worship. I was *in* Bethlehem tonight. I experienced the Nativity story in a new way."

Dick hesitated only a moment before he agreed. The man was a friend and colleague, not to mention the fact that he outranked Dick. So the next morning he showed up as Jesse of Bethlehem at his counting table at the basic trainees' chapel, and watched as 200 men filed into the seats. Well acquainted with basic trainees, he knew that they have to run everywhere they go. And he also knew that when they have a chance to sit down, most of them fall asleep almost instantly.

As he began his presentation, part of his mind noted with surprise that 200 basic trainees kept their eyes riveted on Jesse of Bethlehem. His first thought was that the coffee must have been pretty strong in the mess line that morning. Afterward, many of the trainees wanted their pictures taken with Jesse of Bethlehem and to have him autograph their chapel bulletins. This was something new. Dick had always fancied himself a reasonably good preacher, but nobody had ever asked for his autograph.

At 11:00 out came Jesse of Bethlehem again. Another 200 trainees paid close attention. By the time he had finished for the second time that morning, Dick got the point. *This is a mode of preaching that I can do. I enjoy it, and people enjoy listening. I can do this!* And for him a whole new way of doing ministry was born.

Chapter 19

"The Vote Was
Pretty Much Unanimous"

That's the last one," Ardis called from the door as Dick carried another heavy suitcase to the car. He and Ardis and the kids were driving to Denver to see his parents. The relationship with his mother, while always somewhat strained, had been pretty good lately, with regular letters and phone calls keeping them connected.

Erik was about 6 and Rikki was 4, and Ardis and Dick wanted their children to know and love their grandparents. It was a long drive, especially for the two lively kids, but they had promised them a day of skiing while they were in Colorado. That helped make the long hours in the car easier for the kids to bear. All went well, and they had a good vacation with the grandparents.

The last day of their visit dawned bright and sunny—a perfect day for skiing. Ardis and Dick loaded the kids and all their gear into the car, and the family took off for Winter Park ski resort, a little more than an hour away.

They returned to his parents' house around 7:00 or 8:00 that evening, all of them tired but invigorated after a good day on the mountain. Ardis was eager to get the kids bathed and tucked into bed before they fell asleep on their feet.

As soon as they walked in the door, they could tell something was wrong. Mom was pacing up and down the living room, extremely agitated and angry. Her attitude was a complete turnaround from the sweet, cheery grandmother of that morning. "I don't know what you two were thinking," she shouted, "taking the kids away on the last day of your visit to do your own thing."

Her words were slurred. It was all too obvious that she had been medicating herself. Dick's heart sank. She must be obtaining prescription drugs from somewhere. He didn't know what had gone wrong that day, but nothing he or Ardis could say placated her in the slightest. As she continued to hurl vitriol at them, his dad hovered in the background, unable or unwilling to intervene.

"We came to visit you, not upset you, Mom," Dick said in an effort to calm her down. "If our presence here is so distressing, maybe we need to leave."

"Then get out!" his mother yelled.

"OK, Mom, if that's what you really want," he said, shocked that she had taken him up on the offer.

"Leave!" she yelled again.

"OK, we'll go right now." By then, it was after 10:00 at night. He and Ardis packed up the car with the kids and all their luggage and drove away from his parents' house, having no idea where they were going.

Stopping to make some calls, Dick finally reached somebody at Fitzsimons Army Hospital in Aurora, on the east side of Denver. Dick knew that installation had guest quarters for active-duty officers. Their guest rooms were full, but with their help, he obtained a discounted room in a nearby hotel. Finally, well after midnight, they settled down for what was left of the night.

The incident crushed Dick. He loved his parents and had strived to stay close to them, but it seemed that there was no way to save the relationship with his mother, especially now that it was clear that she was abusing prescription drugs.

He had no doubt that the jealousy thing was the real reason for the problem. Ardis and Dick had gone off and spent the whole day together. Mom always felt threatened by his wife. Dick believed his mother liked Ardis—loved her, in fact—but Mom's innate sense of inferiority constantly caused her to compare herself unfavorably to other people, his wife in particular.

The continuing up-and-down nature of the relationship with his mother frustrated him. His personality was so different from hers. When he had a problem, he dug in until he discovered a solution. It might take all of his ingenuity to find it, but for him, that was part of the joy and the fun of a challenge. This mother-and-son relationship just didn't respond to his usual problem-solving style. No amount of love or creativity could fix it.

Back at Fort Leonard Wood, the busy round of life continued. A combination of guest speakers, programs, and classes for both women and men made the family life center one of the most popular spots on the installation. Chapel attendance at Lieber Heights continued to grow, too. Active programs for children and youth contributed to its success, resulting in consistent higher attendance than the main post chapel.

Dick invited the Heritage Singers, a well-known Adventist choral group, to visit the post one weekend. They arrived in their bus and did several concerts, each time to standing-room-only crowds. When they gave a concert at the Lieber Heights chapel, Dick and some volunteers prepared a meal for the group after their concert. They had decided on spaghetti, thinking that would be easy. They had a huge vat of spaghetti ready, and plenty of sauce—enough to feed the singing group and all those who had lent a hand with the event.

People began lining up for their food. Vickie Mabry, Dick's assistant, had the big kettle of spaghetti all ready to drain when she realized they had no strainer. "Dick, we don't have a colander. How are we going to drain this spaghetti?" she wailed.

What shall we do? he thought. He looked around the kitchen for something to use. Then he got an idea. Opening the refrigerator, he removed the food from three of the metal-rack shelves. After rinsing the shelves under hot water, he laid them on top of each other, criss-crossing the wire grids, and that became their strainer. It was awkward, but it worked. Ingenuity won out again. They had nicely drained spaghetti, well-fed Heritage Singers, and extremely clean refrigerator shelves.

The years at Fort Leonard Wood were a good experience for the whole Stenbakken family. Isolated as they were, they had to be creative and find their own amusements. They enjoyed canoeing, hiking, and backpacking. Rikki and Erik had their own little backpacks and their own stuff to carry. Even Kandi the poodle had a side pack to carry her own dog food.

The little Adventist church they attended was in Waynesville, about five miles off the post. The pastor had more than one church in his district, so Dick often took the pulpit on Sabbath. The congregation consisted mostly of local people whose children were grown and gone, but there were a few families—mostly military—with school-age children.

They began to discuss how great it would be if they had their own church school. Their children were being bused to an Adventist school about 45 minutes away in Rolla. But they had no building for a school, and no money to construct one.

Dick learned that the Army was closing down some old wooden frame buildings on an unused part of the post. He wasn't sure what the buildings had served for, although Fort Leonard Wood had housed German prisoners during World War II. The structures could well have been remnants of that era. The base offered them to anybody willing to tear them down.

It was a good deal—the Army would get rid of the buildings, and someone would salvage the usable lumber. Dick and some of the guys from church drove out to the back side of the post to have a look. There they found a good-sized building in reasonably decent shape. It needed some work, but the structure was sound and the roof was good.

He went to the post engineers. "I'd like to have this building for the Adventist church."

"Sure, Chaplain, fill out the paperwork and it's yours, as long as you tear it down."

"But I don't want to tear it down; I want to move it."

"You can do whatever you want with it, Chaplain, as long as it is gone in two weeks."

After obtaining a permit from the county to move the building, Dick found a mover who was willing to relocate the building for $1,200. He brought the information to the church board, and it looked as though the project might end right there. People wanted to see it happen, and $1,200 was a fraction of the cost of a new building, but the congregation just didn't have the money.

They had discussed the matter in the presence of a woman hardly anybody knew—a nurse who had been attending only a short time. When she felt impressed to write a check for the full amount, the project was back on track.

The members prepared a block foundation, and the building soon sat right behind the Adventist church. Dick, Ardis, and other church members spent many hours of their off-duty time helping to get it ready to serve as a school. It required painting, rewiring, and the addition of a bathroom and a small kitchen area. The congregation found a teacher, and that fall the little one-room school opened with 10 students, two of them named Stenbakken.

As the months turned into years, Dick's long-distance relationship with his mother slowly recovered from that terrible night when she had told her son to take his family and leave. Phone calls resumed, although often marred by his mother's growing prescription drug addiction.

Conversations with his father were necessarily constrained, but it was apparent that Dad had become Mom's full-time caregiver—forced to monitor his wife's every move as her behavior became more erratic. Her health began to fail, and she had a couple brief hospitalizations, because of congestive heart failure.

Then one day Dad called. Dick knew, as soon as he heard his father's voice, that something was wrong. "She's in the hospital again, son. And she's not doing well at all. You'd better come."

Dropping everything, Dick caught the next flight to Denver. Dad picked him up at the airport, a relieved smile on his face. "I just talked to your mother's nurse. She's doing much better. Let's get something to eat before we go to the hospital." Father and son had a meal at Dad's favorite Mexican restaurant, and had just returned to the house when Porter Hospital called. Dick's mother had quietly passed away.

Dick called Ardis right away. Recovering from a racquetball injury, she had her left ankle in a cast. But in her usual strong, self-sufficient style, she bundled up the kids, took a bus from Fort Leonard Wood to the St. Louis airport, and flew to Denver to be by his side.

The funeral was at Olinger Mortuary at Speer Boulevard and Sherman Avenue in Denver. Celia had been 81 years old. In death she seemed to be peacefully sleeping—the lines of insecurity and discontent finally erased from her face. She had lived a long life, but only in death had she achieved the peace that she had been seeking.

The elder Stenbakken continued to live in the house on South Downing Street in Denver. Dick and Ardis helped him dispose of Mom's things, and, as they had suspected, they found numerous bottles of Seconal and other prescription drugs, filled at many different pharmacies, along with multiple prescriptions from various doctors—some even in the name of his uncle Ray, who had been dead for years.

A frustrating sense of failure compounded Dick's sorrow. Despite all his best efforts and his deep love for his adoptive parents, he had been unable to ease his mother's sadness. He reflected that his parents' problems had doubtlessly influenced his decision to work with marriage and family life issues, and he was grateful for the opportunities the family life center gave him to reach out to hurting people. As he laid his mother to rest, he asked God to continue to guide him as he strove to help others find the happiness that had eluded Celia Stenbakken.

Dick returned to Fort Leonard Wood after his mother's funeral somehow energized and ready to roll up his sleeves and get back into the day-to-day running of the family life center. But although he still had a great deal to accomplish there, he soon learned that a change was in the wind.

At a chaplains' training event the new installation chaplain, Colonel Gene Allen, made an announcement. "I need an administrative chaplain to help me pull all of our programs together. I'm looking for an administrator who can handle money, help me do long-term planning, organize events— in other words, help us all to work together more tightly as a unit." Then he asked each man to write down the name of the chaplain on the post most suited to do the job.

Dick didn't give the matter a further thought, but the next day Allen called him into the office. "Well, Dick, the vote was pretty much unanimous. Your peers want you to be the administrative chaplain."

Dick was flabbergasted; it was the last thing he had expected. Everybody knew he was a hands-on guy and enjoyed being where the action was— where the people were. Administration was a desk job. Surely the colonel didn't intend to turn him into a desk jockey! "Sir, I'm happy doing what I'm doing."

"This is input from your peers, Dick," Allen responded, effectively putting an end to any further discussion. "They unanimously voted you the administrative chaplain, and I agree." That was that. A new chaplain would be taking over at Lieber Heights. Dick was changing jobs.

The first time since he became a minister (other than school) that he didn't have a pulpit, it was hard to let go of the hands-on aspects of ministry. He'd put a lot of sweat equity into the family life center. It was hard to stand aside and watch another chaplain put in charge—hard to watch the new guy build on what Dick had started. But his ministry footprint was about to become much bigger.

Gene Allen was a good leader, but Dick soon noticed that he went to a lot of meetings off installation. In fact, some of his subordinates called him the "ghost chaplain." While he had the final say in everything, he looked to his staff for the nuts and bolts of the day-to-day operation. Dick was going to have to figure out much of his new job on his own.

No courses at the seminary had prepared him for such responsibilities. He had had no training in systematic long-term planning and budgeting. But he had to start somewhere. Going to the post exchange, he scrounged a huge mattress box. After cutting it open so that he had a large blank piece of cardboard, he drew a great big calendar on it for the next year and put it up on the wall. Then he began pinning notes to it, and took it from there.

Soon he was doing budgeting, time planning, and personnel management. As he developed administrative skills, he began using abilities he hadn't known he had. It was a learn-as-you-go experience. Budgets were particularly nerve-wracking. If you didn't get the money right, somebody wouldn't be able to do ministry.

Dick had always loved learning about systems. He had some background in the dynamics of family systems and knew how the military worked as a system, and now he had an opportunity to get into the workings of the chaplaincy system. Up to this point his ministry had been one-on-one—preaching, teaching, and counseling—but now he began to understand that good, solid administrative work could also be a rather spectacular ministry. Enabling ministry for others was a ministry in itself.

Not long after that, Chaplain Allen moved on. The Pentagon's chief of chaplains had selected him to be president of the Army chaplain board, a sort of chaplains' think tank. Responsible for long-term planning, it had its headquarters at Fort Wadsworth on Staten Island, New York.

Dick himself was due for a move and a promotion. He had been at Fort Leonard Wood for more than three years. Making major would be an important milestone. While he was too immersed in his work to give promotions much thought, he knew that only 60 to 65 percent of guys made major on the first shot. If you didn't get promoted by the second go-around, your days in the Army were numbered, and it was time for you to think about reentering civilian life. Then his superiors selected Dick for the six-month career chaplains' advanced course at Fort Wadsworth. That was good news. The program was the next step in the promotion process.

It was January 1977, and once again he and his family were on the move—heading east from Missouri to New York. Departing a house on a military installation was no small undertaking. It had to be left spotless. Dick and Ardis and the kids moved into their travel trailer in the carport for their last few days at Fort Leonard Wood, and cleaned the house thoroughly, even scraping wax off the bathroom's tile floor with a razor blade.

The four Stenbakkens headed across the country, towing their trailer behind them. On their last night on the road they were in Pennsylvania's Pocono Mountains when they heard a weather report.

Forecasters were predicting a big storm to hit New York City by noon the next day. They drove as late as they could that night, and started out again at 5:00 the next morning, hoping to beat the storm, but it wasn't long before they were battling blinding snow. Announcements of road closings crackled over the car radio, and sure enough, they soon found their way blocked. Locating a back road still open, they somehow made it to a major route leading into New York.

They arrived at Fort Wadsworth on Staten Island just before noon, in the midst of a full-blown blizzard. Dick stopped to call his new sponsor, who happened to be his old friend Chuck Savely, for directions to their preassigned post housing. Chuck phoned headquarters to pick up the keys, only to learn that they were closing immediately because of the weather. He insisted that they stay open until he could get there. Then he met the Stenbakkens outside their townhouse with the keys in hand.

The place was empty—with not a stick of furniture—but it was warm and had running water. Dick found a place to park the trailer at the top of the street behind them. From there it was a straight shot to their back door. Slipping and sliding, they carried their suitcases and travel trailer mattresses down. They were home!

The storm shut down New York City for more than a week. The snow was more than a foot deep, and it wasn't going anywhere. The weather delayed the truck with their household goods. The family slept on the pads from their travel trailer, and for several days, they lived on the food they'd brought with them.

They'd been in their townhouse for about a week when an MP knocked at their door. "Is that your trailer parked up there, sir? That's not a parking place. You're going to have to move it."

Dick just grinned at him. "You shovel it out, and I'll move it." The trailer sat there all winter.

Two weeks after they arrived, the moving van finally showed up with their furniture. A lot of snow still covered the ground. The driver pulled the truck right behind the family's trailer. Then he climbed out of his vehicle, looked around, and scratched his head. How in the world was he going to move furniture down a slippery ice- and snow-covered street?

Ardis and Dick had a big wooden toboggan, a gift from her parents. The movers stacked some boxes on the toboggan and slid it down to the back door. That worked, so they used it to haul bigger things. They tobogganed everything down the hill, including the piano.

Dick found the chaplains' advanced course useful and rewarding. He entered the training with a lot of hands-on experience in pastoring, counseling, mentoring, leadership, and, most recently, administration. His promotion came through during the course, and he became Chaplain (Major) Dick Stenbakken.

When the advanced course ended, the personnel director from the chief of chaplains' office, Cliff Weathers, visited Fort Wadsworth to inform each graduate of their next assignment. Chaplain Weathers was the quintessential Southern gentleman. Dick had no idea where he would be going next, but he was hoping for a decent assignment. Shaking Cliff's hand, he settled into the chair across from the man's desk.

"Dick, I think I've got an assignment you're going to like," Cliff began. "The chief wants you to serve on the Army chaplain board in charge of family life." Dick couldn't believe what he was hearing. He knew that the man who had just vacated that job was a lieutenant colonel. Dick was a brand-new major, and yet he was being asked to step into a senior position on the staff of the chief of chaplains! His utter surprise must have showed on his face, because Cliff leaned back in his chair and laughed.

"No, really, Dick. You know Chaplain Allen, you work well with him, you know your craft, you've shown you have administrative skills and abilities, and we all know that you work well with family life. The chief wants you to take this job."

Dick took a deep breath. This was definitely moving into the fast lane. And he was only 37 years old. With the gift of hindsight, he was beginning to see how the dots were connected, bringing random events and individual decisions into a clear pattern of the Lord's leading.

Ten years before, the Adventist Church had asked him to become a chaplain. He'd made regular Army when lots of guys were getting cut. Next he'd had a year of superb training in family life, then a utilization tour at Fort Leonard Wood, which had allowed him to develop the skills he'd learned and which also led to the chance to enter administration. Even Chaplain Allen being named president of the Army chaplain board was part of the pattern.

Now the Army was inviting him to serve in the chief of chaplains' office. He'd be the most junior man on the board—the most junior man in the chief of chaplains' office, for that matter. No doubt about it, this was pretty heady stuff.

While he knew he had a strong inner drive to achieve excellence in whatever he did, most of these opportunities had found him. He hadn't sought them out. Maybe some people would attribute his success thus far to being in the right place at the right time. Or you could call it divine guidance. He preferred the latter. Once again, he felt an inner assurance that he was where God wanted him to be, doing what God wished him to do.

And somewhere in the back of his mind, Dick realized that he wanted very much to make full colonel. Never before had an Adventist chaplain served in the Army as a full colonel. (One had gotten promoted to that rank upon his retirement.) Dick wanted to see that barrier broken.

Chapter 20

"He Has Plenty of Bananas"

Swinging his legs out of bed, Dick winced as his feet hit the icy floor. His new assignment hadn't required a move, so the family had remained at their quarters at Fort Wadsworth. Their 1930s row house had many quirks, not the least of which was the sometime lack of heat.

For some strange bureaucratic reason, Fort Dix, another Army installation miles away in New Jersey, controlled the temperature of all the buildings at Fort Wadsworth. Fort Dix was further inland and didn't get as cold as Fort Wadsworth, which was right on the water. Cold mornings were the rule of the day every fall until Fort Dix got around to firing up the furnaces for the winter.

The house wasn't exactly luxurious. Within a few weeks of their arrival the sewer had backed up, flooding the kitchen with filth. The kitchen floor was so rotted out in front of the sink that you could actually see into the basement. Ardis called the post engineers, and they sent a workman over. "Oh, yeah, that needs to be fixed," he said, and headed back out the door.

"Wait a minute!" she called after him. "That's why I called you." Months went by, and they didn't hear any more about the matter until one Sunday morning when the family was eating breakfast. From the dining area window they could see a parade of men, carrying large sheets of plywood, heading down the hill to their back door.

"We're here to fix the floor," their foreman announced. He looked around the kitchen and the adjacent living room, including the wall-to-wall bookcases overflowing with books. "Oh, you've got a problem. Our contract calls for us to put new floors in the entire house. You're all moved in."

"No, I don't have a problem," Dick replied. "You have one. We asked only for a repair to the kitchen floor. And we're not going to move those books."

The workmen grumbled, but they took down the bookcases and

removed all the books. Then they moved all the furniture and rolled up the carpets. By the end of the day they had completed the task of laying plywood and tile over all the floors. Sawdust covered everything in the house, but the bulk of the job was done—until the next thing went wrong. It was that kind of house.

Dick's new responsibility as the member of the Army chaplain board in charge of family life was for long-term planning for all marriage and family life ministries in the entire Army, all around the world. Wherever soldiers were, balancing the demands of a military career with family responsibilities presented unique challenges. His job was to determine the needs of and find the resources and materials for family life centers and for all chaplains working with families.

Early on he put his finger on a problem. Army chaplains didn't have all their specialties logged into their personnel files. The military was just beginning to recognize the importance of marriage counseling and family life centers as a part of chaplaincy.

For the past few years the Army had been training chaplains at the master's level in family life and therapy, but they hadn't recognized it as a specialty or a career path. Once chaplains with family life and counseling training had completed their year-long utilization tour in the field, the Army lost track of their expertise. Most chaplains went on to other aspects of their profession and didn't serve as family life center directors.

Dick understood that if Army family life centers were going to succeed, they would need chaplains as directors, trainers, and supervisors as they rose through the ranks. The military should employ their education and experience in meaningful ways. Dick set about working with the Pentagon's chief of chaplains' personnel people to make it possible.

He enlisted the help of Tom Smith, who had been a fellow chaplain at Fort Leonard Wood. Tom had taken the same extended training in family life that Dick had done at Fort Lewis. Then he had gotten out of the Army and earned a Ph.D. in family studies. With Tom's help Dick wrote up a new policy, recognizing family life chaplaincy as a special career path. It required a unique designator—a military specialization code—that would go into chaplains' files and follow them throughout their career. Then the personnel people could look at a person's record and know that the individual had special training.

Dick submitted this policy to the Pentagon's chief of chaplains, who tweaked it and signed off, making it a part of the Army's permanent regulations. The policy still operates in the military today. His work changed the face of the Army chaplaincy, particularly as it related to family life ministry. Army marriages and families are still benefiting from those changes.

Next he built a database of all Army chaplains who had already had education in family life programs and would be willing to serve again in family life centers. Then he thought back to his own training at the American Institute of Family Relations in Hollywood, and another idea occurred to him.

He had had to hustle up his own civilian clients in order to complete the practicum part of his master's program. What if he could find other master's level study programs adjacent to Army posts?

Dick pinpointed several suitable counseling and family life training sites close to military installations, where chaplains could go to school and do their practicum and supervised counseling right on their installation. It would not only provide a needed service to the post's personnel, but also lighten the load of the post's chaplains and allow them to serve as mentors. Such changes would eventually alter the whole direction and shape of family life ministry in the Army.

Next, he turned his attention to another problem. Family life centers were starting to multiply around the Army, but it had no guidelines for what a center should look like or how it should operate. Once again, he wrote a detailed policy, outlining standards for the establishment and continuation of a family life center.

He had been serving on the chaplain board for about two years when one day he received a phone call from the board's president, Chaplain Gene Allen. "Dick, we're being asked to come to Washington to brief General Max Thurman, the Army's deputy chief of staff for personnel, on your proposed policies for family life centers."

The Personnel Department gave ultimate approval for all policies related to people. Its chief was a four-star general. The man was about as high up the totem pole as you could go. Only the Army's chief of staff was higher. "Dick," Gene continued, "this policy's your baby. I told Thurman you'd be going to the Pentagon to brief him."

Dick almost swallowed his Adam's apple. Although still a very junior major, he would be briefing the four-star chief of personnel of the Army? And he knew he wouldn't be making his presentation to the general alone. There would be a roomful of brass.

Dick knew a little about the reputation of Max Thurman, the Army chief of personnel. Reporting directly to the chief of staff of the Army, he was known to friend and foe alike as "Mad Max." Thurman was an exceptionally focused, dynamic man—a bachelor reputedly married to his work. It was said that he was so full of energy that he didn't have a desk in his office. Instead, he stood up when he worked, using a specially built podium.

An extremely congenial person, Thurman had recently come to the personnel office from the recruiting command, where he had been in charge of recruiting for the entire Army. He had come up with the "Be all you can be" slogan—one of the Army's most effective recruiting campaigns ever. Dick had met him briefly on one of his trips to the Pentagon. The man was brilliant. And now he wanted to be brought up to speed on Dick's policy book for family life centers! Dick made sure he was thoroughly prepared.

When he walked into the oak-paneled conference room, the first thing he noticed was that the full colonels were seated against the walls. *You know you're breathing rarefied air when full colonels are among the lesser mortals, seated at the back of the room,* he thought to himself. Around the huge, highly polished conference table, ensconced in large burgundy leather chairs, were generals—one-star, two-star, and three-star generals, each identified by a brass name plate on the table. Max Thurman was seated at the far end of the table opposite Dick.

Dick took a deep breath and began his presentation. Confidently and quickly he warmed to his topic. After all, he had spent several years doing family life ministry, and in the past couple years on the board had put together a whole system for family life centers, writing policy and setting up educational processes. Dick knew what he was talking about.

He described for the assembled brass what family life centers were doing and outlined their needs in terms of support from the Army's various commands. Then he reviewed the policies he had written to ensure their systematic operation. When he had finished, he was excused, but Max Thurman asked him to wait outside. "I'd like to talk to you briefly after I dismiss the group, Chaplain."

After the meeting had ended, General Thurman invited him back in for a one-on-one discussion. The chief of personnel asked astute questions and probed for more details. As Dick was about to leave, Thurman said, "Dick, I'd like you to get me what you think are the six best books on family ministry so I can get up to speed on family needs." Promising to do so, he had no doubt that Thurman would examine all six books thoroughly. *He's probably a speed reader too*, he thought.

Sometime later, when Dick was at the Pentagon on other business, he ran into Max Thurman again. The general instantly recognized him, called him by name, and thanked him for the books. Dick was impressed. The man had a profoundly deep focus on his work. He gave off such an aura of respect and competence that you knew immediately he was somebody you would never want to mess with. And yet he was without a doubt one of the warmest people he had ever had a chance to work with.

Dick wore several hats on the chaplain board in addition to his primary responsibility for family life. He served as its assistant administrator and also as deputy funds administrator. When Gene Allen was away, which was often, Dick signed off on orders in his place. And when the funds person was absent, he signed off on money matters, including travel.

Since Dick himself did a lot of traveling, it meant he occasionally signed off on his own travel requests and approved his own expenditures. Each of the seven board members was an expert in his specific field. Consequently they did training for chaplains all over the United States, as well as overseas, particularly in Europe. So, in a sense, Dick had the authorization to send himself anywhere at any time.

And travel he did. Several times he went to Germany to do training, as well as Japan. And he trekked all over the U.S., visiting almost every stateside Army installation at least once during his time on the board. He attended civilian conferences related to family life ministries, such as the annual meetings of the American Association of Marriage and Family Therapy. He also made frequent trips to the locations where the Army was moving its family life master's level training to be sure the programs met its needs.

The Air Force and the Navy each had a chaplain board, and periodically the three boards got together to compare notes and share ideas. Dick could not have imagined any richer experience in terms of understanding systems. He was working not just within the chaplaincy system, but within Army personnel systems. Also, he contrasted both with the similar but different systems used by the Navy and the Air Force. Some days he had to just shake his head. He was a long, long way from Worland, Wyoming!

Dick helped manage a $2 million annual budget—a sizable sum in the late 1970s. While staying within the budget, he developed ideas, resources, and materials for use by chaplains at Army installations all over the world, both for their own professional development and for their work with military families. Drawing from many sources, he brokered materials to supply the entire Army chaplaincy system with resources related to marriage, family life, and counseling. Even while planning for current needs he developed a long-term strategy for the future.

Audiovisual materials were just beginning to explode in quantity and variety. One of Dick's fellow board members specialized in screening and selecting such resources. The new James Dobson *Focus on the Family* films were well suited for use in family life centers.

The board purchased multiple sets on 16-millimeter film for distribution all over the world. Looking ahead, they specified in the purchase order that the Army would have the right to copy the films into other media. Sure enough, videotape soon replaced the 16-millimeter format, and the Army had the authority to transfer the films to videotape with no additional fees. This single farsighted decision saved the military many thousands of dollars.

Occasionally Dick ran into a stumbling block. For instance, one of the major command chaplains—a full colonel in charge of 10 or 15 of the largest military installations in the country—contacted Dick. "Don't start sending stuff directly to my chaplains," he ordered. "Send the materials to me, and I'll decide if they're appropriate for my people."

"Thank you for the suggestion, sir," Dick responded. "But my job description says I am to send materials directly to the field. I'd be glad to send you copies so that you can recommend them." Although outranked, Dick stuck to his guns. In effect, he was saying, "I hear what you're saying, but in order for it to work the way you want, you'll have to take it up with your superiors."

The argument continued for a while, generating more smoke than heat, until the two ran into each other at a meeting. "Well," the colonel said to him, "I've been rough on you. I know you're doing what you're supposed to do. We need to figure out a way to work together. Let's have lunch."

Dick accepted. "I'll pick up the tab," he said. The two men had a meal together at a nearby café. When the check came, Dick opened his wallet—only to discover he didn't have a single cent on him. No cash, no credit card, nothing. Horrified, he'd never been so embarrassed.

The colonel laughed it off. "That could happen to any of us," he chuckled. "I make more money than you do—I'll pick it up." Dick never heard another word about the colonel's need to screen all his materials, although the man did remind him about his empty wallet every time they met.

Every organization, military or not, has its own corporate culture, and the chaplain board was no exception. None of its members or staff wore uniforms. Their office cubicles were designated by their specialties, not their rank. The Army had selected all the members of the board because they were extremely creative people—people who could think outside the box. They enjoyed each other's company. The man at the top, Chaplain (Colonel) Gene Allen, was an affable guy. He enjoyed a good joke, practical or otherwise.

Allen was especially fun to travel with. He and Dick, dressed in sober dark suits and ties, were in an elevator one evening, in Alexandria, Virginia, near the Pentagon. The elevator stopped, and a young couple got on. Gene leaned over to Dick and in a loud stage whisper said, "Dick, I still can't believe you left the gorilla in the room by himself!"

"Oh, don't worry about it, Gene," Dick replied. "I told you, I do it all the time. He has plenty of bananas, and I left *Lassie* playing on the TV. You know that's his favorite show. He'll be fine until we get back from dinner."

Then they enjoyed the consternation on the faces of the two strangers, who tried to look as though they hadn't heard the peculiar conversation. Sometimes creative people just enjoy being creatively silly.

Not wearing uniforms had a certain freedom—freedom to have fun together on occasion, and sometimes freedom to disagree. The chaplain board was a ministry team working toward a common goal—supporting Army chaplains and their work throughout the world. They represented a variety of denominations, including Seventh-day Adventist, Baptist, Presbyterian, Lutheran, and Catholic. The whole experience made Dick see Army chaplaincy, and his own role in it, in a different way.

One day he was preparing materials for a major Pentagon briefing. The collating function on the copying machine had broken down, and Dick was on his hands and knees, collating stuff on the floor. Bill Forman, the board member for religious education, walked by, stuck his head in Dick's cubicle, and said, wonderingly, "Well, would you look at that!"

Glancing up from his task, Dick assumed his colleague was referring to his unorthodox collating method. "I'm not talking about you, Dick. Look there," Bill said, pointing to the wall of the cubicle.

Throughout his entire career Dick had had a painting of Christ on his office wall. It depicted Christ with open, reaching hands. When Dick looked up from his knees, he saw that the afternoon sun was hitting a white marble windowsill, then reflecting off the marble and focusing a single ray of light directly on the face of Christ.

As Dick studied the picture, the office around him receded. The light must have struck that picture in that same way every day, but he had never noticed it. *I'm so busy doing His work that I didn't take time to look at Him,* he thought. Stopping everything, he knelt there on the floor for a long moment, looking at the softly illuminated face of Christ. He would never forget the lesson of that sobering moment.

Dick was still a member of the chaplain board on May 13, 1981, when Pope John Paul II was shot at St. Peter's Square at Vatican City. He was in Kansas, running a weeklong workshop conference for family life chaplains. The group was gathered together, just before noon, when they received word about the assassination attempt. The pope had been hit four times and had lost a lot of blood. Some feared that he might not survive.

The news shook the entire group, but the Catholics among them were especially stricken. One priest, his eyes filled with tears, asked Dick if he would offer a prayer. Dick felt honored to do so. Following his prayer, others prayed also, lifting their hearts to God for a wounded fellow pastor.

Later, when he reflected on that moment, he thought to himself, wonderingly, *How many times has an Adventist pastor been asked by a Catholic priest to pray for the pope?* He had been asked, and he had been privileged to respond. Once again, it had been impressed on him, regardless of rank or religion, when you got together to do ministry, a singleness of purpose transcended a lot of things that would otherwise block camaraderie.

Ministry wasn't about doctrine or standards. It was about doing what Christ would do—responding to human issues and human needs. Whatever your denomination, it didn't matter when a fellow human being was hurting and asking for prayer.

That was the sheer genius of military chaplaincy. People respected you for who you were, not because of the denomination you represented. Many times he'd known a particular chaplain well, but if someone asked about his denomination, he'd have to stop and think. You were a good person and a good pastor—or you weren't.

That was the ethic under which the chaplain board worked, and for four years Dick had the magnificent experience of being a part of that. During those four years he was instrumental in changing the entire direction of military ministry to families. Once again, looking back, he could see that the Lord had put him in the right place at the right time.

His family had some adventures of their own while living on Staten Island. They attended the Staten Island Seventh-day Adventist Church, located in a pleasant residential neighborhood, and the kids went to the church school in the basement. The students were primarily Hispanic, with some Pakistani, some Indian, and some Black families.

The two Stenbakkens were the only Caucasians in the school, and they soon learned what it was like to be in the minority. They responded well to the cultural shift and learned to love and respect people of all ethnic backgrounds—a gift that would serve them well in later years.

Sometimes the whole family would travel with Dick. Being "Army brats" had its advantages. Already at their young ages, Erik and Rikki had lived in lots of different places, traveled extensively, and observed many different walks of life. One of their favorite trips was to the big Barnes and Noble bookstore in downtown Manhattan. It had a great bargain section there. Books with dinged corners sold for pennies on the dollar. They'd come home triumphant, toting grocery bags full of books bought with their own money.

While he was so close to New York with its major universities, Dick wondered if it was time to work on his doctorate. Although he had three master's degrees—two from Andrews and the third in family counseling—he still wanted to get a terminal degree.

Ardis and he talked about the possibilities. Dick investigated several schools, including Rutgers and New York University. Columbia University tested him, and he scored high enough to qualify for a Ph.D. program in psychology, but they wanted him to resign from the military and be a full-time student. It didn't take him long to weigh that possibility. Put his family in jeopardy to get a doctorate in family studies? He didn't think so.

Besides, he reasoned, a doctorate in psychology from a secular university might not be all that comfortable for Adventist administrators. So he kept looking. Then he discovered that Columbia's Education Department offered a doctorate specializing in family and community education. That looked too good to be true, but further investigation revealed it to be amazingly in line with his current assignment on the chaplain board. He talked to Gene Allen about it.

Gene fell right in with the idea. "That's fine," Allen agreed. "It's a win-

win. These courses appear to be directly related to your assignment. So go for it." Dick could spend two afternoons a week at Columbia.

The Army agreed to pay 75 percent of the tuition, as long as the coursework would help with his current assignment. The GI Bill would pick up the remainder. Books, transportation, and other incidentals would come out of Dick's pocket. Enrolling shortly after getting the board position, he took two courses per term, attending classes from 4:00 p.m. to 9:00 p.m. two days a week.

The program also expected him to do independent study. He came up with a plan to conduct an evaluation of a new parenting training program, recruiting chaplains at 10 or more Army installations across the country to use it for a specified time in a controlled situation. They would then evaluate it, with Dick providing mentoring and supervision. When he made the proposal to his advisor, his professor responded, "This could be a magnificent study, but can you actually coordinate all this?"

"Absolutely!" Dick responded. "That's my job!"

One day he received a letter from Columbia. "We have reviewed your file and course materials, and it appears that you have already surpassed our requirements for a master's degree in education," it read. "Would you like us to issue it?"

Wow, he thought, *that's a no-brainer.* All he had to do to get his master's in education from Columbia was to check a box on a form and sign his name. That made four master's degrees, but who was counting?

It was an incredibly busy time. Dick was working full-time and going to school virtually full-time. Midway through his four years the chaplains' school moved to Fort Monmouth, New Jersey. The chaplain board and the school had always been colocated, but the new installation didn't have enough housing.

So he and Ardis bought their first house, and the kids transferred to a nearby church school in Collingwood Park, New Jersey. With house payments and the extra expenses related to his education, money was tight. With all their expenses, the family was running almost $100 a month in the red. A major's pay and the high cost of living in northern New Jersey didn't add up.

One day he noticed a sign on a community bulletin board. A local nondenominational church needed an interim pastor. They offered a small stipend for someone to preach a sermon once a month. He took the job. While he didn't have the time for it, it was a way to earn a little extra money.

Besides, he was starved for a pulpit. Despite the exciting ministry he was involved in, he was still a preacher with a passion to share the gospel. He started preaching at the Bayshore Community church the next week, and it wasn't long before he was taking their pulpit every Sunday.

Ardis looked for work, too. She accepted a job cleaning the church school. It humbled him to know that his wife was cleaning toilets so that he could finish his education. Then she found another part-time job at a craft shop in the mall. Later she taught school and served as acting principal for a while when one of the church school teachers became ill, but still they were running behind every month. Yet somehow they made it through.

Then his four-year term on the chaplain board ended. In the Army you knew when you took a job that it wasn't yours for life. It lent a sense of urgency to what you did each day. He had also managed to complete all his coursework and submit his proposal for his dissertation. All that remained to finish his doctorate was to write the dissertation itself.

Dick had had a marvelous experience being a part of the chaplain board. Working with people of that caliber had had its effect. He had learned that if you want to make a difference in this world, you can do it—but you have to be serious about it.

The people in the chief of chaplains' office had been that kind of people. He had watched them, listened to them, and learned from them. It had been an indescribable growth opportunity—personally, professionally, and spiritually. Now, once again, it was time to move on.

Chapter 21

"Well, Chaplain,
You Give Us No Choice"

Dick leaned back in his office chair at Fort Monmouth and looked out
the window at a bleak and wintry New Jersey afternoon. *It's so cold
out there the icicles have icicles*, he thought. He was on the phone with
Chaplain (Major General) Kermit Johnson, the current chief of chaplains
at the Pentagon.

The subject under discussion was Dick's next rotation. Johnson was
retiring soon and wanted to get the matter of the assignment settled before
he left. "You know, Dick, you've done a great job on the chaplain board,
but you really need to take a boots-on-the-ground assignment next. You
haven't had an overseas tour since Vietnam."

"Well, sir, I go where you send me."

"OK, Dick, let me think about it. I'll get back to you."

When Johnson called back, it was with the surprising news that Dick
had two assignments to choose from. That was a pretty remarkable state of
affairs for a major. Usually, the Army just shipped you where they needed
you.

"We can send you to Germany," Johnson began. Dick's ears perked up.
He and Ardis had always wanted to do a tour in Germany. They had loved
the country ever since their European road trip in the Karmann Ghia right
after the seminary. The drawback was that Erik was now high school age.
In Germany he might have to attend a military boarding school, and his
parents wouldn't be terribly enthusiastic about that. Still, the country was
tempting.

"Or," Johnson continued, "there's been a request for you to go to Hawaii
and start a family life center." Starting a new center appealed to Dick. He
loved nothing more than building something from nothing. Erik could
attend the Adventist high school there. As for living in Hawaii—he glanced
out the window again at the snowy landscape—Hawaii wouldn't be too
bad. His decision was easily made.

Next came the now-familiar packing-up-and-moving phase. Finally they waited at the airport check-in counter, surrounded by a mountain of baggage. The agent took a good look and jokingly asked, "Are you people *moving* to Hawaii?"

"Yes, in fact, we are!" Dick replied. They stopped over in Denver for a few days to visit Ardis' parents and Dick's dad before continuing on to Oahu. Then, about six months from the date he had received the assignment, Dick and his family stepped off the plane in Hawaii, catching a whiff of fragrant plumeria blossoms wafting on a warm, gentle breeze.

Their chaplain sponsor met them with leis, then took them immediately to the post housing office near Aliamanu Military Reservation. "We're sorry, sir, but we don't have anything currently available on the reservation. It's possible that you will need to live off the installation," an official told Dick.

Dick set his jaw. He didn't want to be difficult on his first day in Hawaii, but that wasn't going to fly. Since he was going to start a family life center in the middle of a housing community, he needed to live where he'd be doing ministry. Prepared for a fight, he made his position clear to the post commander.

"Well, Chaplain, you give us no choice. We're going to have to put you up temporarily at the Hilton Rainbow Towers on Waikiki Beach."

"That won't break my heart!" he replied, thinking how his family would respond to that news. And he was right. The kids were ecstatic being a 50-yard dash away from the finest stretch of beach on Waikiki! They all enjoyed the swimming, the shops, and the hotel restaurants. The family reveled in high-rise hotel living for a couple weeks.

Then they learned that they would have to relocate. Evidently the Army considered the hotel too expensive for a longer stay. Fortunately, they were able to move into a condo right across the street from the hotel.

Meanwhile, Erik began classes at Hawaiian Mission Academy, an Adventist high school in Honolulu, and Rikki started school at the nearby Hawaiian Mission Elementary School. Altogether, they lived on the beach at Waikiki for about six weeks. By then their house was ready, their household goods had arrived, and they moved onto Aliamanu Military Reservation.

AMR, as everybody called it, consisted of housing for 2,600 military families, spread across the shallow bowl of an extinct volcanic crater. Officers lived around the crater's rim, and the enlisted family housing filled the vast caldera in the center. It was a beautiful place to live, surrounded as it was by verdant green mountains.

From almost anywhere on the reservation you could look up and see the Army's Tripler Medical Center, a collection of massive coral pink buildings nestled on the emerald slopes of Moanalua Ridge; or look down and see the sparkling waters of Pearl Harbor. Light, misty rain showers fell almost every morning and evening, and rainbows were a daily occurrence. The three-mile main road around the crater's edge was a favorite of runners and joggers. It was no wonder they called it paradise.

AMR was unusual in that it was not attached to any one military installation. It was like any suburban subdivision, only all of its residents were military families—mostly Army, although some Air Force, Navy, and Marine families also lived there. Fort Shafter, the headquarters of the United States Army of the Pacific, was a few miles away.

The area had almost no public amenities at the time—no churches, no family facilities. The only shopping consisted of the Shoppette, a gas station-convenience store-PX.

Quickly Dick realized that the place, although beautiful, was going to present some unique challenges. That impression deepened when he began the search for office space. Eventually he negotiated the use of a couple rooms in a condemned residence—deemed unfit for family housing because of its cracked walls. The installation commander, a female lieutenant, and her NCO had their headquarters in two of the four bedrooms. Dick and his assistant made their offices in the other two.

Dick paid his first visit to Chaplain Tom Carter, the command chaplain for all Army posts on Oahu—the man who had put in the request that brought Dick to Hawaii. "Chaplain, what do you want me to do at Aliamanu?" he asked, clipboard in hand and pen at the ready.

"Well, Dick, I want you to get a family life center up and running, with religious education, parenting classes, youth programs—you know the drill," the command chaplain replied." Dick suppressed a smile. He knew the drill, all right, having written the book, so to speak. But there was a problem.

"Chaplain, there are no buildings available. There isn't a single space on the whole installation suitable for use as a meeting place," he said, stating the obvious.

"Yeah, you're right. Then you'll have to figure out how to get one."

"What's my budget for that?"

"Budget? There's no budget. Draft up something—tell me what you think you'll need for a building and equipment." The command chaplain wasn't as uninterested as he sounded. He knew Dick wouldn't give up until the family life center became a reality. Then he made sure Dick had sufficient funds to set up his offices and start working. The rest Dick would have to figure out for himself.

Dick left the command chaplain's office scratching his head. *No facilities. No budget,* he thought. *Starting from scratch is one thing, but this is ridiculous. Well, the good thing is that anything I do will be an improvement.* He sent a prayer heavenward, knowing that he was going to need help with this one! And then that familiar sense of joy and anticipation that any new ministry project generated in him began to spread through him. With God's help he'd make it happen!

First, he began to explore the reservation, asking questions as he went. Lots of young families lived there, so there were many children of all ages. He learned that a Navy family named Hoard was providing, on a volunteer basis, the only religious education.

The Hoards ran a kind of traveling Vacation Bible School on the back of a pickup truck. They would pull up somewhere, such as the parking lot of the Shoppette, unload their easels, set up felt storyboards, and teach Bible stories. Kids knew where the truck would be ahead of time, and they would flock there to hear the stories and do the crafts and activities.

Dick also learned that the military had used the crater as an ammunition storage depot during World War II, which accounted for one unusual feature. Dotted around the crater's edges, below the rim, were massive, inch-thick reinforced steel doors about eight feet wide. They led into huge human-made caves, known as the Aliamanu bunkers, cut deep into the volcanic rock.

All were locked with heavy iron padlocks. Most were abandoned, but some still served for storage. The Boy Scouts had received one of the bunkers to use for their den meetings. That windowless cave was the only public gathering space in the whole AMR.

As he looked around, Dick continued to pray about what could be done. The needs were huge. *I gotta start someplace,* he thought. Finally he decided to pick an event as a focal point to plan toward, and settled on Easter—about six months away. While wrangling furniture, equipment, and supplies for his office, he kept on thinking, praying, and planning.

Requisitioning a typewriter, he asked for an IBM Selectric. The typewriter was delivered to headquarters—and stayed there. When Stenbakken heard that it was in, he requested that it be sent on to him. "Sorry, Chaplain, we need it up here."

Even a chaplain can get his hackles up, especially when somebody appropriates what's rightfully his. Dick took out a DF (a distribution form—Army talk for an interoffice memo) and printed a message on it in crayon. "I need to get my typewriter," he wrote. "If it is impossible to give me the typewriter I asked for, I need several cases of crayons. The points are wearing down on the ones I have."

When he gave the note to his assistant, Sheila, to deliver, she rolled her eyes. "You're not going to send that up to headquarters, are you?" She thought he had lost his mind. But when she saw that he was deadly serious, she delivered it herself. And two days later he had his typewriter.

Dick chuckled when the typewriter showed up. Not long before, he'd been working at a Pentagon-level job, consorting with generals, and now he was scrapping for a typewriter. Life had its twists and turns. So far the Army had given him quite a ride, teaching him much at each step of the way. But he knew what the system could do and how it could support you if you understood how to use it. *I'm here to do good ministry, and I'm going to help the system help me do it,* he thought. Little did he know how much he was going to need all his knowledge, skill, and ingenuity to get the job done.

While he worked on the other aspects of the start-up of a family life center, he continued to plan the Easter event. It would be an outdoor Easter sunrise program. The setting was ideal, and it would serve as his introduction to the community. He thought back to the Christmas program he'd given at Fort Leonard Wood, when he'd told the Nativity story in the persona of an innkeeper. This time he would relate the Easter story as a Roman centurion who had witnessed the Crucifixion.

In his spare time he made himself a set of Roman armor. After finding an old brown Naugahyde tablecloth, he cut it up and riveted it together to look like banded leather armor. It wasn't even remotely accurate, but he didn't know that. Taking a construction helmet, he turned it backwards, mounted an Army-issue whisk broom on top, spray-painted the whole thing gold, and he had a passable Roman helmet. Finally, he made a sword out of a flat piece of metal he obtained in the Army craft shop.

He wrote the presentation and prepared flyers. Locating a big open field with a hill on one side, he got up before dawn one morning to figure out exactly where the sun would rise over it. Then he built a big wooden cross and set it on the top of the hill, sited so that as the people seated down below watched, the sun would come up right behind the cross.

To provide the music, he paid the excellent Aiea Adventist Church choir $50. With his assistant, Sheila, he handed out flyers all over the reservation, inviting people to bring their lawn chairs and beach mats and watch the sunrise service. Everything was in readiness for his debut Aliamanu performance, and what he hoped would be the launch of a successful ministry.

The night before the program, it started to rain about midnight. It continued all night long. Dick was already jumpy enough, but the rain made him even crazier. Although he prayed hard, his faith was being outweighed by a sense of impending doom. Every 15 minutes or so he woke up and lay listening to the sound of the rain hitting the roof. *I'm dead*, he thought. *With this much rain, that whole field is going to be a sea of mud. My Easter program will be a total disaster!* At last Dick got up about 4:30 a.m. to find that the rain had finally stopped.

Donning his helmet and armor, he headed out to set things up the best he could, mud or no mud. To his surprise, the ground was just fine. *"O ye of little faith,"* he thought, smacking himself on the forehead with the heel of his hand. *The ground is volcanic. The rain soaks right through it, like water pouring through sand.*

It was a beautiful Hawaiian predawn, damp and cool. Dick climbed the hill and stood next to the cross, watching as the people arrived. He remained so still, the crowd thought he was a mannequin. Then, as the sun slowly rose behind him, he walked down the hill and began to speak. Every eye was fixed on him as he told the story of the Crucifixion from the point of view of an eyewitness.

While he was speaking, he noticed a familiar face in the front row. Needing a tunic of some sort to wear under his homemade armor, he had gone to a thrift shop at Fort Shafter. As he was looking through the racks of clothes, a clerk approached him. "What are you looking for, sir?" she asked.

"I need a dress," Dick replied, distractedly flipping through garment after garment. Before the woman could respond, his eyes lighted on a nice cream-colored A-line number, just right for what he needed. "This is it! This is perfect!"

"What are you going to do with that?" the incredulous sales clerk asked.

"Do with it? I'm going to wear it, of course. I'll be wearing it Sunday morning at the Easter sunrise service at Aliamanu."

"If you're going to wear that, I'm going to be there!" she replied. And there she was. That 50-cent purchase started Dick's extensive costume collection.

Close to 100 people attended the Easter sunrise service. After the presentation Dick walked around among the crowd, shaking hands, still in Roman armor. It was a good beginning. People were starting to know who he was. But how in the world was he going to continue a ministry for these people, with no place to meet?

Dick had been looking around for land where he could put any kind of building, assuming he had one. He found a likely place on the edge of an open field, across from a couple of the bunkers. Although a little isolated, it looked like it would be a pretty good spot. He went to the installation commander. "If I can wrangle some building materials, could I put a building here?"

"Sure, why not? But how are you gonna get a building?"

"I don't know. But I'm working on it."

The commanding officer shook his head. "OK, Chaplain," he said, not unkindly. "You work on it."

It was time for the Stenbakken praying-networking-scrounging machine to shift into high gear. Dick knew an Adventist Navy chaplain named Herman Kibble who was attached to a Seabees unit at Port Hueneme near Thousand Oaks, California. Port Hueneme is the West Coast home port of the Seabees, the Navy's mobile construction force.

On a hunch, he called Kibble. "Herm," he said, after the usual greetings, "I'm looking for a couple prefab metal buildings—you know, those Butler Buildings the Navy uses. You guys got any of those to spare? What's the possibility of my getting my hands on a couple?"

"Let me check around." A few days later Herman called back. "You're not going to believe this, Dick, but we have a bunch of those unassembled buildings here that our guys are trying to get rid of. I think they're 40 feet by 80 feet. You know, they come as a self-contained kit. Everything's there, the doors, the windows, all of it. You just have to provide the footings and foundation. I have no idea how you would arrange to get them—but I think you can have them if you can find a way."

Dick went back to his commander. "I think I found some buildings. But the problem is the Navy isn't going to give them to the Army, but the Seabees in California will give them to the Seabees in Oahu. Sir, I'd sure like to get those buildings. Would you be willing to ask the Oahu Seabees for them?"

"Sure, we'll ask for them," the colonel replied. And he did.

Now Dick had the promise of some buildings, but they were still in California. How was he going to get them to Hawaii? He called good old Herman Kibble again.

"Herm, what can you do to help me get my buildings shipped?"

"Let me look around; I'll see what I can do." Before long he was back on the phone. "Not going to be a problem. The Navy has ships going back and forth all the time. I think we can get them on board for free."

Dick had his buildings and a means to get them to Hawaii. In the meantime he needed a concrete pad to put them on. You couldn't just set them on dirt. This time he schmoozed the engineers at Fort Shafter, a couple miles up Highway H1. The housing division of the Army owned the AMR, and the Army engineers at Fort Shafter were responsible for supplying construction and maintenance support for the housing.

"OK, guys," he broached the subject after he'd established some rapport and filled them in on his plans for a family life center. "If I can get some Butler Buildings, will you guys give me the money for the foundations, plumbing, and wiring?"

The engineers were skeptical. "Where you gonna get the buildings?"

"That's my problem. I'll find the buildings if you'll put your money into the support." The engineers looked at each other. "Oh, yeah, sure, Chaplain. If you get the buildings, we'll do it." Dick had the distinct feeling they were simply trying to get rid of him, but they had given their word.

One important rule of the praying-networking-scrounging machine, he had learned, was to get everything documented. He took a large three-ring binder with him everywhere he went. Whenever he talked to somebody, he'd haul it out and make notations, recording each conversation with the time and date, so he had a careful record of every commitment. Those records would come in handy.

Quite a while later Dick got the long-anticipated phone call from the people down at the Navy dock. "Chaplain, your buildings are here."

"OK, great!" Hanging up, he then called the engineering office at Fort Shafter.

"The buildings are here," he announced, cheerfully. "I need two five-ton flatbed trucks to pick them up. We're ready for engineer support."

"What buildings?" came the bored reply.

"Those buildings I talked to you about months ago." He referred to the records in his binder, making sure the man on the other end of the phone could hear the paper rattling as he turned the pages. "The buildings we discussed on such and such a date, at such and such a time."

"Oh, yeah, Chaplain, now I remember."

"OK, good. They're sitting on the dock at the Navy yard. I need trucks to get them up to AMR."

"Well, I don't know, Chaplain." The voice on the other end was obviously reluctant to commit.

"Call me when you can get them." The buildings sat on the dock for about two weeks, with Dick phoning the engineers every other day. Nothing happened.

That does it. I'm done with the engineers, he thought. He called a transportation unit at Fort Shafter. Because his assignment in Vietnam had been with a transportation unit, he knew how they worked.

When someone answered the phone, he plunged right in. "They're bugging me to get those buildings off the dock," he began.

"What buildings?"

Dick explained his need. "You got it, Chaplain. We'll pick 'em up this afternoon. Don't worry, we'll pick them up at 1:00. Where you want us to put them?"

Then Dick called the engineers back. "It's your property—you tell me where to put the buildings."

The engineers specified an open lot, and the transportation crew delivered the two building kits and unloaded them. And there they sat.

Dick thanked the transportation unit guys and the engineers. "OK, now we need to have a plan to get them built." The engineers acknowledged that they had agreed to provide support, but nothing happened.

Again he waited a couple weeks. Then he went back to the Army commander, a full colonel.

"Sir," he said, "those buildings you asked for from the Seabees have arrived. But they're just sitting over here. I think you're going to have to call the Seabee commander back and tell him we can't use them."

The colonel looked at Dick as if he had just been shot. "What do you mean, you can't use them?" he barked.

"The engineers aren't returning my calls. I can't get answers from them about the schedule or the money to get them built. If we're not going to use them, we need to give them back."

Dick knew full well that there was no way that the officer would tell his counterpart at the Seabees, "Sorry, we can't use what you just gave us." He'd die first. Dick understood how the system worked. And the colonel knew he knew. "OK, Chaplain. Sit down."

The colonel reached across his desk and grabbed his phone. He called the commander of the engineers, a lieutenant colonel. The two men were on a first-name basis, but both of them clearly knew who outranked whom.

"I want the chaplain's buildings built immediately, and I want you to call me back not later than 4:00 this afternoon with a plan to get it done," he bellowed. Although he interjected a few more colorful words, they didn't obscure the message in the slightest. The colonel didn't even say goodbye before he slammed the receiver down.

Then he smiled at Dick. "I think we can get this done, Chaplain. Let's not give the buildings back."

Dick concealed his delight. "Thank you very much, sir," he said, rising from his seat. "I appreciate your support."

Then things started happening. The engineers found the money for cement and poured the slabs. The Seabee team arrived, surveyed the site, and started putting up the two metal buildings. Dick asked to have them sited about 40 feet apart.

"As long as you're pouring the cement," he asked, "why not put a patio between the buildings? And while you're at it, could you put some bolts in the corners, so we can add some posts to support a canopy?" That created a third usable space. The engineers were cooperative. One phone call had changed their attitudes completely. Dick duly logged everything into his three-ring binder.

They brought electricity in from a power pole across the street. Some empty ammunition storage caves were right across the road from the new buildings. Two of them were locked and secured, and the third was the one being used by the Boy Scouts.

Finding out which Army command "owned" one of the remaining bunkers, Dick got permission to use it as a storage area. When he could not discover the owner of the other bunker, he "unlocked" it with a drill and a sledgehammer and claimed it for the family life center also. Possession, after all, was nine-tenths of the law, even in the Army.

So now Dick had a chapel, a religious education room, classrooms, offices, an outdoor space, and two windowless bunkers for additional classrooms and storage. And the large paved aprons outside the bunkers provided plenty of room for parking. The family life center facilities were shaping up nicely. All that remained was to find the money to furnish and equip them. Dick obtained some "temple tax" money from the chief of chaplains' office at the Pentagon. (When you take up an offering in an Army chapel, 10 percent goes to the chief of chaplains' office for special initiatives and projects. That's the "temple tax.")

So he had the money in hand for carpeting and seating for both buildings. But he didn't want pews—not even for the chapel. The buildings needed to serve many purposes. He preferred stackable, padded chairs for flexibility and comfort.

Having seen exactly the right chair in a catalog of items authorized for military purchase, he went to Schofield Barracks to order them. "I need 120 of those chairs," he said, showing the purchasing agent the catalog.

"Sorry, Chaplain. Those chairs are not approved for chaplain use."

"But I have the money from the chief of chaplains to buy these chairs!"

The purchasing agent shook his head. He wasn't budging an inch. "I can't order them. They're not on your allowable list."

That was a new one on Dick. He hadn't run up against this particular problem before. "What do I need to do to get them?"

"There's no way, Chaplain." The purchasing agent showed Dick the TDA—the table of distribution and allowances—that he worked from. "If you're not authorized to buy a certain kind of item, you can't spend government money to do it, even if you have the money already appropriated. I can't go down and buy a diesel truck. I'm not authorized to have one. The TDA won't allow it."

"What do I do to get the TDA changed?"

"Forget it. Only the Pentagon can change it." The agent relaxed, relieved that he was about to get this doggedly persistent chaplain out of his hair.

But Dick wasn't finished. "OK, what's your phone number?" Noting it down, he said, "I'll be back."

"Yeah, sure, Chaplain" was the weary reply.

Back in his own office in the house with the cracked walls, Dick called Chaplain Gary Councell in the chief of chaplains' office at the Pentagon. Gary was a fellow Adventist chaplain who just happened to be in charge of writing the TDA for all Army chaplains.

"The chief has given me money for furnishings for our new family life center, Gary," he explained, "But the TDA won't let me buy the chairs I need. Can you get it changed?"

"Sure, Dick, I'll put in an interim change right now." And then he took down the information on the chairs Dick wanted.

"Thanks, Gary. Here's my purchasing guy's phone number. Will you let him know?"

"No problem, Dick. Good to talk with you!" Councell hung up the phone.

Dick drove back to the purchasing office at Fort Shafter. The agent looked stunned. He had just gotten a call from the Pentagon, making an interim change to the TDA, authorizing the exact chairs Dick required.

"Any questions?" Dick asked.

"Yeah, how'd you do that?"

With a grin he pointed heavenward. "You could say I've got connections in high places," was all he said.

Dick had never had so much fun. At every turn he had encountered roadblocks—things that hadn't been done before. The project had been a challenge, but it was just the kind of thing he relished. With the Lord's help, he'd used all his ingenuity, all his talent, all his wit, and all his charm, not to mention most of his connections, but the AMR family life center was now a reality.

The new facility was an immediate hit. The lights were almost never turned off, because it was the only place on AMR where you could have a meeting. The stackable chairs and folding tables were constantly being rearranged for different uses.

Soon Dick and his assistant were running a full slate of family life programs and events. He hired Brenda Hoard, she of the pickup truck Vacation Bible School, as a full-time director of religious education. Brenda developed a creative program for kids, with every kind of craft and activity. It wasn't long before the 100-seat chapel was filled beyond capacity, with two Protestant worship services every Sunday morning, and a religious education program (Sunday school) between them.

Chapter 22

"We've Made a
Name for Ourselves"

While Dick was focusing on getting the family life center up and going, his family was thriving in the Hawaiian sun. Who wouldn't, in a land of sun-drenched beaches, wild waves, and cascading waterfalls? But more than sunshine kept them happy and busy.

Erik and Rikki loved their schools and were involved in many activities. Ardis taught English as a second language at Hawaiian Mission Academy after completing her master's degree in secondary education with an emphasis in English at the University of Hawaii on the Manoa campus. Her thesis project focused on teaching the Bible as literature in the public school.

The whole family was active in the Seventh-day Adventist Church in nearby Aiea. The church membership was a delightful blend of races and cultures, including a large number of Japanese, some of whom spoke little or no English.

The church was known for its fabulous potluck dinners, held every Sabbath after services. It always had two serving lines, one just for Japanese fare. Rikki and Erik, already quite cosmopolitan teenagers, were being exposed to many new cultures, learning more about the food, backgrounds, and interests of their Hawaiian friends.

Weekends were always busy. Dick and Ardis had developed a relationship with the Aeia church choir, beginning when they had provided the music for his first Easter presentation at AMR. He and Ardis did similar programs with them many times, traveling with them to various islands.

Dick taught a Sabbath school class, served as an elder in the church, and often took the pulpit at Aeia or another Adventist church. One particular weekend he led or participated in 13 different events. Sometimes, with a busy Sabbath schedule and an equally full Sunday calendar, he was glad to see Monday come so that he could rest up a little!

Weekdays were nearly as full, however. In addition to his pastoral duties, many of Dick's responsibilities were administrative, including managing budgets and logistics for the various programs of the family life center. And, in addition, he was doing at least five or six hours of counseling every day.

His military congregation understood that he was a Seventh-day Adventist and worshipped with his family on Saturday. The people were delighted when his wife and children attended services with the Sunday congregation, but did not expect that they would do it regularly. Rikki and Erik knew this was Dad's job. It was his passion—like breathing—but he understood that his kids needed more space, and he and Ardis made sure they got it.

Not long after they started holding religious services in the Butler Buildings, he and Brenda Hoard devised a unified approach for all the religious activities at the family life center. They started with a "Through the Bible" theme. Dick would preach from the book of Genesis, for example, and they would prepare and distribute family worship materials on the same topic.

The religious education or Sunday school classes would also follow the theme. This allowed them to teach the Bible in a systematic way to many people who had only a rudimentary idea of what the Scriptures actually contained. The people loved the approach, and both services on Sunday morning had every seat filled.

Dick followed up that series with another, "Bible Personalities," which gave him plenty of opportunities to showcase his first-person narratives. The people got so involved that even the volunteer who did the floral arrangements designed the flowers around that week's theme. Dick was especially delighted when he arrived at the church on the morning he was doing a presentation on Moses, to find floral arrangements depicting a baby in the bulrushes and a burning bush.

It wasn't many months before the expanding programs and growing congregations at AMR had outgrown the little prefab metal buildings completely, and he began to dream of a more permanent edifice. The buildings were functional and served their purposes well, but they were not really what you'd think of as a true military chapel. Dick was aware that the Pentagon's chief of chaplains had a long-term building plan to put new chapels on military installations. But nowhere on that list was there one for the Aliamanu Military Reservation.

Also, he knew that the Army had a special program called the Chapel of the Year. It was a line item in the Pentagon's budget that made provision for one new chapel each year not in the regular building schedule. It was based on filling an acute need—one that had emerged that nobody had anticipated. He thought Aliamanu fit that bill.

Dick talked to his command chaplain, Lieutenant Colonel Tom Carter, and then with Carter's successor, Lieutenant Colonel Herm Kizer, about the possibility of AMR getting the Chapel of the Year. He thought the idea had several things going for it, in addition to the obvious need. For one thing, Dick himself had just come out of the chief of chaplains' office, so he knew the right people. Pointing this out to his boss, and then warming to his subject, he leaned forward in his chair.

"And for another thing," he urged, "the AMR Butler Buildings chapel has achieved a certain degree of notoriety. Whenever anybody comes to visit us from the chief of chaplains' office, our buildings are on their must-see list. They've all heard about our setup, and they want to see it for themselves. They shake their heads and wonder how in the world we were able to create something out of nothing. We've kind of made a name for ourselves.

"So," he concluded, "we have that good will at the top of the heap. That makes it easier to approach them with our request." Then he leaned back, and he and Tom Carter looked at each other for a moment. Suddenly Chaplain Carter grinned. "Let's go for it!"

So they made an application for the Chapel of the Year. The process was long and laborious, the red tape unbelievably difficult. They waited for months while their application underwent review by all the necessary levels of command through the Army system. It had reached the office of the secretary of defense when it hit a snag. Somebody in the OSD had a family member—an officer—living at AMR. That individual picked up the phone and asked his relative, "Do you guys really need a chapel?"

"No, we don't need a chapel here," the person replied. "There are at least a half dozen military chapels scattered around the island, not to mention hundreds of other religious facilities. We can go anywhere we want."

When Dick heard about it through the grapevine, he knew that that one comment could sink the project like a stone. They'd have to do something to counteract it. And he recognized a serious flaw in the officer's argument. Up on the edge of the crater, where the officers lived, there was a car or even two for every home. But for the enlisted soldiers' families, living down in the crater, a household was lucky to have one car, and even more so if it ran.

The soldier would need the car to get to work, often leaving the spouse and kids stuck. Living in AMR without a car was like existing on the dark side of the moon. The families had no way to get anywhere and nothing to do. The AMR chapel served their needs—and not only as a chapel, but as a family life center—a community gathering place with programs for moms, teens, little kids, and so much more.

But sure enough, the damage had been done. The powers that be turned the project down. Dick and others sent out a request to reconsider. Then he received a letter from the office of the secretary of defense. "In order to reconsider your request," it read, "we need to have the name, address, phone number, and worship schedule of every religious facility within a 25-mile radius."

Dick was livid. A 25-mile radius covered the whole island of Oahu! He drafted a short letter in reply. "I can comply with your request," he wrote, "but it will take seven and a half man years of labor. However, please consult the attached." Then he gave the letter to his assistant to process. "Where's the attachment?" she asked.

Dick handed her 30 yellow pages torn from the Honolulu phone book. "You're not going to send them that!"

"I most certainly am."

They resumed the waiting game, but it looked as if the project would never happen. Dick heard that a swimming pool was on the drawing board for AMR. A swimming pool? This was Hawaii, with water in every direction. A swimming pool was needed—but a chapel wasn't?

It was frustrating, but he had never walked away from a challenge, and he wasn't about to start now. Aware that military officials have a strong political desire to remain on friendly terms with members of Congress, he devised a plan. He would go to every single meeting and event held in the Butler Buildings and the adjacent caves and make a pitch.

For several weeks he was even busier than usual, shuttling from Scout meetings and book clubs and Tupperware parties to youth groups and knitting classes and exercise sessions. He attended military briefings and Catholic Masses and went to men's groups and women's groups. And he showed up at every kind of community gathering.

At every event, he talked about the needs for a new meeting center and chapel in AMR, about the Chapel of the Year program, and the snag their application had encountered. Explaining what it would take to influence the right people to make the right decision, he came prepared with pens, paper, envelopes and stamps, and, most important, a list of congress members from every state in the union.

"Now, I'm not asking you to write a congressperson in your home state," he'd conclude, "because it would be against Army regulations for me to do that. But if you feel moved to do so, help yourself to these supplies. And if you do choose to write your congressperson, you might want to send a copy of your letter to Senator Daniel Inouye." Everybody knew who Daniel Inouye was—Hawaii's beloved senior senator who had lost an arm fighting in Italy during World War II.

Soon congress members from all over the country began receiving letters from their constituents concerning the need for a new Army chapel at a little place most had never heard of, called Aliamanu, Hawaii. Legislators want to stay on the good side of their constituents, so most had someone on their staff follow up by contacting the office of the secretary of defense.

More than 50 congressional inquiries started. Military people didn't want to blow off 50 congress members, either, and suddenly the OSD became much more positive toward the project.

About the time Dick's tour of duty in Hawaii was due to end, he received word that all agencies had approved Aliamanu to build the Chapel of the Year. He put in for a one-year extension of his tour. After leadership granted it, he became involved in the initial design and development stages for the new facility. The project expanded to include not only a brand-new 350-seat chapel and family life center, but a first-class child-care facility as well. When he left Hawaii after four years, three chaplains replaced him—a full-time family life center director, a pastor, and an associate. (Later Dick returned for the ribbon-cutting ceremony when the multimillion-dollar facility opened. Something had definitely been created from nothing.)

Then it was time for his rotation out of Hawaii. In typical gracious Hawaiian fashion, friends and coworkers came to the airport to see the family off. The crowd was huge. Teachers and students from Hawaiian Mission Academy, fellow church members from Aiea, parishioners and neighbors from Aliamanu, and colleagues from the military all crowded around, placing flower leis around their necks in the time-honored Hawaiian custom.

Soon Dick and his family couldn't see over the stacks of flowers. Their friends loaded their arms with more flower garlands. They boarded the plane covered in so many flowers that they couldn't sit down. The

Stenbakkens offered flowers to the other passengers, and the flight attendants appeared with garbage bags to hold the overflow. It was a charming way to end their four rewarding years in Hawaii.

About a year before the end of his Hawaiian tour, Dick had received a promotion to lieutenant colonel. He knew that when his tour was up, he would be moving on, but of course, he didn't know where. Then administration selected him for a division chaplains' training course. In terms of leadership, moving into a division chaplain's position was a little like a preacher becoming a conference president.

A division chaplain supervised 30 or more chaplains and many more support staff. The job would be a combination of boots on the ground mixed with administrative duties. If you did it well, your chances of reaching full colonel were good. It was an opportunity that many chaplains eagerly hoped for, but you couldn't apply for it. It came to you.

His selection for the division chaplains' course was something of an anomaly. The military chose most division chaplains from the ranks of what were called "line assignments"—guys that had worked directly with troops in combat zones or at least in overseas installations. Dick had been a family life chaplain—had even spent a tour at the chief of chaplains' office. He hadn't had any boots-on-the-ground experience since his assignment at Fort Lewis.

Then, too, some people had suggested that his specialization in family life might be a career killer, but he knew it was what God had called him to do, and he was willing to accept the fact that it might not put him on the fast track to promotion. And now he was being selected for the division course. That meant he'd be going back to chaplain school for additional training, and after that, who knew? Not every chaplain selected for division training actually got the job.

Chaplain Tom Carter, Dick's first command chaplain in Hawaii, had risen to full colonel and had moved from Hawaii to Fort Polk, Louisiana. When he realized that Dick, now a lieutenant colonel, was up for reassignment and had been appointed for the division chaplains' course, he contacted the chief of chaplains' office at the Pentagon and asked for him by name to be his division chaplain. Dick was visiting his father in Denver when the call came from the chief of chaplains' office. "Congratulations, you got a division."

When he heard his new post was in Louisiana, he had mixed emotions—it was an honor and a privilege to be getting the division job, but—Louisiana? That was about as far away from his dad and Ardis' parents as you could get. He called his wife.

"We got a division!" he announced.

"That's wonderful, honey. Where?"

"Fort Polk, Louisiana."

"You're kidding! Where? Get serious."

"No, honey, really. We've been assigned to Fort Polk, Louisiana."

A long pause. "Well, we're military. We go where they send us, don't we?"

Slowly he hung up the phone, his mind in a whirl. Gradually the whirling slowed down, and he began to focus on the situation at hand. *I'm here in Denver,* he thought. *Fort Carson, just a few miles away at Colorado Springs, is the home of the fourth infantry division. I know the installation chaplain there, Tom Downes.*

He smiled inwardly. The man was a good guy and a great friend. A Catholic priest, he was also a family life specialist, like Dick—one of the very few Catholic chaplains in family life. *I think I'll give my buddy Tom a call,* Dick thought.

"Tom, what's the rotation like for the fourth division?" Dick asked, once the usual pleasantries were out of the way.

"It's empty."

"You have anybody named coming in?"

"No, I'm still waiting for the chief of chaplains' office to tell me. Why do you ask?"

"Well, I'm selected for Fort Polk down in Louisiana. But with my elderly father here in Denver, I wouldn't mind being closer to him."

"Hey, I'd love to have you!"

"So, Tom, would you be willing to call the chief's office and say that?"

"Absolutely! Sure, I'll do it right now."

A short time later Dick received another phone call from the chief of chaplains' office. "Chaplain Stenbakken, we just had a call from Tom Downes at Fort Carson. We know you're already assigned to Fort Polk, but Chaplain Downes has asked for you by name. Would you be interested in going to Fort Carson?"

Dick expressed his interest in Fort Carson. Matt Zimmerman, the current chief of chaplains, was traveling in Europe and Asia. His staff contacted him for the final approval. Such assignments required the personal approval of the chief of chaplains, a two-star general. Once they'd chased him down and obtained his authorization, the chief of chaplains' office phoned again.

"Chaplain, you're going to Carson. We'll get somebody else for Fort Polk." Dick was relieved and thankful. Once again, by God's grace, he had known the right person in the right position at the right time—a situation that gave him exceptional input into his future assignment.

Fort Carson, Colorado, was the perfect place for the whole family to be. Rikki would be a high school junior and Erik a college freshman. Both Campion Academy and Union College were nearby, and Dick would be close to his father. And not only that, but some years before, Ardis' parents had retired and moved to a place in the mountains west of Loveland, only a couple hours away.

And Dick had recently learned that Tom Carter, the chaplain who had asked for him to come to Fort Polk, had since moved on to another assignment. *If you tried to write this as fiction,* he thought to himself, *nobody would believe it!*

They arrived at Fort Carson in 1986. The installation didn't have enough housing for all personnel, so he and Ardis found a house to buy just north of the post. They closed the loan on a Tuesday, and on Wednesday they shampooed all the carpets.

The people next door, an Army major and his family, made them welcome, bringing over sandwiches and lemonade. The truck with their furniture arrived on Thursday. As they unpacked, Erik packed up his stuff, and on Friday morning he left for Union College in Lincoln, Nebraska. Ardis and Dick were driving Rikki up to Campion Academy in Loveland, Colorado, that same day. They planned to stay overnight there. The new house was still filled with unpacked boxes—and a black cat named Kukui.

Dick walked over and knocked on the neighbor's door. "I hate to impose on you folks," he said, "but would you mind taking care of our cat for a day or two?"

"Sure, we'll be glad to," they replied. So he gave these people, whose names he barely knew, the cat food and the key to their house, containing everything they owned, and he and Ardis and Rikki took off for Loveland. That's what it meant to be a military family. You had a bond, and you trusted each other.

Chapter 23

"Well, That's One
for the Books"

On one of his first mornings at Fort Carson, Dick decided to go out for his usual early-morning run. Staying in good physical condition wasn't an option in the Army—it was mandatory. Regulations required him to keep his weight under certain standards and to take regular physical training tests—including running, sit-ups, and push-ups.

So he thought he was in pretty good shape as he put on his running shoes and headed out on a beautiful, cool morning. At first he cruised along, enjoying the fresh morning air. But after only a quarter of a mile, he suddenly ran out of oxygen and began gasping for air.

That was his reintroduction to what it was like to live at 6,000 feet above sea level. It was a big change from Hawaii! He struggled back home, and from then on did much shorter, slower runs. It took a few more weeks to get acclimatized.

His new job took some getting used to as well. It was a far cry from the pastoral role he had filled in Hawaii. As a division chaplain he had a handful of major-level chaplains reporting to him. Each of the majors was responsible for a brigade. Each brigade had a chapel, and each major had three or four chaplains under him.

Dick's position was both administrative and hands-on. The military expected division chaplains to be planners, executors, budgeters, trainers, and mentors. The training for the job had been, in typical Army fashion, both intensive and practical. The classes consisted of creating an entire Army installation on paper.

The virtual Army post filled two big three-ring binders and included fictitious maps, addresses, and phone numbers. In a typical afternoon lab session each student received a sealed envelope. Inside was a problem or situation, such as "Chaplain, you have just received word that three chaplains have died in combat, and you need to replace them." Each student had to write up the steps they would take to resolve the situation within the setting of the virtual Army post and according to military protocol and regulations. They had resource books to consult to find the right solution. If you got it wrong, the problem came back to you until you solved it correctly. Meanwhile, the trainers handed you more problems, and you were under pressure to do the right thing in the right way in each situation. Make a few mistakes, and the problems would start to stack up. It was relentless.

When Dick completed this training process, however, he felt equipped to cope with any situation that arose. The course had done what it was supposed to—given him the sense that he knew what he was doing. It allowed him to feel comfortable in his new job.

The training could not cover every possible situation, as he soon found out when his phone rang at 3:00 one morning. On the other end of the line was one of the brigade chaplains under his command, Chaplain (Major) Krishna Ajjarapu, a native of India. His chapel was down at the south end of the installation—one of the old cantonement chapels, a small, white-painted wooden building dating from the 1930s.

"Good morning, sir; how are you today?" Chaplain Ajjarapu said politely.

Privately Dick thought, *Well, I'd be better if I hadn't been awakened at 3:00 a.m.*, but he returned Krishna's greeting in the same courteous manner.

"I'm very well, thank you, Chaplain. What's happening?"

"Well, I am sorry to say, sir, that a car has driven into the chapel."

The little chapel sat at a sharp bend in the road. Some driver, possibly under the influence of something stronger than milk, had failed to make the turn and had actually put his car halfway into the chapel at 3:00 in the morning.

Dick couldn't fault Chaplain Ajjarapu for his 3:00 a.m. call. Early on, he had had a little talk with the chaplains who reported to him. "If something happens in your area, good or bad, you should be the first person to know about it, your spouse is the second, and I need to be number three. I don't want to get my news through the grapevine." Ajjarapu was just following orders.

"Do I need to come?" Dick asked him.

"No, sir. The driver was not badly injured. There's no fire, and I've put a sheet of plastic over the hole in the wall."

"Fine. I'll meet you there in the morning, and we'll decide what needs to be done. Thanks for calling." *Well, that's one for the books—or one that wasn't in the books,* he thought as he turned off the light.

Fort Carson was close enough to Denver that he was able to see his father more frequently. Dad was still living alone in the house on South Downing Street and appeared to be managing quite well, but when Dick began to delve into his father's finances, he discovered a tangle of multiple bank accounts. A diligent saver, Dad had certificates of deposit in various amounts in 12 different banks. As a result, he spent a lot of time visiting his money—going from bank to bank, renewing the CDs one at a time when they reached maturity. As the years went by, however, he tended to forget what he had and where he had it. Dick was able to step in and help his dad consolidate his finances. Often Dick had occasion to thank the Lord for putting him at Fort Carson—so he could be close to his father when he was needed.

Fort Carson offered plenty of opportunities for boots-on-the-ground contact with the troops. Bob Bernard, another of Dick's brigade chaplains, was accompanying his unit on a trip to the National Training Center at Fort Irwin in the Mojave Desert of California. They were going out to do field training, and he invited Dick to spend some time with the troops. It was the first of several desert training trips Dick would make during his tour at Fort Carson.

The unit was Armor and Infantry, Heavy Division. It had armored personnel carriers and quite a few large pieces of equipment. The men and some of the equipment made the journey by train. Other pieces of equipment got airlifted in.

When Dick arrived, he learned that Bob's jeep had been destroyed. Dropped from a plane, one of its two parachutes had wrapped itself around the other. Although it was a maneuver the Army had done successfully repeatedly, it had failed this time. The jeep had hit the ground so hard that the wheels sheared off the fenders. Chaplain Bernard picked him up in a borrowed jeep.

When they arrived at the training center, the men had already set up a tent city. Dick would share a tent with Bob. Immediately Dick realized that the Army had not chosen the Mojave Desert location for its salubrious climate. It was so hot that the soldiers could throw their MREs, or ready-to-eat meals, onto the hood of a jeep for a few minutes, and enjoy a piping-hot meal.

When the sun went down, cooler air came down from the mountains.

The change was welcome, but when the cool air met the heat still radiating from the sand, severe windstorms resulted. Around 2:00 or 3:00 in morning you'd make a trip to the latrine and find yourself in a battle for your life, caught in the middle of a howling, sandblasting windstorm.

The troops would conduct mock military battles both during the day and at night. Sometimes at night Dick and Chaplain Bernard would be careening around in their jeep in absolute blackout conditions. One night their driver ran the jeep over some concertina wire, which hung up under the vehicle. It took several hours to cut away the concertina wire and remove it from the jeep.

One day a mock artillery barrage began in the headquarters area. Mines planted in the ground created huge explosions. The men ran for foxholes, diving into ditches to escape. One of the officers had seen Dick's trick foot (the one he could turn around facing backward whenever he chose) and made a suggestion. "Chaplain Stenbakken, here come a couple of new doctors. They're pretty green. Why don't you crank that left foot around backward and tell them you broke it jumping into a ditch?"

Always game for a practical joke, Dick flipped his foot around and hobbled into the medical tent, supported by two soldiers. The doctors got all excited. Although it was supposed to be a mock battle, now they had a real patient—an officer, and a badly injured one, too. Everybody had a good laugh at the medics' expense.

There was nothing lighthearted about the training, however. It was serious stuff. Later, at the time of Desert Storm, when Dick heard TV commentators pontificating about how American soldiers weren't prepared to fight in the desert, he had a good laugh. He knew that was baloney. American troops were well trained. They knew exactly what to do in a desert.

Colonel Wesley Clark was the brigade commander on one of Dick's visits to the desert. That was long before Clark became a household name, but even then he was an impressive man. The youngest full colonel in the entire Army, Clark had finished first in his West Point class and had gone to Oxford University as a Rhodes scholar. He was an intensely brilliant, focused person, but, at the same time, extremely personable. A four-star general before he retired, he would even make a brief run for president of the United States.

But at the moment he was out in the Mojave Desert with his troops, doing mock battle at the National Training Center. Recently he had been the commander of OPFOR (opposing forces) at Fort Irwin, and those same troops were now confronting his brigade as the opposition forces in the mock battle. Using Soviet-style equipment and uniforms, they were impersonating the bad guys, and they acted the part with gusto.

Eager to show Clark how well he had trained them, they wanted to defeat him in battle, and he realized it. He called all his commanders together. "You know the OPFOR are going to do everything they can to beat us, because they want to show off," he said. As he looked around at his men he saw them nodding and grunting their assent. Yeah, that was exactly what they were expecting, and they were ready for it—raring to go.

Then Clark spoke again. "Let me make something very clear. Our job is to train, not win or lose. But even more important, our number one job is safety. Everybody here is somebody's father, son, daughter, husband, wife—and we will keep safety number one. Winning is not number one. Safety is number one."

What a guy! Dick thought. *What a privilege it was to serve with people like that.* The Army wasn't perfect, but it was filled with people who inspired him. Clark might have been expected to have a cocky, arrogant attitude, but he didn't. He was there for his people.

On another trip to the Mojave with Chaplain Sam Adamson, the two conducted a field worship service. The desert heat was searing. The two men had brought along a gigantic watermelon—the biggest specimen they could find—stowed in ice in a Coleman cooler in the back of their jeep.

The plan was to break out the watermelon at lunchtime, after the worship service, but 70 guys showed up for the service. Those pieces of watermelon were going to be on the small side. And another problem immediately surfaced. As the men lined up for this cool treat, Sam looked at Dick. "I've got nothing to cut this thing with!" he said.

"I got a knife," spoke up the first sergeant, pulling a wicked-looking Bowie knife out of a sheath strapped to his leg. He handed it to Dick, who took it gingerly. With its long, highly polished blade and curved point, it was a frightening object. Dick wondered if he could wound himself just by looking at it. But it sliced through the watermelon like butter, and Dick easily cut the melon up so that everybody got an ice-cold chunk. He handed one of the first pieces to the first sergeant, but the man wouldn't take it. "I'll wait until the men have all had a piece," the noncom said. "They come first."

What a privilege it was to serve with people like that, Dick thought.

Chapter 24

"He Didn't Run Over Anybody"

Chaplain, you wouldn't be planning to be in the headquarters building in the next five minutes, would you?" the commanding general's secretary said over the phone. Dick's office at Fort Carson wasn't in the headquarters building, but it was only a short drive away.

"Yes, yes, I was, as a matter of fact. I plan to be there in about two minutes." The secretary hadn't said, "You're needed immediately in the commanding general's office," but the message was clear. Dick didn't ask why—he just dropped what he was doing and hightailed it over to headquarters. Something was up.

Early in his Army career Dick had learned that cultivating relationships with the civilian staff could often be the key to doing good ministry. Senior secretaries were government service workers—it was a civilian job. Commanders and generals would come and go, but the secretaries stayed in the same position forever. Their knowledge of the Army and protocol was encyclopedic. They knew more about what was going on than anybody. Dick had made it a point to befriend such important people, and always took a minute to talk with them when he was near their offices.

A couple minutes later he entered the headquarters building and stopped by the secretary's desk for a chat. "What's going on with you today?" he asked. The two hadn't talked more than 30 seconds when they heard a big, booming voice call, "Is that the chaplain out there?" William Hall, a two-star general and the commander of Fort Carson—top man on the installation—had heard and recognized him speaking just outside his door.

"Yes, sir!" Dick responded.

"Chaplain, please come in. I need to talk to you." Dick stepped into the general's office.

"Please shut the door, Chaplain." General Hall, a tall, wide-shouldered

Black man, was standing with his back to Dick, apparently looking out the window.

Sensing that something was terribly wrong, Dick waited quietly until the general turned around and began to speak. The man's voice, usually deep and powerful, was strained. It didn't take long for Dick to get the picture.

The general had just returned from a training exercise. Three sergeants had been doing demolition training, attempting to blow up some ordinance. They had used a huge pipe bomb called a bangalore torpedo.

When it didn't go off as planned, they had moved in to find out why, and while they were huddled around the thing, it exploded, blowing the three soldiers to bits. The wife of one of the men was eight months pregnant. To General Hall, the men were like his own sons. He cared about his troops that much.

When the secretary heard what had happened, she had called Dick right away. God used her to open the door to ministry for him—a ministry that was needed immediately. No doubt the general would have called him eventually, but thanks to his good relationship with a vigilant secretary, he was able to support the commander as the man dealt with his own loss, as well as with contacting the families of the troops that had been killed.

Accidents were a fact of life at Fort Carson, both on the post and at the National Training Center in the Mojave Desert. Combat training was as much like the real thing as the Army could make it. Thus, there was always inherent danger. The somber truth was that dealing with the aftermath of injuries and death was a part of an Army chaplain's job.

A bad accident during a mock battle at the NTC in the desert involved Fort Carson troops. A soldier had inadvertently turned the turret on a tank, which had smashed into the head of one of the men inside. The injured man was airlifted to Loma Linda Hospital—the nearest trauma center to the accident.

Word went back to the post at Fort Carson, and the soldiers' unit chaplain broke the news to the wife that her husband was in critical condition. The Army helped her make arrangements to fly out to Loma Linda immediately. Before she could board the plane, however, the chaplains' office received word that her husband had died and arrangements were being made to ship his body back to his home of record on the East Coast.

The problem was, even though the chaplain knew the man had died, the Army had not officially declared him dead, so he couldn't release the information to his wife. It was an ethical and moral dilemma.

The deceased man's unit chaplain called Dick. "What do I do? We can't tell her, but we can't let her go. What do I do?"

"Tell her not to take that flight. If she asks why, say that there are other arrangements that need to be made. Don't lie to her, but don't let her get on that plane."

The official notification of the soldier's death finally came through, and with the chaplain's help, the grieving wife was able to change her plans, taking a flight east to the funeral, rather than west to the hospital. Once again, it had fallen to chaplains to balance compassion with protocol and come up with a solution.

One Sunday the whole post was abuzz with the story of the kid who had stolen a tank that morning and driven it up Interstate 25. Evidently the young soldier had decided that he wanted to get out of the Army, and pretending to be crazy seemed like the best way to him. So he did the most insane thing he could think of—he stole an M1 Abrams tank, a piece of Army equipment that weighed about 65 tons.

Somehow the kid slipped under a wire fence and got into the tank. Trained as a tank driver, he had no problem starting up the vehicle and guiding it straight through the locked gate.

A military policeman armed with a .45 pistol guarded the gate, but his gun was no match for a rolling tank. Leaping out of the way, he got on his radio and called someone to take his place as guard. Then he jumped into his car and followed the tank—right up onto the interstate where it lumbered north, headed for Denver. The MP trailed at a safe distance, radioing reports back to the post.

Informed of what was happening, the post's tank commander put things into high gear. They had no way to stop the tank, short of bombing it from the air. Instead, he positioned a five-ton flatbed truck on the freeway, traveling just behind the guard. Then he notified the Colorado Highway Patrol and asked them to clear the road ahead.

The kid drove that tank about 70 miles—all the way to the southern outskirts of Denver, where he turned off into a residential neighborhood—and ran out of fuel. MPs surrounded the tank, got the kid out, and took him into custody. Soldiers loaded the tank onto the flatbed truck and immediately hauled it back to Fort Carson.

Anticipation and trepidation ran high at the Monday morning staff meeting following the incident. What would General Hall say about losing a tank and seeing it driven up the freeway? He had total authority and could demote or fire people right on the spot. Everybody held their breath as he came into the room.

"I suppose you're wondering what my take is on yesterday's event," he opened, gazing around at the assembled officers with a stern expression on his face.

"Yes, sir," a couple brave people spoke up. The general paused for dramatic effect.

"I have several things to say," he continued. "Number one, we train our drivers well. That kid never left the road. He didn't run over anybody. I commend the trainers for that.

"Two, we train our MPs correctly. That young sergeant was smart enough to get out of the way, and smart enough to follow the tank and get on the radio. I commend the trainers for that.

"Three, there was no ammunition on board, so there was no great danger. The ammunition was correctly locked up. I commend you for that.

"Number four, we have a great maintenance program. That tank didn't throw a track. It performed perfectly at top speed, all the way to Denver. I commend our mechanics for that."

Then Hall smiled. The relief in the room was palpable as people realized there would be no tirade, no bloodletting. "Let's not have a repeat of this," he concluded, and then went on with the staff meeting.

Now, that's a leader, Dick thought to himself.

At Fort Carson, Ardis was busier than ever before. As her husband rose in rank and assignments, she carried more responsibility among the chaplains' wives' group. Dick's immediate superior, Chaplain Tom Downes, asked her, as the wife of the next senior chaplain on the post, to lead the chaplains' wives' group and to represent the chaplains at officers' wives' organizations.

Fortunately, Ardis was well prepared for such responsibilities. She had a master's degree and plenty of experience working with both chaplains' and officers' wives. Taking a major role in the team ministry of all the chaplains and their spouses on post, she worked closely with the command leadership group at Fort Carson.

Ardis had honed her administrative skills by serving in various capacities in the officers' wives' club. Because it was an official organization, all board minutes and budgets had to go to the Army's judge advocate's office for review and approval. Working within that framework, she quickly learned to manage board meetings and organizations.

In addition, she held a paid position as an instructor at the Army Learning Center on the post, which gave her firsthand knowledge of the various units of the Fourth Infantry Division. She knew which groups were away on training missions and what major events were coming up. As she learned more of the inner workings of the installation, she understood more clearly the pressures that affected both soldiers and their spouses.

The two Stenbakkens shared their parallel perspectives with each other. So much of what made them effective was their ever-deepening understanding of Army culture—its people and relationships. Together, they made an effective ministry team, as they had done since their first pastorate in Wyoming. And, although they didn't know it, all those experiences were preparing them both for further service in the future.

When Dick had been the division chaplain at Fort Carson for 24 months—six months longer than that particular tour usually lasted— it was time for him to move on and turn the job over to the next guy. The chief of chaplains at the Pentagon was now Major General Norris Einertson. Dick had worked with Chaplain Einertson when Dick was on the chaplains' board, and knew him fairly well.

A Lutheran chaplain at Fort Carson, Gordon Peterson, was retiring. Einertson, who was also a Lutheran, received an invitation to Fort Carson for a staff visit, and to officiate at both Peterson's retirement ceremony and the change of command from Dick to the next division chaplain, John Bauer. Norris agreed to come.

Dick had charge of setting up the protocol and making all the arrangements for Einertson's visit and the two ceremonies. The change-of-command ceremony took place in the chapel, and the farewell dinner for Chaplain Peterson was scheduled for the evening of the same day at a restaurant in Colorado Springs.

It was Dick's responsibility to chauffeur the chief of chaplains to and from the event. Ardis and he enjoyed taking the chief to the dinner, but during the event, Einertson pulled Dick aside. "Dick, would you mind dropping Ardis off on the way home, before you take me back to Fort Carson?"

I wonder what's up? Dick thought, but he didn't ask. He told Ardis what was happening, and she had the same question. Neither of them had a clue, but they did as the chief asked.

Later that evening, as he drove Einertson through the darkness toward Fort Carson, the chief of chaplains was silent. Then Einertson cleared his throat and said, "Dick, I've been thinking. I'd like to see you be the cadet chaplain at West Point."

Dick's heart skipped a beat—in fact, several beats. He peered straight ahead and concentrated on keeping the car on the road. This was unheard-of. West Point had not had a military cadet chaplain since the time of Abraham Lincoln! The United States Military Academy, oddly enough, used civilian clergy, hired by the military, to run their cadet chapel. The other branches, Air Force and Navy, had always had military chaplains as their cadet chaplains, but not the Army.

From somewhere seemingly far away, Dick was aware of the chief's voice again. "Would you be interested in doing that?"

"Sir, it would be an absolute honor," he managed to say. In his mind he pictured the 3,400 cadets at West Point and the soaring arches and ornate stone carvings of the Point's massive Gothic cathedral-like chapel.

"Well, what I want to do, then," Einertson continued, "is put you at West Point, so that when you become a colonel, you'll be in position to take over the chapel there."

Dick gripped the steering wheel. He was a lieutenant colonel, hoping at some point to be promoted to colonel, and now the chief of chaplains was saying *when*, not *if*, you become one. *This was too much to take in!* Dick struggled to make an appropriate reply and not go berserk. Later he remembered nothing about dropping the chief back at his quarters and driving himself home.

"Ardis, you'll never believe the conversation we had," he called when he opened his front door that night.

But the move to West Point never happened. When the commandant of the United States Military Academy, a three-star general, heard that the chief of chaplains, a two-star general, wanted to put a military cadet chaplain above West Point's civilian chaplain, he put his foot down. A major general can't tell a lieutenant general what to do. The turn of events disappointed Dick, but still, he would remember that night for a long, long time.

It reminded him of something he had seen in his record at the Pentagon, just before he made the move to Fort Carson. He would periodically review his personnel file to see that everything was in order. Not many people did that, but it was his right, and he wanted to be sure it contained no errors.

While looking through the file, he had come across a letter from the chief of chaplains, nominating him to be a White House Fellow.

Out of approximately 1,000 applicants, between 12 and 20 get selected for that honor each year, and he hadn't been one of them—he had never even been aware of the nomination. While he didn't know much about White House Fellows, he did know that Colin Powell had been one. And he was honored to know that the chief of chaplains had submitted his name.

Dick achieved an important personal goal while at Fort Carson. He and several other chaplains had received invitations to a luncheon with a man named Lawrence Aylesworth, a clinical psychologist and a Ph.D. A man of Asian heritage, Aylesworth had piercing dark eyes and a build like a football player. Later Dick learned that the man was a martial arts expert, but at their initial meeting he was struck more by his powerful intellect than his physical strength.

During the lunchtime conversation Dick commented that he was still kind of stuck on his doctoral dissertation. Aylesworth quizzed him about the subject matter, and then asked, "What are you doing Thursday afternoon at 4:00 p.m.?"

Dick had no specific plans for Thursday. "Bring what you've done so far to my office," Aylesworth said.

Dick shook his head. "I can't afford you."

"No, this is a privilege. Just bring what you've got. It'll be fun for me."

Aylesworth became Dick's mentor through the rest of the dissertation process. He met with him regularly and coached him step by step—pushing him when necessary—and he got him over the hump. It wasn't long before Dick was able to send the finished product to Columbia University.

The response came back in due time: "Good work here, but we think you ought to take a totally different direction."

What? Incensed, he fired off a letter. "I want to remind you that you gave me written approval to follow this protocol, which is exactly what I have done. If there is a problem I'd like to take it up with the regents of the university." Evidently that did the trick, because he received no further suggestion that he make radical changes.

Then it was time to go to Columbia University to defend his work. Aylesworth coached and encouraged him through the process. All went well, and in due time Dick was finally entitled to put Ed.D. (Doctor of Education) behind his own name. He would never forget the man's kindness and support.

Dick lost his father during his tour at Fort Carson. He and Ardis had been driving up to Denver every couple weeks to look after Dad, who was in his 90s. It was getting harder and harder for him to manage on his own.

Then he had a bad fall and broke his hip. Help came right away, thanks to the "I've fallen and I can't get up" device he wore around his neck. He survived the surgery and was recovering well, but then he had what was probably a massive heart attack and passed away. Oliver Stenbakken had been 93. Dick knew that was a ripe old age, but of course, he still mourned for the man who had been his father.

As Dick's tour of duty at Fort Carson neared its end, division chaplain Tom Downes retired, and for the past few months of his tour Dick served as the deputy installation chaplain until Chaplain Bob Ennis, Tom's replacement, arrived.

Ennis, a Catholic and a full colonel, had just completed service on the promotion board for full colonels when he arrived at Fort Carson. He and Dick had lunch together. Dick knew the senior man couldn't divulge anything about his work on the promotion board—but he couldn't help asking him, "What do you think of my chances?"

Ennis looked off into the distance, not at him. A smile tugged at the corners of his mouth. "What do you think the chances are of the sun coming up in the east?" he said quietly. Then he resumed eating his lunch.

Well, that was a pretty strong confirmation, but still, Dick knew how competitive promotions were. There were only so many slots to fill. Of the group of chaplains who had gone onto active duty at the same time as he, only about 15 percent eventually made full colonel.

In the chaplain corps at large, usually less than 5 percent of chaplains became full colonels. Some left after their initial three-year commitment. Others were uncomfortable sharing a pulpit with clergy of other faiths. A few just didn't make the grade. Dick hadn't been sure he would become a career Army chaplain when he started, but he hadn't realized then how much he was going to love the work. Now he very much wanted to know whether he would make full colonel.

Everybody knew when the promotion board would announce its decisions. Two days before the date, Chaplain Ennis was called up to the main personnel division office. When he returned, he walked by Dick's office and flipped a little four-inch-square folded piece of paper onto the desk as he passed.

Dick opened it up. It had the number 10 on it. When you're approved for promotion, your priority promotion date is set based on your time in grade. That number 10 told him that his promotion to full colonel had been approved. Ten was his priority number.

A few days before Bob had given him that beautiful number 10, Dick had gotten a call from the chief of chaplains' office at the Pentagon. "Dick, if you were to come out on the full colonel's list, would you be interested in being the command chaplain at Fort Richardson in Alaska?"

While he recognized that it was a rhetorical question, still the question itself affirmed his being promoted to full colonel. He went where the Army sent him, but by this point in his career, the orders were usually broached as a question. Of course he'd be interested, and he said so. Actually, Dick was thrilled about such a posting. He loved the great outdoors, and he had known people who had served in Alaska. Oh, yes, he would absolutely be interested.

Chapter 25

"Don't Stand Too Close to the Old Man!"

"Oh sure, I can tell you how to get to Fort Wainwright from here, Chaplain. It's easy. You turn right at the stop sign, follow the road to the next traffic signal, and you're there." It was everybody's favorite joke on newcomers to Fort Greely. One hundred miles of frozen tundra stretched between the stop sign and the traffic signal.

Fort Richardson, home of "America's Arctic Warriors," was a sprawling Army post located just outside the city of Anchorage in south-central Alaska. As command chaplain at Fort Richardson, Dick was responsible for all the chaplains and all the religious activities for the Army in Alaska, which meant not only Fort Richardson but also Fort Wainwright, near Fairbanks, more than 300 miles farther north, and Fort Greely, at Delta Junction, 100 miles south of Fort Wainwright and one of the coldest areas in Alaska. Dick would be at the top of the ladder—a ladder whose rungs were spaced far apart.

It was a sizable increase in responsibility, and he was grateful for the additional training he received prior to taking the assignment. That was one of the things he continued to like best about the Army. They didn't send you to school to reward you for what you had done—they prepared you for what you were about to do. Every time the system had selected him for a new responsibility, it had equipped him to do the job.

By the time Dick and Ardis left Fort Carson they were "empty nesters," with both Rikki and Erik away at Union College in Lincoln, Nebraska. Ardis stayed behind to try to sell the house in Colorado Springs and to pack up their belongings and ship them to Alaska.

On one of his first trips to the PX at Fort Richardson Dick bought an Alaska state map, thinking he'd learn his way around and impress Ardis when she arrived. Opening the map up, he spread it out on his bed in the visiting officers' quarters.

He took a look at it and then peered at it more closely. Had he gotten a defective map? It had hardly any roads on it! When he checked for a copyright date, he realized that it was a 6-year-old map. *Dummy!* he thought. Obviously he had bought an old map. So he went out and purchased a brand-new map, came home, and opened it up—and it was identical to the old one. There just weren't that many roads in Alaska!

Fortunately, his mode of travel in Alaska was often by air. The commanding general at Fort Richardson had a twin-engine Beechcraft U-21 at his disposal, and the little plane made the trip nearly every day from Fort Richardson to Greeley and Wainwright. Dick hitched a ride and visited one or the other of the two outpost installations about once a week.

Alaska was an incredible place to be, and Dick enjoyed the gorgeous scenery. It was magical to fly right by Mount McKinley or, as it is also called, Denali. Dick saw it at dawn, at dusk, and in bright sunlight, and it was always a thrill.

On his first Sabbath in Alaska he found a Seventh-day Adventist church in the Anchorage phone book and showed up for Sabbath school. Having never been to Alaska, he didn't expect to know anybody, but somehow he wasn't surprised when somebody tapped him on the shoulder and said, "Hi, Dick!" Turning around, he saw 'Nita Yeager Hinman, a classmate from Campion Academy. She and her husband invited him home for lunch. It was great to belong to such a widespread church family.

When Ardis and the household goods arrived, they moved into a house on Birch Hill, the most senior officer residential area on the post. Dick wasn't a full colonel yet, but in every way he found himself treated like one while he waited for his turn on the promotion list. Their brick ranch-style house had a garage, most unusual in government quarters, but essential in a place where you scraped ice off your windshield at least six months of the year.

Their neighbors were the commanding general of the post, his deputy, and the commanders of the various divisions and their families. Military people tend to connect with each other and form a tight community, and Alaska was no exception.

In addition to humans, Dick and Ardis soon found that moose were also frequent visitors on their street—sometimes even coming onto the porch to nibble the geraniums.

Before long Ardis was active with both the officers' wives' club and the chaplains' wives' group. As always, such organizations provided a built-in system for developing friendships and learning about the post, as well as opportunities for service.

Dick's new responsibilities encompassed all areas of ministry. They were administrative, but also pastoral. As always, mentoring others was a top priority. One of his first tasks was to tackle the budget for all the Army chaplains and their ministries in Alaska. He called his five command chaplains together. They arrived at the meeting expecting him to tell them what their budgets would be for the coming year.

But he did something a little different, asking each man to talk to his subordinate chaplains and find out what their needs were, and then help them triage and rank the needs. It turned budgeting from a top-down method into a bottom-up process and provided new opportunities for chaplains at each level to mentor those who reported to them.

The whole team, from the lowest chaplain on the totem pole on up, had input into the budget. Then the command chaplains got together to shape the final figures, giving and taking until they had something everybody could live with. They'd do this quarter by quarter—adjusting and reallocating each time, so that everybody's needs received equal consideration.

The first time they met to hammer out the budget, one of the command chaplains didn't show up. The others wondered what would happen. "We'll go ahead and plan the budget," Dick said. "We'll divide up the pie, and we'll assume that if you're not here, you don't need a piece of the pie."

That chaplain and his subordinates had no budget for the next quarter. He never missed another meeting. The command chaplains, instead of being competitors for the funds, learned to cooperate, managing their money better and doing smarter planning.

Sometimes the job presented Dick with an unexpected challenge. The top officer on the post—the installation commander—was a two-star general. Looking every inch a military man, he had close-cropped dark hair, a loud voice, and dark, flashing eyes. He was an intense person whose bearing made him seem even taller than his six feet.

It didn't take Dick long to discover that in spite of his many good qualities, the officer was the most foulmouthed man he had ever met. At one of their staff meetings, Dick counted 216 hard-core expletives and gutter expressions.

The general's language troubled all his commanders. One even muttered to Dick, on their way out of a staff meeting, "If we're ever in combat together, don't stand too close to the old man!" But none of them had the courage to confront him. After all, he wrote their reports and rated them—and all were hoping to wind up as one-star generals themselves. If you upset the guy who wrote your report card, it would nail shut the door to promotion.

Dick was one of those subordinates, but as the command chaplain he believed it was his responsibility to deal with the situation. He informed the deputy commander, a one-star general, of what he planned to do.

"You'll be walking into a buzz saw, Chaplain," the man said, raising his hands, palms out, and shaking his head. "I want no part of it."

"I'm not involving you," Dick responded, aware that the deputy commander was also hoping for promotion. Still, the man was a professional, and he offered some good pointers on how to handle his interview with the installation commander.

Dick met with the two-star general. "Sir," he began, "I appreciate your leadership." Then he told the boss about some specific things he had seen the chief do that were positive—ways the man had helped him both personally and professionally. "But specifically, sir, I need to talk to you about your language."

The general blew it off, almost contemptuously. "Well, I suppose my words may come across a little strong to a chaplain's ears, but I use that kind of language to make my point."

Taking a breath, Dick replied, "Sir, I've been on active duty almost 23 years. I've heard these terms before. It demeans the uniform you wear and the office you hold. I'm not the only one who feels this way. Many of your commanders have told me informally they're concerned as well."

At the next staff meeting the general didn't change a thing. Every time he'd swear, he'd glance at Dick, as if to say "It makes no difference to me what you think."

Dick thought about what to do next. Nobody in Alaska outranked the man. So he called Hawaii and talked to the command chaplain for the U.S. Army of the Pacific, of which Alaska was a part. This chaplain worked for the Commander of the U.S. Army of the Pacific—a three-star general responsible for writing reports on Dick's superior.

General Johnny Corns, Dick knew, was a gentleman in every sense of the word. If Corns had overheard one of those staff meetings, he would have relieved the Alaska commander of his command on the spot.

Although Dick never knew exactly what transpired between the two generals, at the next staff meeting his commander pulled a small tape recorder out of his briefcase, switched it on, and announced, "From now on, for purposes of history, we are going to record all staff meetings." Then he turned and looked directly at Dick, his eyes cold and hard. From that point on, the strongest word he ever uttered in a staff meeting was "darn."

When the buck stops at your desk, sometimes it calls for hard decisions. Leadership and authority offered more opportunities to mentor, but they also meant dealing with more problems. Chaplains might be ministers and officers, but they were also human.

One day as Dick conducted a visit to Fort Greely, a sergeant asked to speak to him. The soldier confided that he and his wife had been having some serious problems, and the chaplain at Greely had been counseling them.

The chaplain had suggested that the man's wife spend some time at a Catholic retreat center down at Fort Wainwright, which she did. Then the sergeant found out that the chaplain had been at the retreat center at the same time as his wife.

Not only that, but he had spent a whole week with the guy's wife, driving around Alaska in a camper. "Now," the soldier reported, his eyes filled with pain and worry, "my wife is going back to the lower 48. We have a car in Salt Lake City that we need to bring up here. She's going down there to get it. I'm concerned, because I've just heard a rumor that the chaplain has offered to fly down and drive back with her."

Dick summoned the individual in question, a major with more than 12 years in the service under his belt. A man of average height with a muscular, outdoorsy demeanor, he had a face that managed to look both square-jawed and weak at the same time.

Dick met with him in the office he used at Fort Greely, asking another chaplain to also be present. Then he told the man what he had heard and gave him an opportunity to explain himself. The chaplain's demeanor was sullen, but he didn't deny a thing.

"Your behavior is completely inappropriate," Dick admonished. "You will not fly down and drive with this woman back to Alaska, Chaplain. Is that clear?" The man nodded. "I've put it in writing," Dick continued. "This is so sensitive that I haven't asked an assistant to type it up. It is handwritten. I want you to sign it and date it. I'll make a copy for you, and I'll keep the original in my file."

The chaplain looked at the handwritten document. It stated that he would not fly down, would not drive back up to Alaska with the woman, and also that he would have nothing to do with her husband—not contact him or harass him.

"If he comes to church, that's OK," Dick added, "but you will not have any contact with this man or his wife, other than at religious services with other people present."

Indicating that he understood, the chaplain signed the document. Then Dick gave him a copy and hoped that would be the end of the matter. It wasn't. Dick got word that he had indeed flown down to Kansas—to "see his mother"—who lived not all that far away from where the woman had been going. Dick called the chaplain's mother. "Oh, yes, sir," she answered. "He was here, but he left about five days ago."

Dick smelled a rat. He went to the military travel agency on post and asked to see the chaplain's flight history. It was an unusual request, but he persisted. "I'm this man's direct superior. This is an emergency matter. I need to be in touch with him."

The clerk looked up the flights. The chaplain had flown down to Kansas where his mother lived, but then had gone on to Salt Lake City and had canceled the rest of his return flight to Alaska. It was all too evident that he had broken his promise and was driving back to Alaska with the sergeant's wife.

About a week later the chaplain called Dick. "Good morning, sir! I just wanted to let you know that I'm back. The trip went well," he announced nonchalantly. Dick had already explained the situation to the commander at Fort Greely and given him a copy of the handwritten document the man had signed. They agreed that the two of them would talk to the chaplain together, and they called him in.

"We know you canceled your return flight, Chaplain," the commander said. "How did you get back to Alaska?" Realizing that he was about to be nailed, the man admitted what he had done.

"I'm sorry," he started to say, but the commander interrupted him.

"Go to your apartment, pack your goods, and be off my installation by sundown," the officer barked. The man was removed from his pulpit, "relieved for cause"—the worse thing you can have on your record in the Army.

Then Dick informed the chief of chaplains' office at the Pentagon of the situation. "We want you to know that this guy has no place in Alaska," he told the official. The Army moved the man out of Alaska, and Dick never saw or heard from him again. It was a miserable way for a chaplain to end his ministry and his Army career, and a sad episode for Dick.

That wasn't the only time he had to remove a chaplain from his pulpit. Fortunately, it didn't happen very often, but when it did, it was painful for all concerned. A Black chaplain led a mostly Black congregation at Fort Richardson. Army chapels were not segregated, but sometimes they evolved more or less that way on the basis of a preference for a particular worship style.

Dick began to hear stories about the chaplain, who had managed to chalk up a succession of improper incidents. The worst was that he had used sexual innuendo in a joking manner from the pulpit; something that was tasteless and completely inappropriate, regardless of worship style.

He had also gone into the PX, apparently in his pajamas, and purchased a pack of cigarettes, choosing the cheaper, generic brand. After he had paid for them, he had reached across the counter and swapped them for a more expensive pack of Marlboros, raising a fuss about having to pay the difference.

On another occasion he had checked out a military van to take a group of his troops on a fishing expedition. That was a perfectly good thing to do—chaplains were encouraged to conduct such team-building events. But he had let the soldiers take the keys to go into town. The men had gotten drunk and had managed to bang up the side of the van. Then the chaplain had turned in the van without filing an accident report, trying to hide the fact that it had been damaged.

That incident cooked his goose with his commander, who was ready to relieve him for cause. Dick went to bat for the man. "Look," he said to his superior, "I have no quarrel with you relieving this man for cause, but I would like to try to rehabilitate him. Don't relieve him for cause, and I'll give you my word that if he messes up again, I'll take care of it."

Dick called the man in for a "chat." His appearance held no clues to his character. Dark-skinned, of slender build and medium height, he wore glasses, and a slightly graying moustache decorated his upper lip.

Dick was hoping to counsel the guy—to point out the areas he needed to improve. But the chaplain was defiant and had excuses for everything he'd done. He stated that his off-color remarks in front of his congregation were perfectly acceptable in a Black church. "You're not pastoring a 'Black church,'" Dick responded. "You are a military chaplain in an Army chapel, and your behavior is inappropriate."

"Chaplain, you all have it in for me because I'm Black. This is a race issue." Dick sighed. His attempt at rehabilitation wasn't going so well. But he had expected that the man would play the race card sooner or later.

Dick looked him right in the eye. "You're right."

The other man's eyes showed his surprise. "In a sense it is a race issue. If you were a White chaplain, you would probably have been out years ago. This is not a Black or White issue. It is an Army issue—it's about being a professional military officer, and you have missed that mark repeatedly."

Still obstinate, the chaplain refused to acknowledge his problems. His next move was to recruit a delegation of Black pastors from the local area to talk to Dick on his behalf.

"I'll be glad to speak with just two of your representatives," Dick told him when he heard of his plan. "But they will need to bring a signed, notarized statement from you, releasing me to discuss all issues related to you. No statement, no deal." He was banking on the guy being smart enough to realize that the interview wasn't such a good idea.

To Dick's utter surprise, two Black pastors from the local town showed up, the signed document in hand. Dick took their measure as his assistant ushered them into his office. Fresh haircuts, neatly pressed black suits—the men looked like exactly what they were—civilian clergy—but something about their bearing said ex-military to him, and he was right. One was a retired sergeant major, while the other man had served about six years. Both men were polite and dignified as introductions were made and hands shaken, but it was clear they had come prepared to do battle for a brother and a fellow pastor.

Dick had the Black chaplain's officer record brief on the desk in front of him. An ORB is an individual's entire military history—three or four pages detailing all assignments, promotions, awards, decorations, etc.—a condensed account of an officer's entire career.

"Pastor," Dick addressed the older of the two men, "you say you were on active duty for more than 25 years. I suppose you received a number of awards during that time. In fact, I'll bet you had salad all the way to your shoulder."

The ex-sergeant smiled. "Yes," he nodded. "I got quite a few decorations." Then Dick asked the younger man the same question.

"Well, I was in for just six years. I have nothing like my brother here, but yes, I got some decorations too."

At that point Dick showed the two men the Black chaplain's ORB.

They knew from experience that if a soldier managed to stand upright and remained reasonably sober and did a mediocre job, he'd always get some kind of award when he left a position. This chaplain had never received an award. It was unheard-of—15 years and not a single one.

"This chaplain has been on active duty for 15 years, and he has received no awards—not any. His problems did not start with me."

The older preacher leaned back in his chair and rolled his eyes toward heaven.

The other pastor stood and offered Dick his hand. "Chaplain, thank you for your time. We have nothing more to say." The two left Dick's office. Dick had no choice but to relieve the chaplain of his responsibilities.

Shortly after that, the Army transferred the man to a post in Germany. A chaplain there would pick him up at the airport. The man had been in the car only a few minutes when he started in about a guy named Stenbakken, the most despicable person he had ever met in his life.

The chaplain who met him was John Bauer, the lieutenant colonel who had replaced Dick at Fort Carson—a man who was almost as close to Dick as a brother. John just let the man dig himself into a hole. Then he said quietly, "That's not the Dick Stenbakken I know."

Personnel problems were the exception rather than the rule. Dick relied on his training and his professional skills to handle problems as they arose, carefully documenting every step of the way.

Nearly all the men he supervised were excellent chaplains. His division chaplain, Lieutenant Colonel David Hicks, was a standout, combining all the qualities of a Christian gentleman with unbridled enthusiasm and energy. His gray eyes were always smiling, his demeanor always pleasant. Even his step had a verve about it—you could sense his energy and focus just by watching him walk down the hall. He was a man who loved life, the Army, and ministry.

"Dave, how do you like your job?" Dick asked him one day.

"I love it," Hicks replied without hesitation. "I love to be with the troops."

"Well, enjoy your time as a division chaplain," Dick told him, "because I see in you leadership potential to go to the highest levels of the chaplaincy, and I'm going to do all I can to help that to happen."

Hicks had an interesting history. A former enlisted man who had come up through the ranks to staff sergeant, he had had a conversion experience, thanks largely to the influence of an Army chaplain. When he got out of the Army, he finished college and the seminary, and then came back in as a chaplain. He had both a pastor's heart and a soldier's spirit. Dick was honored to be able to mentor him and write the well-deserved excellent Officer Efficiency Reports that would help to guarantee his future success.

When the Army later promoted Hicks to serve at the Pentagon as a deputy chief of chaplain—a one-star general—Dick was there at the ceremony. His protégé and friend had passed him in rank. Chaplain Hicks retired a few years ago as the Army chief of chaplains and a two-star general, only the second Black chaplain in history to achieve that rank.

Dick also had several occasions while in Alaska to use the old scrounging-praying-schmoozing machine that had worked so well for him in Hawaii and other places. About a year before he left there, the opportunity came to start up a new troop chapel at Fort Wainwright. The post had an old cantonment chapel that could be renovated, but all the furnishings in it were deplorable, especially the pews. They were literally falling apart.

Poking around, he discovered an Army National Guard chapel that was closing down somewhere in the Midwest. It had burned a few years earlier and been completely refurbished afterward, including all new pews and other furniture. Now the Army had closed the reservist installation, and the chapel was sitting there, padlocked. Dick contacted the appropriate authorities and asked for its contents.

"If you'll pay the freight to get it from here to where you want it, we'll release it to you," they told him. "But, of course, you'll need a written authorization from your commander."

"Can you hold it for a couple weeks, while I get things lined up?" The answer was in the affirmative, and Dick researched the costs for the shipping—by train, boat, and truck—to get the contents of the chapel, including a set of beautiful stained-glass windows, to Wainwright.

Then he tackled the installation commander. "It's going to cost about $60,000 to furnish that cantonment chapel at Wainwright," he told the man.

"We don't have that kind of money, Chaplain!" came the immediate reply.

"I know, sir. Here's another alternative. We can get an entire, brand-new set of furnishings from a defunct post in the lower 48 that will fit our chapel for around $10,000—the cost of freight to get the stuff here. If we were to buy it all new, we'd still have to pay the same amount for freight. All the Army down there is asking is that you write a letter requesting the stuff. What would you like to do?"

The commander gave Dick a look that said, *That's a dumb question.* "OK, I'll sign the letter. But you'll need to write it."

Opening a folder, Dick extracted the prepared letter and placed it on the desk. The officer just shook his head. He knew that Dick had worked things up the channel quietly—anticipating his approval. The commander liked the idea that his staff knew what they were doing. And Dick loved working within the system to make extraordinary things happen.

Ardis and Dick made several trips home to Colorado during their Alaska tour. Rikki spent some time working in Costa Rica as a student missionary. Erik was a senior at Union College and was considering working on a master's degree in Florida. He was dating Gelerie Arafiles, a Filipino girl. Erik called one day and mentioned that he and Gelerie were planning to come to Colorado to spend Thanksgiving with Grandma and Grandpa Dick—Ardis' mom and dad. When they hung up the phone, Dick looked at his wife. "We're going to Colorado for Thanksgiving," he said. "I want to meet this girl before the wedding."

"Wedding, what wedding?" his wife asked in surprise. Nobody had said anything about an engagement, much less a wedding, but Dick had picked up something in Erik's voice, and he knew that Gelerie had stolen his son's heart.

"We need to meet this girl," he said again.

They had a great family time together. One evening, toward the end of their visit, Erik and Dick were working on a project together in Granddad's workshop. "Well, Dad," Erik said, "what do you think of Gelerie?"

"If you let this one get away, don't come home," he said, with a grin. Gelerie had stolen his heart too.

Chapter 26

"Would You Be
Willing to Accept?"

Wanta fly a little closer to the mountain?" the pilot asked. It was a perfect bluebird day in Alaska, without a cloud in the sky. Dick was hosting General Matt Zimmerman, the current chief of chaplains, who had just arrived at Fort Richardson for a staff visit. They were using the commander's plane to fly up to Fort Greely. Dick had made the trip innumerable times, but this time he wanted to show off Mount McKinley for his visitor. They flew in a circle completely around the summit—an utterly breathtaking experience. They were so low they could have waved to climbers, had there been any that day.

After their visit to Greely, he and the general took off by helicopter to head back to Wainwright, and as they flew over the tundra, Dick spotted a huge grizzly bear. He tapped the pilot on the shoulder and pointed down.

The pilot dropped the helicopter, not low enough to harass the bear but so that they could get a good look at it. It was a huge chocolate-brown creature, nearly four feet tall at the shoulder. The bear heard their noise and ran for cover—moving faster than any horse.

Those were typical of the many experiences that made Dick's time in Alaska so much fun. On another occasion he was walking back from a staff meeting on a day when there had been a recent snowstorm. The sidewalk had been shoveled and scattered with salt.

As he passed the main post chapel he noticed the Catholic priest in his black cassock standing in the doorway, and right in front of him, at the bottom of the steps leading up to the chapel, was a moose, on his knees, head bowed, obviously licking up the salt. "Father," he called. "I've heard Saint Francis was pretty good with animals, but he was nothing compared to you!"

One Sunday morning, about 18 months before he was due to leave Alaska and only a few months after Dick had received his promotion to full colonel, he received a phone call that would rearrange his life. The man on the line was Matthew Bediako, a vice president of the General Conference of the Seventh-day Adventist Church. Dick knew him from various church-related events.

"Dick," Bediako said after the usual greetings, "we want you to know that we have voted you in as the director of chaplaincy ministries for the world church. Would you be willing to accept?"

Needing to sit down, Dick reached for a chair. Had he heard correctly? After all, he hadn't worked for the church directly since his fledgling pastorate in Wyoming. Ministers who served at the highest levels of the church almost always got chosen from within its own leadership ranks. His career had taken a completely different turn. This was unheard-of—his mind whirled.

When he found his voice, he replied, "Well, I'd definitely be interested." Then he continued, "Elder Bediako, you may not know that I've been a full colonel for only a few months. If I were to retire from the Army with less than two years in grade, I'd do so as a lieutenant colonel, not a full colonel.

"My guess is that you'd prefer to have a full colonel in that position. That would mean I wouldn't be free to accept your position for another 18 months." He fully expected the conversation to end there. Surely the church would not be interested in waiting that long.

"Well, Dick, we want you as the director of ACM, and we understand the importance of you retiring as a full colonel. If you'll accept the job, we'll hold it open for you until you can get here." *Hold a job open for 18 months?* Dick thought. That was unheard-of too.

Dick knew that the Adventist Chaplaincy Ministries Department of the General Conference was a fairly new organization. It had developed out of a request by a group of Adventist military chaplains meeting in 1971—an event he had attended.

Up to that point there had existed something called the National Service Organization, which had dealt specifically with military issues. Dick's invitation to become a chaplain had come through the NSO. The organization served as the agency responsible for providing denominational endorsement for Adventist military chaplains (a prerequisite to military chaplaincy). It also issued their ministry credentials and provided an avenue for direct access to the upper echelons of church leadership.

Other kinds of chaplaincy ministries, including health care, education, and correctional facility chaplains, had no such organization—and there were more of those chaplains than military ones.

At their meeting in 1971 the military chaplains had recognized such a need and made a request to the General Conference that it establish a Chaplaincy Department that encompassed all chaplains at the highest church level. It resulted in the Adventist Chaplaincy Ministries Department, or ACM.

When Dick took the phone call from Matthew Bediako, the ACM was still in its infancy. Dick was the first military individual the denomination invited to be a part of its leadership. He already knew the men who formed the current leadership team. Bud Bracebridge had become director when the first director, Charles Martin, retired. Martin Feldbush, the associate director, was the first person on the ACM leadership team with a health-care background. Now Bud had fallen ill, precipitating the need for a new director.

Dick and Ardis prayed and thought long and hard about the opportunity. They weren't tired of the military—far from it. He would have been content to stay for his full 30 years. But the opportunity to continue serving the military and the church by opening doors for others to serve as chaplains—that wasn't something you took lightly.

Financially, he knew that leaving the military at this point in his career would be expensive. Exiting the Army before serving a full 30 years would significantly reduce his Army retirement pay.

By policy, the church's defined benefit retirement program excluded retired chaplains from receiving any church retirement. And the denomination's pay scale didn't compare favorably to that of an Army colonel. Dick figured his salary would get cut in half. If you looked at it purely from a financial standpoint, his leaving the Army didn't make any sense at all.

What did make sense, though, the more he thought and prayed about it, was for the church to choose a high-ranking ex-military individual to serve as the head of the ACM.

Then, through more prayer, came the conviction that the Lord had molded him—had guided his experience and training to prepare him to serve the denomination in this capacity. Dick and Ardis made up their minds. They would leave the military, and he would accept the position at church headquarters.

"You name the date!" Matthew Bediako said when Dick called him with the news. They agreed on July of 1992.

On July 27, his fifty-second birthday, Dick, having fulfilled his three-year tour in Alaska, signed out of Fort Richardson. For the last time he went to the logbook and wrote his name, rank, Social Security number, and the date and time.

Then he walked out of the front door of the post headquarters in civilian clothes, turned, and smartly saluted the flag one last time. No longer was he in the Army. For nearly a quarter of a century he had pursued his passion for ministry within a system that had fit him like a glove.

He had appreciated the attention to ethics, the camaraderie, and the support he had found in the military. It was an emotional moment—leaving the career that had so engaged his heart, soul, and mind for more than 23 years.

His Army career was over, except for the formal retirement ceremony. That would take place at the Pentagon, some weeks after his arrival in the Washington, D.C., area. (Interestingly enough, the ceremony was held at the exact spot in the building where the plane would hit on September 11, 2001.) Dick would receive the Legion of Merit award at his retirement ceremony, given for superior service.

But for now he and Ardis were on the move again—as they had been every three or four years of their entire married lives. They drove to Haines, Alaska, where they boarded the Alaska Ferry for Seattle, Washington. Then they headed south by car from there. His prediction had turned out right. They had a wedding to attend. Erik and the lovely Gelerie were getting married in Pasadena, California.

Next they went to Colorado for a visit with Ardis' parents, as well as for a big family reunion at Glacier View Ranch. Erik and Gelerie spent several days of their honeymoon attending the reunion. Dick thought it said something rather fine about her, that she would happily use part of her honeymoon getting to know her new husband's many relatives.

Finally it was time to drop Rikki off at Union College for her senior year and start for Maryland and the headquarters of the Seventh-day Adventist Church. The offices were located in Silver Spring, Maryland, a suburb of Washington, D.C.

Dick and Ardis had already done their house-hunting in the area. Finding a nice corner lot in the nearby leafy suburb of Columbia, they had arranged with a contractor to build them a house. It was nearly ready by the time they arrived.

For the first time in 23 years, no sponsor met them. No one was assigned to welcome them to the new situation and ease their transition into the new neighborhood and job. Somebody showed Dick where his office was located and handed him a key. Someone else checked with him to be sure his name would be spelled right on his office door—and that was pretty much it.

For Ardis, there was no officers' wives' club, nothing that instantly integrated either of them into their new community. *The church could learn something from the Army,* Dick mused. It wasn't the first time he had had that thought, and it wouldn't be the last.

Dick soon learned that he would have to make some adjustments to his thinking as he transitioned from Colonel Dick Stenbakken, a command chaplain in the U.S. Army, to Dick Stenbakken, a departmental director of the church's General Conference. No doubt the fact that he had been working outside the church organization for more than 20 years highlighted those differences.

The first and most obvious adjustment had to do with rank. When you walked onto an Army post—even if you had never been there before in your life—you immediately knew where you fit into the system. All you had to do was glance at the insignia on another person's sleeve or collar, and it told you exactly where you stood in relation to that individual. As time went by, of course, you'd develop relationships that went far beyond rank, but initially you could tell at 20 paces how to relate to each person you met.

Dick hadn't realized how much time such a system saved. At the General Conference rank wasn't apparent. That didn't mean that it didn't exist—far from it—but its clues were much harder to decipher. A definite pecking order did exist, but it was up to the new guy to figure it out.

A more subtle difference was that at church headquarters you didn't have the same kind of direct authority that rank conferred on you in the military. You developed authority by the committees you served on, the relationships you cultivated, and by your ability to persuade others, but it was a whole other kind of clout, wielded in an entirely different way.

And another thing—in the Army rank had had its privileges. It could be something as simple as a reserved parking spot. Your car had rank, too. Woe be unto anybody who parked in the colonel's parking space! Dick hadn't thought he was spoiled by those kinds of privileges, but he had to admit, being just one of the gang was different. Not a bad thing—just different.

The Army had expected 24-hour-a-day accountability. As a division chaplain at Fort Carson, and later as the command chaplain in Alaska, he had been available around the clock. The chaplains he supervised were aware that if anything of consequence came up, they should notify him immediately, day or night. The ranking Army chaplain in Alaska, he always got contacted if anything serious happened.

After he began working at the General Conference headquarters building, there were no more emergency calls. When he walked out the door at the end of the day, that was that. It was an odd sort of loose-ends feeling at first.

It also felt strange not to have to sign in and out. As an Army officer he had been required to sign out any time he left the installation—for travel, even for a vacation. The first time he went on a trip for the General Conference, he was at the airport, about to board a plane, when he suddenly broke out in a cold sweat—he hadn't signed out! That took some getting used to.

All such differences were simply evidences of two very different corporate cultures—not so difficult to adjust to, even interesting sometimes. But one big difference was more challenging for him. By the end of his first week at church headquarters he had begun to visualize all the various departments and ministries within the building as a "collection of silos."

The silo metaphor was not his invention, of course. It was common use in the corporate world for an organizational unit that lacked the motivation or desire to communicate with or work with other units.

The Army had no tolerance or time for silo building. Dick was accustomed to getting things done by using his ability to connect with people, and by building relationships across the various disciplines in the Army. That was how the military operated—through cross organization.

No doubt it had something to do with the importance of communication and cooperation in combat. Infantry, artillery, transportation, medical, chaplaincy—everybody knew how they were going to contribute to the major effort. Everybody knew what everybody else was doing and how they were going to support each other. In battle that kind of cross organization was a matter of life and death. The Army had a saying: "Lone rangers come back in body bags."

At the General Conference Dick sensed that the system encouraged more barriers than bridges. Little cross connection existed between departments and individuals. People tended to stay in their own lane. They didn't often share information across departments or coordinate their activities.

This element of the General Conference corporate culture frustrated Dick. For him, ministry had always been about relationships. He had spent his Army career working across all sorts of barriers: different denominations, different races, different ranks. He understood the need to be productive—to be accountable to his superiors. But if you didn't connect, what was the point?

Leaving his second-floor office in the General Conference headquarters building, Dick roamed the halls, learning his way around, introducing himself to everybody. He used every excuse possible to interact with people throughout the vast maze of offices and cubicles—avoiding the interoffice mail and delivering his own memos, even bypassing the phone when he could substitute a personal visit. He was determined to build relationships and connectivity.

Dick had been at the GC for only a few months when he was asked to plan an employees' Christmas worship program. "Sure, fine," he responded. By then he had been walking around long enough to know quite a few people in the building. Now he had a whole new excuse to cross connect.

"Hey, I'm putting the Christmas program together—whom do you know around here with special talent?" he asked wherever he went. Soon he had recruited a whole bunch of willing people from all over the building. They collaborated on the program, rehearsed together, and did a fine job. The Christmas program was a big success.

"How'd you do that?" someone asked him after the program. "You had people from all different departments—secretaries, directors—all working together!"

"Is that unusual?"

"Oh, yeah!"

Dick just shook his head. *What's up with these people?* They were all in the same place with a common goal—what was so unusual about working together? He was amazed that people were amazed.

When he arrived at the General Conference, Dick had known a few of his coworkers—some from college, some from the seminary. But the big surprise came when he attended his first Military Chaplain Endorsers Conference. *Why, I know at least a third of the people here!* he thought, looking around at endorsers from other denominations.

It appeared that other churches also made good use of ex-military chaplains. It was as if he had never actually left the military—he was still working with people he had done so with before. There was no "who is this new Adventist endorser guy?" Within a year he would be elected chair of the group.

At the GC his routine office work didn't differ a whole lot from his job in the military. Dick was still involved in writing budgets and planning retreats and building an organization. He and his associate, Marty Feldbush, worked together to develop a global understanding of chaplaincy as a career field.

North America had well-established policies and guidelines for the chaplaincy, but many places around the world lacked wide-reaching chaplaincy directives or policies. Dick did a lot of international travel; helping leadership in the worldwide church understand the concept that chaplaincy was a real career track that people should train for and master, one that they would want to remain in long-term in order to mentor other people.

Wherever the church was growing rapidly, in such places as Africa and parts of Asia, chaplaincy as a ministry profession was expanding also, and an urgent need existed for an international system of policies and guidelines. Some areas required one kind of chaplaincy, while other parts of the world demanded something completely different. Dick's job was to ascertain the needs in each country and work with the leaders in the field to develop policies that fit their requirements. It took a lot of one-on-one schmoozing, often working through interpreters. Dick marshaled all his people skills and experience for the process.

Marty was a meticulous detail person and good at writing policy. He and Dick worked together well. They developed a system of guidelines and directives for various kinds of chaplaincies, including health care, correctional facilities, and educational institutions.

Dick learned that some divisions of the world church had no Adventist military chaplains at all. In Korea, which had a huge military establishment, the church had never approached the military to put Adventist chaplains in place, so military chaplains weren't an issue there.

Instead, the church in Korea needed more and better-trained campus and health-care chaplains. "Let us help you write some policy for your chaplaincy programs," Dick suggested to the Korean church leaders, "so that if a minister is a chaplain in a Korean hospital, and he moves to the U.S., there would be some consistency to the requirements in both countries."

In essence, Marty and Dick were knitting together the fabric of an integrated chaplaincy structure for the Adventist Church. Building on the good leadership of the past, they were committed to creating cohesive systems for the ever-expanding numbers of Adventist chaplains worldwide.

Rachel Child was the administrative assistant on the ACM team, joined later by Linda Scales. The four team members had abilities that complemented each other well, and they had a wonderful time working together.

Child was a whiz at budgeting, and she kept an eagle eye on their department's finances. One morning she walked into Dick's office with the budget statement in her hand and a puzzled look on her face.

The ACM budget was a hybrid affair, with the General Conference of the church contributing half, and the North American Division contributing the other half. The NAD acted as banker, managing the funds according to Dick's directives, but they had no authority to remove funds from the account without his knowledge or permission.

"Dick," Rachel handed him the statement, "$20,000 is missing from our account." She showed him the line item, and sure enough, he saw an unexplained withdrawal of $20,000.

"I'll be right back," he said, pushing back his chair.

"Where are you going?"

"To the treasurer's office, of course," he replied over his shoulder. He was already halfway down the hall, propelled by a tsunami of righteous indignation.

Juan Prestol was the NAD treasurer. Dick flew by Juan's secretary and marched into her boss's office, waving the statement in his hand. Although Dick held Prestol in high regard, he would not let anyone mess with ACM's budget.

"I've discovered that the NAD has removed $20,000 from our budget. How dare they take money out of our budget without consulting me?" Dick was so angry he was practically dancing around Juan's desk.

Prestol looked up from his work, his serene brown eyes taking in the furious Dick Stenbakken. "I don't know how that could have happened, Dick," he said quietly.

"I don't know either," Dick responded, a little bit of the wind going out of his sails. "But it needs to be fixed."

The next morning he arrived in his office a few minutes early to find Juan Prestol standing beside his desk, still wearing his overcoat and gloves. "I owe you a letter of apology, Dick."

"No, you don't. I just want to understand what happened," Dick responded, his anger gone.

"I have restored that $20,000 to ACM's account. It will never happen again. And my letter of apology will be on your desk before noon today."

"Juan, your word is as good as gold to me," Dick protested, feeling a little embarrassed now. "I don't need a letter." But he had a letter of apology, signed, sealed, and delivered to his office before noon that day, and he never had another incident in which his budget was in any way manipulated without his knowledge.

That's not to say that no other episodes reflected less-than-perfect cooperation and communication between departments. One time the North American Division's nine union presidents had a meeting to discuss overall budgets. Dick was not even aware of the session.

Money was tight, requiring some belt-tightening. The presidents took a careful look at all expenses and voted to withdraw funding for field operations for ACM's three military centers. Located in Korea, Germany, and Japan, the centers were managed by ACM and funded mostly from the NAD's budget. They were the "homes away from home" for North American Adventists serving overseas in the military.

Leadership notified Dick that he should make plans to shut the centers down. "Put me on the agenda for their next meeting," he requested.

"But they haven't invited you to attend" came the reply.

"I'll be at that meeting. They're not going to close down part of my department without my knowledge or consent." The military man was reasserting himself. Dick might have been wearing a tie and a conservative pin-striped suit, but his underwear was still olive green. When it came to protecting those centers, he was Clark Kent stepping into the phone booth.

Dick met with the union presidents at their next meeting and presented his case for keeping the centers open. At this meeting the union treasurers were also present. For some reason they had not been there when the vote to close the centers took place. As it happened, many of the treasurers were ex-military and had fond memories of off-duty time spent in the center in Frankfurt, or Seoul, or Okinawa, and they understood their importance. They were appalled that the church would even consider closing the places. After a rather lively discussion, the group rescinded the vote. In fact, the unions voted a larger contribution to the centers than before.

Dick was sympathetic to the need to tighten budgets, and he and his team looked for creative ways to fund the centers and at the same time lighten the load on the NAD. They heard about the fact that in Korea, for example, no tithe from the country could go to the General Conference. By law, all money collected in Korea had to stay there.

"Why don't we fund some of the operation for the Seoul Center out of Korean tithe?" he suggested. It turned out to be a good plan, and money from Korea paid almost all of the costs for the Seoul Center.

One time he learned about another money problem. Military personnel stationed in foreign countries could return their tithe through the local church where they were posted, but they could not get a valid receipt that they could use to show a charitable donation when it came time to file their U.S. tax returns. Dick suspected that many soldiers did not pay their tithe regularly because of the problem.

Dick talked to Treasury. "What if we made it possible for overseas military personnel to pay their tithe through ACM—then we can give them a valid receipt?"

The NAD agreed to give the plan a trial. ACM posted the information in *For God and Country*, its newsletter. Tithe money soon began to flow into ACM. Dick inserted a tithe envelope in the newsletter, and even more money came in. One soldier sent in $10,000—he had been saving his tithe up because he wasn't sure how to pay it. A portion of the money went to support the three overseas military centers.

When Dick took over ACM, the United States and Canada had about 300 Adventist chaplains. Less than 50 of them were active-duty military, and another 50 or so were reserve National Guard. Most of these chaplains were being supported by OPM—"other people's money."

The church didn't pay the salaries of military or federal prison chaplains—the government did. Nor did the church fund health-care chaplains. Those chaplains were representing the church, doing ministry, and returning millions of dollars in tithe, but their salaries did not come out of church funds. You had to admit that it was a pretty cost-effective way to do ministry.

Chapter 27

"You've Got Two Adventists and Three Rabbis . . ."

Travel was a big part of Dick's life as the head of ACM, and it offered its challenges as well as its rewards. Dick was on a bus in Africa one Christmas Eve, heading from Kenya to a special service in Arusha, Tanzania. The occasion would honor Adventist college graduates unable to attend their graduation ceremonies, because they had been held on the Sabbath.

All went well until they got to the Tanzanian border. There armed border guards stopped them and demanded a "toll" of $300 in American money. It was a shakedown, pure and simple, but there was no way around it.

Dick and the others on the bus took up a collection, but they were still $100 short. They tried negotiating, but nothing worked. Since they had no way to get money on Christmas Eve, they would have to spend the night on the bus, sitting at the border.

Then he remembered that some months before he had taken a brand-new $100 bill, folded it up small, and tucked it into his wallet "in case of emergency." He had forgotten about it, but this certainly qualified as an emergency, so he dug the money out of his wallet. That did the trick, and the bus full of people was soon on its way, driving through the night to reach Arusha by daybreak.

On another occasion he and Marty flew to Detroit to conduct a chaplain recognition service, planning to leave directly from it to catch a flight to Tokyo. As Dick got up to do his part of the program, he left his leather folder containing his passport and ticket on the front pew of the church.

When they reached the airport, he realized he had left the folder behind. He had neither ticket nor passport. They called back to the church and caught the pastor, who quickly confirmed that the folder was right where Dick had left it. "Can you drive as fast as you can to the airport?" Dick pleaded. "I'll be at the curb in front of United Airlines."

It seemed like forever before the pastor pulled up and handed the leather folder to him. The counter agent escorted him through security, bypassing a blocklong line of waiting customers. They raced through the Detroit airport and arrived at the gate, and Dick ran onto the plane, plunking himself into the only empty seat. And some back at the GC headquarters thought that people who traveled had all the breaks!

While Dick was learning his way around the General Conference and the world church, Ardis was busy too. She and Dick had been in the Washington, D.C., area for about a year when Rose Otis, the current director of women's ministries for the world church, hired her to provide some editorial assistance.

At first the job was part-time. Then it became half-time, and finally full-time. Eventually the denomination elected her the associate director of the department, working with Rose and then with Dorothy Watts. When Watts returned to India with her husband, Ardis moved into the position of director of women's ministries for the world church.

Everything in Ardis' background seemed to have been tailor-made to prepare her for the extraordinary position. Her bachelor's degree in English, her master's degree, her teaching experience, and her extensive work with women's groups in the Army had all had a part to play. She had also done considerable Bible study and research into women's issues.

As with her husband, her position required a great deal of worldwide travel. She and Dick were occasionally like the proverbial ships that pass in the night. Sometimes they saw each other only at airports, but both Stenbakkens believed, as they had many times before in their dual careers, that they were in the place where God wanted them to be, doing what the Lord wished them to do.

One Thursday afternoon Dick received a phone call. Two Adventist chaplains were currently enrolled in the Army basic chaplains' course, preparing for active duty. And one of them needed help with a problem.

"Elder Stenbakken, they are scheduling a field exercise here on Sabbath, and we've told them we can't do it. We've asked that the Sabbathkeepers be allowed to do this physical training on some other day, but they have refused our request." The young chaplain went on to explain that in addition to the two Adventists, three Jewish rabbis faced the same problem.

"OK," Dick said, "let me call you back." He phoned Gil Pingle, the commandant of the chaplain school and an old acquaintance, for a friendly chat. "Gil, what's the deal here?" he asked. "You've got two Adventists and three rabbis, all of whom feel that their religious convictions prevent them from doing this field exercise on the Sabbath. What can be done to reschedule this? I mean, you're teaching the chaplains about religious accommodation, right? What better opportunity to demonstrate it than to accommodate these men's religious needs?"

"We train the way we fight" was Pingle's unbending reply. "We're not going to make any accommodations."

"OK, Gil, we'll be in touch," he concluded, thinking to himself, *That wasn't exactly a friendly chat.* His next call was to the chief of chaplains' office at the Pentagon. He breathed a prayer before asking to speak to the deputy chief, his old friend and mentee, Dave Hicks, who was now a one-star general.

"Dick!" Dave's deep booming voice came through the phone. "How ya doin'?"

"Not too well, Dave. I've got a problem. As of today the U.S. Army is going to get no more Seventh-day Adventist chaplains—not active-duty, not reserve, none. And those that are already in the pipeline, I'm going to shift to the Air Force and Navy."

A puzzled silence. "What's wrong, Dick? What's going on?"

"Dave, I cannot, as an endorser, knowingly put people into a system in which I know they will not have religious accommodation for Sabbathkeeping. If our people are not valued, we can't put them into that system." Then he explained what was going on at the chaplain school.

"Just a minute, Dick," Dave said. Then he put the current chief of chaplains on the phone, a two-star general named G. T. Gunhus. Dick and Gunhus had worked on assignments together and knew each other fairly well. Dick reiterated the story. "G. T., I cannot endorse chaplains for the Army if the Army is going to treat them like this. Ethically, I just can't do it."

"Stay by your phone, Dick," G. T. stated.

"I'll be right here."

Twenty minutes later the commandant of the U.S. Army chaplain school called Dick back. "Well, Dick," he began, "concerning our earlier conversation, we've looked at the matter again, and we think this would be a good opportunity for us to demonstrate the importance of making a religious accommodation. We will schedule the Sabbathkeepers to do their field testing at another time."

"Thank you, Gil, for that enlightened decision," Dick responded with great courtesy. "We appreciate your extending this religious accommodation and teaching chaplains about its importance."

Thirty minutes later he got another phone call from the chief's office. "Dick, by any chance, did you get a call from Pingle?"

"Yeah, I just talked to him."

"You're welcome," Dick's old friend, Chaplain (Brigadier General) Gunhus, said.

As it turned out, it poured rain on the Sabbath of the scheduled physical training, and the Army had to cancel the exercise for everybody. So everything got rescheduled. Later Dick learned that the unfortunate commandant of the chaplain school had endured a thorough dressing down from his superiors. No more religious accommodation issues troubled the chaplain school.

It was one of many occasions that Dick was thankful for God's leading, and for his military background. Having been on active duty and knowing the chief of chaplains and his deputy personally, as well as understanding the Army system, had made a difficult situation much easier to resolve.

Another such situation surfaced at the Air Force Academy. A junior cadet there had received a large number of demerits for failing to attend Saturday football games and other sporting events. The academy considered sports as part of the team-building curriculum and mandated attendance.

The cadet had instead spent his Saturday mornings at the Adventist church in Colorado Springs. Not all his demerits were directly related to his Sabbath activities (some came from being late to class and other minor infractions), but more than 80 percent resulted because he chose to attend church on Sabbath mornings.

The Air Force Academy chaplain alerted Dick and suggested that he needed to make some contact at the Air Force Academy. Dick made plans to fly out to it and to take Mitch Tyner, a General Conference attorney, with him.

Dick talked to the Air Force Academy chaplain, a full colonel. He knew that as the endorser for the Seventh-day Adventist Church he would receive the same courtesies as a one-star general. "I understand there is a hearing scheduled for this kid. I'm going to be there. Please make arrangements for me to stay at the VIP housing. I'll need two rooms. I'm bringing our corporate attorney with me."

"Your attorney can't go into this hearing—and for that matter, neither can you," the Air Force Academy chaplain replied.

"I know, we just want to be there to support our cadet, and to see if any follow-up action is needed."

When Dick arrived on the Air Force Academy campus, he met with the one-star general who was the commander of cadets. "This is not a religious issue—it's a discipline one," the general stated.

"I beg to differ." Dick had a copy of the kid's demerit list. "Here, look at the record," he said, running his finger down the row of dates. "Eighty percent of these absences occurred on Saturdays. That's when this kid is in church. It *is* a religious issue!" Then he changed gears. "Do you have Jewish cadets here?"

"Yes, of course."

"Do they get demerits for going to religious services on Sabbath?"

"No, of course not!"

"Then why can't you accommodate a Seventh-day Adventist?"

Dick actually received permission to attend the hearing and was invited to speak. "This young man is academically fit," he reasoned. "He has done well in every way, and as I look at the list of demerits, the vast majority of them happened because he is going to church rather than to ball games. You're making religious accommodation for your Jewish cadets, so why not for another Sabbathkeeper?"

Dick also explained that the young man, who was Korean—an American citizen whose parents had immigrated to the United States—no doubt was aware that in his ancestral homeland many Adventists in the military were being forced to do things on Sabbath that were against their religious convictions. Many had been imprisoned when they refused. So the cadet came from a culture in which people accepted going to jail rather than violate the Sabbath.

The Air Force Academy chaplain also spoke at the hearing and gave a good exposition on Adventist beliefs. Then the members of the hearing asked him and Stenbakken to step out while they discussed the matter.

"We'll be waiting right outside the door," Dick said. The group debated for more than an hour, and then asked both chaplains and the young cadet to come back into the room.

"We have examined your situation carefully, and we are going to remove all demerits on your record that occurred on Saturdays," they told the young cadet. "Furthermore, we are going to institute a policy that Seventh-day Adventists or any other Sabbathkeepers who go to worship services in lieu of sporting events will all have equal opportunity to do that,

224 THE MAN WITH THE REVERSIBLE FOOT

without incurring demerits." So they changed their regulations right there on the spot.

Dick's presence at the hearing had spoken volumes. Just his being there had conveyed a message: *This is an international church organization standing behind a cadet's religious convictions.* The presence of the church's attorney reinforced that message even more strongly. *This organization is prepared to make this case a high-level legal issue if that becomes necessary.*

Sometimes you just had to put all your cards on the table faceup.

Chapter 28

"This Is Mine!
It's Not Going Back!"

The Stenbakkens' daughter, Rikki, had recently become engaged to Jason Welch, a fellow employee at Christian Record Services for the Blind, a Seventh-day Adventist ministry in Lincoln, Nebraska.

Dick liked the young man. Rikki's intensity, brains, and drive had frightened the socks off most guys, but not Jason. Although a brilliant student, his laid-back, easygoing personality was the perfect foil for Rikki. Dick was looking forward to the wedding of his only daughter—sometime in the future.

Her petite frame masks an intense personality that possesses many of her father's traits of character, including his quirky sense of humor. She and Jason called Dick one spring evening when she was still living in Lincoln. "Dad, Jason has something he wants to tell you." Her boyfriend came on the line and hemmed and hawed. He talked about the weather and hemmed and hawed some more.

Then he blurted, "Rikki and I have decided to elope—in fact, we're getting married this weekend."

I'm gonna kill him was Dick's first reaction. Then he thought, *No, he's going to be my son-in-law, so I can't kill him.* His next thought was *Ardis is going to go ballistic!* Then he heard Rikki giggling in the background. At the same moment he realized that the day's date was April 1.

"April Fool!" the two young people chorused. They had caught him, the family jokester, flat-footed at his own game. *Well,* he thought, *I guess some things really are genetic.*

Rikki loved languages. She had started teaching herself Latin as a little kid, and she was fluent in Spanish. As a student missionary for a year in Costa Rica she had helped run a radio station. Then she'd spent time in Spain and six months in Chile working for the Adventist Development and Relief Agency.

After college she wanted to do a master's degree in international studies. Accepted into a program at American University in Washington, D.C., she moved home and lived with her parents while completing the program.

Rikki did an internship with Macro International, a marketing and opinion research firm, and then went straight to work for them after graduation. Jason became a physician's assistant. The couple married in 1998 and now live in Maryland with their two children. And Rikki still plays jokes on her father, but she's never succeeded as well as she did on that April Fool's Day.

When Dick had been at the General Conference a few years somebody at the top levels of administration conceived the idea to conduct a world study about the effectiveness of its various departments. Some thought such departments should not be hands-on—should not provide services directly, but rather should serve only an administrative, policy-setting function. The researchers prepared a general questionnaire and sent it out to all parts of the world church to gather data. But they did not inform the directors of the departments in question that such a study was taking place.

It wasn't long before Dick and other directors began getting calls from their counterparts in other areas of the world. "What's this study all about, and who is doing it?" people asked.

"Hey, what's going on here?" the directors quizzed each other. "We're not against administration asking questions about our effectiveness, but we're right here—we could work with them on this."

Feelings were running pretty high. A rumor even floated around the offices that some of the departments might get eliminated. People felt that the study was being done behind their backs and that it indicated a lack of trust on the part of the General Conference administration.

Dick figured that the survey would undermine any progress that had been made toward team building at the General Conference. He made an appointment with GC president Bob Folkenberg. When he arrived at Folkenberg's office at the appointed time, he had an inert training hand grenade hooked to his belt under his suit jacket.

Folkenberg was a gracious, genial man, and he greeted him warmly. The two men had known each other since their seminary days. Dick launched right into the matter of his concern. "Bob, there's a situation you need to be aware of that is quite explosive. It could do some real damage to your leadership and to the church."

"What's this about, Dick?"

"Well, let me illustrate it," Dick replied, pulling the hand grenade off his belt. "Here, hold this," he said, handing the grenade to him and pretending to drop it, while keeping his finger through the ring on the cotter pin. Instinctively Folkenberg grabbed for the grenade, and when he did, Dick pulled the pin.

The president's usually jovial expression changed to one of horror. "This isn't real, is it? This is not a live grenade, Dick, is it?"

"No, Bob, it isn't real. If it had been, both of us would have been dead in four seconds." Dick held up the cotter pin, which was dangling from the index finger of his right hand. "But there's a situation in this building that is just as explosive, and you're the only one who can put the pin back in that grenade."

Dick had gotten his boss's attention. He went on to tell Folkenberg that many of the directors in the building were concerned that a major study about the value of the work of their departments was being conducted without consultation with them, and the situation would not get better unless the president addressed it with the directors.

At 3:00 that afternoon Bob Folkenberg summoned all the departmental directors to the third-floor presidential committee room for a meeting with him. A lively discussion followed as directors from family life, chaplaincy, women's ministries, youth ministries, communications, health ministries, stewardship, Sabbath school, children's ministries, education, personal ministries, and other departments expressed themselves.

"Just let us know what's going on. We're willing to work together to make whatever changes or improvements are needed, but don't do something like this without even consulting us." The directors felt that the departments they ran were the fabric holding the church together. The church was about doing ministry, and their jobs were to facilitate such ministry.

"We don't want to downplay the importance of good policy—we need good policy," someone added. "But you never run into a person who says, 'I'm in the church because of a good policy.' They say, 'I'm in the church because of a teacher, or a chaplain, or a youth pastor, or a friend who took a personal interest in me.'"

The church administration backed off on the study. No doubt it had seemed like a good idea at the time—but the one-size-fits-all approach and the lack of communication with the affected departmental leaders had rendered it pointless. The GC told church leaders around the world not to worry about responding to the questionnaire. "If we do a study, we'll work with each department to make sure the questions we ask are appropriate to the department," administration explained. "After all, we're all on the same team."

Dick put his defanged hand grenade back in his bottom desk drawer. That kind of thing worked only once. Besides, another situation had arisen that needed his immediate attention.

Joel Klimkewicz was a young marine deployed to a ship in the Persian Gulf. The ship's chaplain was a Seventh-day Adventist, and in addition to the regular Protestant worship services he conducted on board ship, he made himself available, as all chaplains do, for personal counseling and Bible study.

Klimkewicz attended the worship services, and, seeking more spiritual understanding, he also met regularly with the chaplain for Bible study. He asked the Adventist chaplain what he believed, and the man responded, showing him from the Bible its teachings about the Sabbath and the second coming of Christ.

Joel and several others on board were baptized—not as Seventh-day Adventists, but in a general faith commitment. His superiors and fellow marines noticed that both Joel's military performance and his personal life underwent a drastic and positive change after his conversion.

When Joel returned to the States, he was stationed at the Marine base at Camp Lejeune, in Jacksonville, North Carolina. One of the first things he did upon his arrival there was to find a nearby Seventh-day Adventist church. He and his wife, Tomomi, attended faithfully and were baptized into the church in 2002.

Things were going well for him, and he was nearly at the end of his second enlistment. Then, after a great deal of soul searching, he came under the conviction that he could no longer carry a weapon. To say the least, he was in the wrong place for such a decision. The Marine Corps has an extremely low level of tolerance for not carrying a weapon.

Everyone who serves in the Marines is a weapon-carrying combatant. The noncombatant medical corpsmen and chaplains who serve the Marines are attached to the Navy. The Marines pride themselves on being a 100 percent formidable fighting force.

Ironically, Joel was an excellent marksman—so good that he had been training other soldiers to use a weapon. Nevertheless, he put in the paperwork for recognition as a noncombatant. He asked for assignments that would allow him to serve without carrying a weapon, and even though his second enlistment period had only six weeks or so to go, he offered to go to Iraq and clear ordinance. Trained to diffuse mines and IEDs (improvised explosive devices), he figured that in such a job a weapon would be in the way. He wasn't afraid to risk his life to save others.

His request, duly filed, went up the line. In the meantime, according to policy, the Marine Corps had to treat him as a noncombatant while his request was pending. Everything went smoothly for a few weeks, but then his request for noncombatancy came back down the pipeline, marked *Denied*.

The Marine Corps brass knew that a lot of soldiers faced redeployment for the second and third time, and they were no doubt concerned that a request for noncombatant status might go viral. So even though Joel was only a few weeks away from ending his second enlistment, his commanding officer ordered him to pick up a weapon. When he refused, the Marines preferred charges against him and set the date for his court-martial.

Joel had two options. He could choose a trial by jury or have his case heard before a judge. Since the jury was likely to consist largely of combat veterans who would not be sympathetic to him, he figured his chances would be better in front of a judge.

Dick had been in close contact with him throughout this process, and he was convinced that the young marine's decision to ask for noncombatant status was based on real conviction. The Adventist Church advocates nonviolence, but leaves such personal decisions up to the individual. Nevertheless, the denomination was committed to giving any individual who chose noncombatancy its full support.

Dick and GC attorney Mitchell Tyner attended the court-martial. There was testimony from Joel's chaplain, from Dick, and from Tyner, as well as from Joel himself. The command presented their side. The judge retired to his chambers, and returned shortly. He pronounced the verdict. Joel was guilty—the equal of a felony conviction.

The court sentenced Lance Corporal Joel David Klimkewicz to six months in the brig. He also received a "bad conduct" discharge—meaning, among other things, that he would lose his VA benefits and his access to the GI Bill for education.

The great irony of the whole situation was that the court-martial itself took place on the very day Joel was scheduled to leave the Marine Corps. It was a ludicrous state of affairs. At every point in which the Marines could have made a wise choice, they had made a foolish one.

Guards marched Joel off to the stockade. His wife was distraught and shaken, but she remained strong. "God will help us," she told Dick, and he promised her that the church would do everything it could.

When he and Mitch returned to General Conference headquarters, they immediately contacted Congressman Roscoe Bartlett, a Seventh-day Adventist legislator from the state of Maryland. Bartlett served on the House Armed Services Committee. Dick knew his chief of staff, Bud Otis. Bud was the husband of Rose Otis, with whom Ardis worked at the General Conference.

The story of the marine court-martialed for his religious convictions on his last day in the Corps spread through the major media—in particular the fact that he had declared his willingness to defuse bombs and IEDs rather than carry a weapon.

Bartlett contacted the commandant of the Marine Corps, firmly requesting a meeting. The commandant was unable to attend, but he sent a one-star general to represent him. The man was a recruiting-poster version of a marine, six-foot-three, square-jawed, broad-shouldered, straight-backed, and taciturn.

Bartlett met with him in a conference room in the congressman's office in the Rayburn House Office Building, across from the Capitol. Both Dick and Mitch Tyner were present as well. They watched and listened as Bartlett questioned the general. Though respectful, the congressman pulled no punches. "This young man wants to risk his life and save others, and you court-martial him?" he asked. "Is this how you want the Marine Corps to be known?"

At the end of the interview, as they were walking out of the room, the general looked Dick straight in the eye. "This would never have happened on my watch," he said quietly. "I get the message." He asked for Dick's phone number and called him an hour later to offer some pointers on how the church could support Joel.

With Congressman Bartlett, the General Conference legal department, and Dick all working with Joel's lawyer, they were able to appeal Joel's case. Kimkewicz did some hard time before his early release, although he was able to conduct Bible studies while in the brig. Eventually the Marine Corps upgraded his discharge to honorable, restoring his VA and GI Bill benefits.

Joel used the GI Bill to attend Southern Adventist University, earning a bachelor's degree in theology. Then he finished a Master of Divinity at the Adventist Theological Seminary. Becoming a civilian chaplain, he and

Tomomi moved to Okinawa, and he managed the servicemen's center on behalf of the Adventist Church. He is now a pastor in the United States.

As rewarding as it had been to help a young man such as Joel, Dick found other aspects of his work at the General Conference equally fulfilling. One of the highlights of his time at GC headquarters was the project he coproduced with Tom Neslund. Tom, who worked with the Health Ministries Department, mentioned a particular burden of his one day. The GC building was located in a suburban area, with hundreds of families living nearby, and Tom thought the denomination needed to find a way to be more involved in the community.

Dick told him about the sunrise service he had done in Hawaii, and the two men began working together on some ideas. It led to Walk Through Bethlehem, a live-action, interactive trip through a bazaar at the time of Jesus' birth, held in the lobby and atrium of the General Conference headquarters building, with volunteers from the GC playing merchants, shepherds, Wise Men, and Roman soldiers.

Visitors wound through the "streets of Bethlehem" until they found Jesus in the manger. The event drew thousands over several nights each Christmas. Afterward they went home with religious materials and a new knowledge that Seventh-day Adventists were good Christian people.

The success of Walk Through Bethlehem inspired Dick and Tom Neslund to collaborate on writing some additional material, and soon Dick had a sizable cast of Bible characters in his repertoire and more invitations to perform them than he could handle. As word of his first-person performances spread, he received invitations to conduct numerous Week of Prayer presentations at churches and other institutions.

Such exposure developed into an opportunity to be a part of a DVD series called Adventist Preaching. Another colleague, Dick Duerkson, had videotaped one of his presentations entitled *The Centurion at the Cross*, which became the first in what would become a DVD series entitled *Faces Around the Cross*, eventually followed by *Faces Around the Manger*, *Miracles of the Master*, and *The Armor of God*. All were (and still are) sold through Adventist Book Center outlets as well as through the Internet and other sources.

All of the renewed attention to first-person costumed presentations revived his interest in biblical apparel and, in particular, Roman armor. He realized that his old Naugahyde tablecloth armor was pretty shabby and far from authentic.

His research led him to a young man named Matthew Amt, who was the leader of a Roman reenactment group in the D.C. area. Dick phoned Matt and told him what he was doing. Matthew invited him to see his armor collection. The two men met and became friends. Amt and his fellow reenactors even helped out with the Walk Through Bethlehem program.

An absolutely fascinating guy, Matt knew everything there was to know about Roman military history of the first century. It amazed Dick to learn that active Roman reenactment groups existed all over the country—and even the world. "I gotta have a set of this!" he exclaimed when he saw Matthew's armor.

Matthew graciously shared plans and material sources, and soon Dick was involved in doing his own research on first-century Roman military history and constructing his own armor. Armed with new insights, he began to see biblical material in a brand-new light. Soon he was thinking seriously about his imagined centurion, the one ordered to crucify Christ. The more he read of first-century military history, the more biblical connections he made, and the more the story expanded.

What's the best way to share this? he thought. Then he had an epiphany. He would write a book. Dick wanted to tell the story in a way that would make applications for today's Christian. That's what he had always hoped to do with his first-person presentations—to pull people into a story in a nonthreatening way, then use the story to illustrate spiritual points. He began assembling material and writing. Pacific Press would eventually publish the book as *The Centurion* in 2009.

Meanwhile, in his workshop the new armor was coming to life. Dick had discovered that you could actually buy full sets of authentically correct Roman armor, but he wanted to make his own, even though he had never worked with metal. *Look, you've got five graduate degrees,* he told himself. *Surely you can figure this out!* Using Matt's plans, he first assembled a complete set using poster board and tape.

The real thing he constructed from 18-gauge soft iron—the same material the Romans had used in the first century. Theirs had been hand-hammered into sheets, and his he rolled out by machine, but otherwise it was the same stuff. Leather straps and rivets held it together—no more Naugahyde.

Dick used a power saw to cut the metal pieces out. The project took more than 100 hours. The finished piece of torso armor, shaped something like the armored vests soldiers and police wear now, extended from shoulder to waist, and weighed 19 pounds.

His original "Roman helmet" had been an old construction helmet turned backwards and spray-painted gold, with two Army whisk brooms mounted on top. That didn't go too well with his new metal armor, so he went back to the Internet.

Finding a site that advertised a Roman helmet from a source in India, he contacted the seller, who turned out to be local—in fact, the company had its office close to where his assistant Rachel lived. The seller agreed to lend him the helmet for a performance, provided he took good care of it.

Rachel picked it up for him and brought it into the office. Dick took one look at the helmet and said, "This is mine! It's not going back!" The owner sold it to him for $125. Combined with a sword he had bought in Alaska, Dick now had the beginnings of a pretty good centurion's outfit.

The collection has grown since then. Dick now has three different sets of Roman armor, two shields, and assorted swords and spears. Also, he has made a collection of real first-century biblical New Testament artifacts, including coins, bracelets, pins, and other items. Some people might call it an obsession, but Dick prefers "hobby," "ministry," or "passion." "Oh, OK," he admits with a laugh, "it's an obsession—but at least it's tax-deductible."

Chapter 29

"An Inch and a Half Thick, You Say?"

Military chaplains are on loan to the armed forces from their religious organizations. Their denominations must endorse them prior to their taking up their duties. Only one recognized name, per religious body, can serve as the endorser.

It was Dick's responsibility, as the director of Adventist Chaplaincy Ministries, to be the Adventist Church's endorser. Endorsement is a professional credential and a prerequisite for chaplaincy. It affirms that the candidate is a member in good standing of the endorsing body and has met its basic ministry requirements. In addition, endorsement also creates a covenant of mutual commitment, accountability, and support between the chaplain and his or her denomination.

The endorsing denomination has the right to remove an endorsement when it deems it necessary, something that happens occasionally in all denominations for one reason or another. For instance, when chaplains move theologically away from their endorsing organization, or when they get into legal or moral trouble, the church has the authority to bring them home, no questions asked.

When a denomination makes such a decision and so informs the chief of chaplains, the chaplain in question must cease all clergy functions. It is akin to a doctor losing his medical license. While it happened rarely among Adventist chaplains during Dick's tenure, when it did it was difficult for all concerned.

A committee that included high-level GC representation as well as legal counsel would make the official decision, but once it decided to withdraw endorsement, it became Dick's responsibility to carry it through.

Such incidents followed a typical pattern, starting when someone called a situation to ACM's attention. In one case, a report came to ACM that an Adventist chaplain was having an affair with an enlisted man's wife, an accusation that it could not ignore. The church had a moral and legal obligation to follow up on it. If the accusations were not true, ACM would take steps to protect the chaplain. And, of course, if they turned out to be accurate, it would involve other procedures to protect the people the chaplain served and the good name of the denomination.

Dick investigated and, in the process, assembled a file that was more than an inch and a half thick. Everything pointed to the fact that the accusations were correct. The chaplain in question had at first vehemently denied everything, but when confronted with the facts, he admitted that they were true.

The ACM committee met, including Bediako and Tyner. Dick presented an overview of the information he had uncovered, and Tyner outlined the legal aspects. The chaplain, who was still on active duty, was present by phone, and the committee invited him to say whatever he wanted. Everything was done to protect the chaplain's privacy, including the shredding of all distributed copies of documents after the meeting.

In the end, the committee voted unanimously to pull the chaplain's endorsement. Dick called the chief of chaplains' office at the Pentagon first, and followed that up with a fax and a formal letter. Then he called the chaplain's commander. She was irate. "What do you mean, you're pulling his endorsement? He's one of the best chaplains I've ever had. From everything I've seen, he's doing a good job. Why are you doing this?"

"It is a serious moral issue," Dick explained. "We have conducted a thorough investigation, and I have a file an inch and a half thick in front of me. If you were made aware of everything in this man's file, you'd probably have to court-martial him, and I know you wouldn't want to do that."

"An inch and a half thick?"

"Yes. As much as it pains us to do it, withdrawing his endorsement is the most expeditious and the least hurtful way to remove him from both the ministry and the military."

"An inch and a half thick, you say?" the commander repeated with a sigh, all the fight gone out of her. And that was the end of the discussion. Dick was glad that situations requiring the withdrawal of the church's endorsement were rare. The vast majority of Seventh-day Adventist military chaplains were godly men and women, dedicated to the Lord and to the people they served.

By now he had been working at the General Conference as the director of Adventist Chaplaincy Ministries for nearly 10 years. He and Ardis were both living life in an Adventist version of the fast lane, traveling widely, and in many ways, at the height of their careers. As they began to think about the next phase of their lives, they were happy to see that their son Erik's own career was going well.

He had graduated from Union College and had completed a master's degree in creative writing at the University of Central Florida. His wife, Gelerie, had also finished her studies in medical technology.

Union College had invited him back to be a part of their public relations team. Soon he found himself editing the college's alumni journal, *The Cord*, and having difficulty getting good, high-quality pictures for the magazine.

Erik had always been interested in photography, ever since his grandfather Dick had given him his first camera and showed him how to help develop photos in his basement darkroom. Soon he was producing his own photographs for the alumni journal and other campus publications.

The Cord began to win national awards, and it wasn't long before other college departments began to call for his work, then even more insistent requests for both writing and photography. So many different college departments and entities made claims on his time and talent that he was overloaded with work.

In the meantime, Gelerie was working as a med tech in Lincoln. She found the work less than challenging, however, and had applied and been accepted to medical school at the University of Nebraska in Omaha—about 60 miles away from where they were living in Lincoln. She was in her second year of commuting back and forth to medical school.

Their lives were hectic, and Erik decided the only way he could get control of his workload was to go independent, so he resigned his job at the college and set up his own agency. It was a courageous move, but it allowed him to prioritize his activities on his own terms. Soon he was doing much of the college's PR work on a contract basis, plus projects for other universities, businesses, hospitals, and industries.

Operating under the name Stenbakken Photography, headquartered in Papillion, Nebraska, Erik had soon amassed a significant body of work, including seven or eight covers for *Christianity Today* and shoots for *National Geographic, Parade, Newsweek*, and many other national magazines. After moving to Greeley, Colorado, he branched out into videography, including a project for Denver public schools.

Gelerie is an anaesthesiologist, part of a doctors' group in nearby Fort Collins, and, like Rikki and Jason, the couple has two children. Ardis and

Dick, having reached a time in life when it is customary to take stock, were extremely thankful for their many blessings, including their strong and successful adult children and their spouses, and their four beautiful grandchildren.

Looking back over the past 10 years or so, Dick had to acknowledge that his work at the GC had been fulfilling. He knew he was making a worthwhile contribution both to the military and to the church. His department was also supporting other types of chaplaincies, something that he and others had wanted to see happen at the GC level for many years.

Together he and Martin Feldbush—Marty with his background in health care, and Dick with his military career experience—were continuing to define and shape chaplaincy into a recognized and respected career field for Adventist clergy on a worldwide basis.

Ardis and Dick began to talk about their eventual retirement. She, too, felt fulfilled and happy in her position as director of women's ministries for the world church. But they had other factors to consider. The heavy travel schedules were beginning to wear on both of them. Ardis' parents were getting older, and her mother wasn't in good health.

Their own health was good, but they remembered some of the retired people they'd seen in Hawaii, hobbling down the sidewalk, dragging oxygen tanks behind them. The Stenbakkens wanted to retire while they were young and healthy enough to enjoy life. Then there was his whole "new" career as a performer on DVDs and a first-person presenter. He needed more time for that.

They both decided that it was best to retire at the peak of their ministry, thus leaving while they still loved the work. They set the date for late 2004, although he would continue to work under a contract basis for a while, and she agreed to maintain her position as editor of the women's devotional book—a major project of the Women's Ministries Department. Their joint retirement ceremony took place in the atrium of the General Conference headquarters building in January of 2005.

It was an open reception, held during the noon hour so that people from all over the building could come by during their lunch period, but the place remained packed for several hours. The GC Conference president Jan Paulsen was there, and many of the vice presidents, but it especially touched Dick that so many of the support staff in the building attended as well. It was a wonderful day and a fitting way to mark the end of one phase of his life and the beginning of another.

Chapter 30

"She Looks Just Like Mom!"

"Dick, don't you sometimes wonder if . . . ?" Ardis let her voice drift off as she looked at their grown-up daughter, Rikki, studying, her tiny frame curled up on one end of the couch, her dark head bent over her laptop.

Rikki, at 5'2" tall, was the smallest of the Stenbakkens. She was petite in every way, from her small hands to her dainty size-2 figure. Still, she was strong and feisty. Even as a child she had always been a little bundle of dynamite, but in stature she was much shorter than her mother or her grandmother.

It wasn't the first time they had wondered if their daughter resembled his birth mother. Dick, of course, had always known he was adopted. As a kid Mom and Dad had taught him that being adopted meant being especially chosen, and so he spent little time wondering about his biological family. As he grew older, he became aware that some adopted children felt driven to find their roots for one reason or another, but it had never seemed important to him.

That attitude hadn't changed in his adulthood, with one added factor. While his adoptive parents were still living, he would never do anything that would make them feel rejected in any way—especially as his mother's health and emotional state became more fragile. He would always honor Celia and Oliver Stenbakken as the parents who raised him.

But not long after his mother died, he was helping his dad sort through some old paperwork when he came across an adoption court order. The name on the paper was Larry Ryan. His first thought was *Mom and Dad must have tried to adopt another child before they adopted me. I wonder why they didn't get little Larry?* Dick felt a bit sorry for this unknown, rejected child.

Then he looked more closely at the paper and realized that the birth date listed was his own. Suddenly his heart rate shot up. *That's me! I'm Larry Ryan!* It took his breath away for a moment. He had never known he had another name. It was a heady moment, meeting himself in this way, but there was also a sense of detachment about it—as though he was an observer and it was happening to another person.

Quietly he put the document under his shirt, made an excuse to go to the drugstore on the corner, and had several copies made of it. Then he returned the original to his dad's files and never mentioned it again. But every now and then he'd think about Larry Ryan. Rolling the name around on his tongue, he would wonder a little more about his origins.

Of course, whenever he filled out a form related to his medical history, he had to leave a lot of items blank. It didn't particularly bother him, but he realized it wouldn't be a bad idea to have some biological history—if not for himself, then certainly for the sake of his kids and his grandkids. And then, every once in a while, Ardis would say, "You know, Dick, you may have siblings out there . . ."

Slowly his interest was whetted, perhaps as much by the challenge of a new area of research as by curiosity. The only legal document he had had for most of his life was a small piece of paper that stated that Richard Stenbakken was the legal son of Oliver and Celia Stenbakken. He had used the form for identification purposes, in place of a birth certificate, and to get a driver's license and a passport.

Now he had the original adoption paper he'd found among his father's things. It listed his birth name and the juvenile court from which he had been adopted. In addition, it also contained a case number, and a judge had signed it. He didn't know it then, but the document was the first piece of an elaborate puzzle that would take him years to assemble fully.

In March 1998 he started the ball rolling by requesting information from the Colorado Department of Health and Human Services. No answer came for three months, and Dick had nearly forgotten about it, when he got a response from what was evidently a very busy and harried clerk, who apologized for putting his request at the bottom of a stack and temporarily forgetting about it. She sent him copies of what they had on file, but all of the identifying information, such as his birth mother's name and her birthplace—or anything else traceable—had been blanked out. Essentially the papers told him nothing he didn't already know—with one exception.

They listed his birthplace as the Salvation Army Hospital and Home in Denver. It was a small piece of the puzzle, but it was something. And that's how the process went, with no big breakthroughs or epiphanies—just the fitting together of one small fragment at a time.

Did a Salvation Army Hospital still exist in Denver? Dick doubted it, and sure enough, he soon learned that the hospital was gone. It had been closed for many years. Then he called the Salvation Army headquarters in Denver and identified himself as a retired Army chaplain to the social worker who took his call.

After some initial schmoozing, he broached the reason for his call. "I'm working on a project, trying to find the birth family of an adopted child," he began.

The social worker, a Salvation Army envoy named Gerald Koch, was no dummy. He had a master's degree in social work and he'd been around the block a time or two. "And how would you be related to that family?"

"OK, fine, I'm that adopted child," Dick admitted. He told Koch what little information he had.

"Well, you have your birth name, and it is likely that in that era a child would have carried the last name of the mother. So it is quite possible that Ryan was your mother's name," Koch said, but he couldn't or wouldn't confirm that it was or it wasn't.

After taking down all the information that Dick had compiled thus far, he said, "I'll look into it," but made no commitment as to how much information he would be able to find or when he would obtain it.

Dick and Ardis were in Denver a few weeks later, buying snacks in a Safeway grocery store for the sixtieth anniversary party for Ardis' parents, when his beeper went off. Finding a pay phone in the back of the store, he returned the call. It was Koch. He started rattling off information. Dick had a pencil but nothing to write on, so he started ripping pieces of paper off the bulletin board by the phone, jotting stuff down as fast as he could.

When Koch took a breath, Dick said, "Gerald, you must have something you're reading this stuff from. I'm taking notes as fast as I can, but I'm missing some things. Can't you send me what you have?"

A pause. "Well, yes, I do have something. Yeah, I can do that. I can send it to you." Dick thanked him profusely, and Koch promised to call him back if he got any more information.

After the anniversary party, Dick and Ardis were just about to step onto a United Airlines plane to return home to the East Coast when his beeper went off again. It was Koch. Dick knew the social worker had found something more, but he couldn't phone him back until they were airborne. It was before cell phones became ubiquitous, and the only way to call was from the seatback phones provided by the airlines. He phoned Koch as soon as he could, but the Salvation Army man was in a meeting and couldn't take his call.

Dick was on pins and needles all the way across the country, speculating what the new information was. He didn't have long to wonder. They had been home less than five minutes when the phone rang. It was Gerald Koch. "Well, I got curious about your situation," he reported. "I hope you don't mind."

Dick rolled his eyes. Mind! It's what he'd been hoping for. "I followed up on some cousins of your mother's who live down in southern Colorado, and made contact with them. I hope that's OK."

"Yeah, that's OK."

"Oh, good. And furthermore, they said they'd be willing to get in touch with you." Then he gave Dick the names and telephone numbers of two cousins.

Thanks to Koch's research, he now knew that his birth mother's name was Frances Ryan. He had learned that she was from a small mountain community called Collbran, about 40 miles east of Grand Junction, Colorado.

When he contacted the Colbran High School alumni association, they told him when she had graduated. They also mentioned that when the class had had a reunion some years before, they had sent a mailing out to her, and it had come back marked "deceased." That information gave him a probable death date for her.

About the same time he was learning this information, he contacted the cousins. "Oh, yes, we remember Cousin Frances. She had had a brother, Larry, who died very young of a massive heart attack." Another puzzle piece slid into place. Now he knew where his birth name, Larry, had come from.

The cousins' mother had remarried, and they had lost contact with the Ryan side of the family, but they sent him some old photographs, one of which they thought was probably their cousin Frances. They also sent another photo, which they said was one of her daughters, Sally.

When the photographs arrived, Dick opened the envelope and looked for the first time into the eyes of the woman who had given birth to him. And he recognized himself. Getting out his graduation picture from Campion Academy—when he would have been close to the same age as his mother in the photo—he placed them side by side. When he compared the noses, the shape of the faces, the eyes—there was no doubt. He had found his birth mother.

The other photo in the envelope he was less sure about. The cousins had said it was a picture of Frances' daughter. The young girl in the photograph smiled out at the world from a face that looked gentle and kind. She was wearing a dark jumper and a white blouse with a demure, lace-edged collar. The back of the photo had one word—"Sally"—and a date, nothing more. Was "Sally" his sister?

The cousins had confirmed that his mother was no longer living. They knew that she had been married, and they contributed another piece of the puzzle—her married name. She had been Frances Ryan Huff.

Dick pulled up the Social Security Death Index on the Internet. Amazingly, it contained about a dozen Frances Ryan Huffs. Although he checked all the birth and death dates, he found no definite matches.

Then he thought of something else. From his work as a chaplain he knew something about Social Security numbers. You could tell what part of the country someone was born in by the first three digits of the number. Only one of the names in the Death Index had a Social Security number that started with 522—indicating Colorado. The Death Index included the address where an individual received his or her last Social Security check. Most were full addresses, but the Frances Ryan Huff from Colorado had only a five-digit number.

The number puzzled him. What was it? Then a little light went off, and another piece of the puzzle slipped into place. It was a zip code—which turned out to be for Sandpoint, Idaho. Calling the library in Sandpoint, he asked for help finding the obituary of Frances Ryan Huff.

"Oh, yeah, we can get that for you," the friendly clerk replied. Within a few hours he had an e-mail with the entire obituary. It described the funeral service, named the funeral home, and mentioned that the deceased's two daughters, Francine Jones and Judy Dyer, had been in attendance. Two more pieces of the puzzle fell into place. Dick knew he had two half sisters. But something else didn't quite add up—the obituary made no mention of a daughter named Sally.

Dick did an Internet search on Francine Jones, but came up with nothing. The same thing happened when he researched Judy Dyer. Then he asked himself, *Where does a newspaper get its information for an obituary? From the funeral home!* So he went online, found the funeral home's information, and phoned them.

He identified himself as a minister and a retired Army chaplain. Again, the person on the other end of the line was gracious. "I'm looking for information on a Frances Huff," he began. "I understand you had the services for her?"

"Oh, yes, we did," the helpful clerk replied. "Her daughter, Francine, made all the arrangements. I think we still have her phone number. Would you like to have it?"

"Oh, yes, that would be helpful."

Suddenly he felt uneasy. Things were moving a little too fast. *How fair is it for me to drop into this person's life after all these years?* He would have been even more concerned about it if his birth mother had still been alive. Believing that Frances Ryan had made the best decision she could at the time, he bore her no ill will. After he talked to Ardis about contacting Francine, they prayed about it.

Then he sat at his desk, looking at the telephone number, thinking, *If I make this phone call, my life and her life will never be exactly the same.* Then his curiosity and his drive to solve the mystery got the better of him. *I'm going to give it a shot,* he thought, and dialed the number. It was October of 1998.

The female voice that answered the phone was strong but tentative. "I'm trying to get in touch with Francine Jones, the sister of Judy Dyer, who lives in Virginia, and whose mother is Frances Ryan Huff. I'm doing research on the family."

The woman on the other end of the line was decidedly cool and unhelpful. Finally he got around to telling her why he was doing the research. He explained that he had been adopted as a child and was searching for his birth family, then outlined the information he had found so far. "I'm following up on a lead that brought me to your name."

Still, he had gotten no real response. This person, whoever she was, was suspicious and questioning. And she seemed to have no intention of cooperating with him in his quest.

Then he tried a new tack. "Does the name Sally mean anything to you?" he asked, thinking of the mysterious photograph the cousins had sent him. He heard an audible gasp on the other end of the line, followed by a prolonged silence. Then the voice spoke.

"If you'll send me that photograph, and if it's the one I think it is, I'll believe you are who you say you are."

"I will certainly send you a copy of it," he replied, "and I'll include some information on myself." Although he didn't understand why, clearly the picture or the name Sally was pivotal for Francine.

The next day he got an unexpected phone call from the Idaho state attorney general's office. "I understand you contacted Francine Jones last night," a deep voice said. "Please tell me about it."

Dick told this official the whole story, ending with "Look, if there is any question, I'll give you the switchboard number here at the General Conference. You can ask for any director in the building, and these people will know who I am."

"No, I believe you're who you say you are," the man replied. "I've been in the investigative business for 25 years, and I know when someone is telling me the truth. I am going to talk to Francine. She'll call you back. I'll let her explain things."

The woman did phone back, and talked to Ardis. She was apologetic about her reticence of the day before. It took several more conversations before Dick got her whole story.

Many years before, Francine had been involved in some serious legal difficulties. Abused, she had gotten caught up in drugs, alcohol, and prostitution. Then she had gone on the run from both the law and her former low-life companions. Eventually she had turned herself in and had served some hard time. The man who had called Dick from the attorney general's office was her former probation officer.

Francine had a three-page-long rap sheet. As she got to know Dick better through subsequent phone calls, more of her story came out. It was like the script for a bad television movie. But not until they actually met face to face did he learn the whole story.

After prison she had wanted to put her past behind her and clean up her life. Her probation officer had befriended her and had helped her change her identity. It sounded almost like a witness protection program. Not only did she change her name, she had even obtained a new Social Security number. She had taken every precaution to become a totally different person—and yet Dick had found her.

Currently she was living in a common-law marriage (which was still viable in Idaho), partly because she couldn't marry her partner legally, since she had no birth certificate—no real proof of her existence. The man she was with had no idea of who she really was. She had been Francine Jones—a woman with no family and no history—for 10 or 15 years when Dick contacted her.

"When you started asking about my mother and my family," she eventually told him, "it scared me to death! My first thought was *They've found me and they've put a hit out on me!*

The young girl she had once been, Sally Huff, had grown up with no idea that she had a half brother. Now he was in her life, and there was finally no doubt in her mind that he belonged there. After all, she'd seen his picture. They had the same nose.

Dick would never forget his first face-to-face meeting with Francine. He and Ardis had flown to Idaho and arranged to meet her in the baggage area at the airport. As they walked into baggage claim, he spotted a small woman at the other end of the large space, coming toward him at a dead run.

"That's Francine!" he told Ardis just before he found himself enveloped in a bear hug. For such a small person she could deliver quite a tackle. Dick, who had managed quite well all his life without blood kin, was surprised at the depth of his emotion. It was a thrill and a shock—something impossible to describe. This was his sister!

The siblings stepped back and looked at each other. Francine was about the same height as Dick's daughter, Rikki—or even a little shorter—and a little rounder. Her hard life showed in her face. A woman who had done everything possible for 10 or 15 years of her life to make herself invisible, she still carried scars and concerns about what had happened in her past.

Francine never would say why her enemies would come after her, and Dick didn't prod her for more information. He was happy to accept her as she was—leaving further revelations totally up to her. Slowly she opened up more. She had been in at least one abusive situation—and she had been hurt in many ways. Still, she was obviously a caring person—quite an achievement for someone who had known little kindness in her life.

His efforts to find his other sister, Judy, ended at a blank wall at first. Francine didn't know where she was, but she had a phone number for her son, Eric—who was about the same age as his son, Erik. Dick called the man, who was friendly, but couldn't help. "My mom was living with us for a while, but one day we came home from work and she was gone. I don't know where she is."

"Well, if she makes contact with you, will you tell her about me? I would love to hear from her, if she wants to call me."

A couple weeks later Dick heard from Judy. Unlike Francine, she was self-assured and assertive on the phone. "So you're my brother!" she began. "How about that!" The two siblings had a good chat on the phone. Later he learned that she had called Francine afterward. "I found our brother!" she announced.

"Oh, that's old news," Francine said. "He called me two months ago." The two sisters hadn't spoken to each other in several years. Dick may have found his family, but it was obviously fractured. His involvement in their lives, though, seemed to be bringing it back together.

Ardis and Dick went to see Judy in Virginia. She too was short, like Rikki, and wore glasses, like Dick, and while she was friendly, her manner was somewhat formal and guarded. They went out to eat and shared pictures. He felt a strong sense of connection, but he also detected that she had a shell around her. As he got to know more about her past, he could understand why.

Learning of his existence had shocked and surprised both of Dick's half sisters. "Mom would never do anything like that!" Judy declared emphatically.

"We don't think you're a half brother, we think you're a full brother," Francine said. They had a hard time regarding their mom, as straitlaced and churchgoing as they had always known her to be, as an unwed mother—and she had never said anything that hinted of his existence.

Except, maybe, one time . . .

It was a small thing—and at the time they hadn't caught its significance. But now that they knew about Dick, the sisters thought perhaps their mother had been trying to tell them something. It happened just before she died. A series of strokes had left her unable to speak. She was a tiny person, small and frail. Francine was taking care of her when she went into congestive heart failure and was hospitalized. It seemed unlikely that she would recover, and Francine called Judy. "You'd better come. I think this is it for Mom."

Judy got on the next plane. "I'm going to the airport to pick up Judy," Francine told her mother. "She's flying out here to be with you."

Mom motioned for a pad and a pencil, and laboriously wrote three letters: B O Y.

"No, Mom, you're confused. It's Judy I'm going to pick up."

Mom just smiled and lay back on her pillow. But she wrote B O Y twice again when both Judy and Francine were with her. When Dick heard the story, he believed his mother had been trying to tell them that they had a brother somewhere. And the sisters agreed with him. They even wondered if Frances had given him her brother's name to make it easier for him to find his family someday.

"Dick, you were the lucky one," Francine told him. Judy said almost the same thing. Neither sister was forthcoming about their childhood. Dick picked up that they had been wards of the state at some point in their lives and had spent time in foster care.

Their father, Elmer Huff, was a cook and a restaurateur, and, from their accounts, also an alcoholic. They had no doubt had difficult childhoods, but they accepted themselves just as they were—and they accepted Dick just as he was. They weren't intimidated by the fact that he was a minister and a retired Army colonel or by his five graduate degrees or by his world travel. He was their brother.

A couple months after their first meeting, Dick visited Judy again. This time he took Rikki along. As they walked into Judy's room, he opened his mouth to introduce his sister to his daughter. Before he could speak, Judy put her hand to her mouth and wonderingly said, "She's the spitting image of Mom!" Her face was white, and she looked as though she was seeing a ghost.

Once Judy got over her shock, the two women—Dick's sister and his daughter—hit it off comfortably. Rikki's outgoing personality made that easy. But Judy would stop talking every now and then and stare at the younger woman. "Oh," she'd say again and again. "She looks just like Mom!"

For Dick, that visit brought his search full circle. He had started by wondering if Rikki resembled his mother. And now he knew.

The next phase of his quest was to find his birth father's family. While he thought his sisters were probably wrong—he wasn't their full brother— the possibility set him to thinking. He had received some papers from the state of Colorado.

Much of the information was blanked out, including his father's name, but he had learned that his birth father was about 35 years old when he was born, and that he was of German ancestry. His health was listed as "good," and his education as "fairly good." It was scant information, but then Dick came across another of those little puzzle pieces. Under "Occupation," someone had filled in the form with two words: livestock commission. That was all he had—no name, no initials, nothing.

When he had first contacted the Salvation Army, they had sent him all the information they had—except for one document about his birth father. When he asked for it, they told him, "We don't release that information." So he contacted them again, explaining that he had already established a good relationship with his mother's side of the family, and they relented and mailed him what they had on his father—with several important pieces of information blanked out, of course.

From those papers he learned that his father's name was Al Greenwalt. That didn't fit with what his half sisters had told him about their father. What's more, the Salvation Army document had a note attached, stating that the father of the child had asked the mother "to sign a document saying he was not the father and would bear no responsibility for the child." What kind of man did a thing like that? Dick still had more questions than answers.

Then one Sunday morning Ardis was reading the newspaper when an ad for DNA testing caught her eye. It was a kit supplied by a company called DNA Security, Inc., in North Carolina. People mostly used the tests to prove or disprove paternity. Dick phoned the company.

"Yes, we can check to see if you and your sisters are full siblings," they told him. Francine and Judy agreed to take the test, and the results came back in due time. They shared both parents, but the third person in the test—Dick—had only one parent in common with them. Elmer Huff was not his father.

Dick's curiosity went into high gear. He researched the name Al Greenwalt on the Internet. Was it Aloysius or Alexander or Alfonso or Albert or Allen? He discovered that Greenwalt can be spelled a dozen different ways. It seemed hopeless—like searching for a needle in a haystack. The trail went cold.

Then in December of 2001 another puzzle piece fell into his lap. In her annual Christmas letter a friend, Linda Vixie, mentioned that she was doing some part-time work, volunteering to register and log historical gravesites in Colorado. Dick e-mailed her, expressing interest in what she was doing and telling her a little about his quest to find his father. "Can you give me any pointers?" he asked.

"What information do you have?" she wrote back.

"Well, his name was Al Greenwalt. He probably lived in Denver, and his occupation is listed as 'livestock commission,'" Dick e-mailed her around the first of January.

Her next e-mail wasn't encouraging. "That's not a lot of information, but let me see what I can do."

Dick didn't hear a thing from Linda for several days. Then, on January 12, she called Dick. "I found him!" she said when he picked up the phone.

"What?"

"I found your birth father."

Dick was floored. Linda had gone into the Denver Registries and had found an Al Greenwalt, living in Denver as an adult with his parents. She knew he was the right man, because the registry listed an occupation—livestock commission. Al Greenwalt and his father were running a livestock business. This Al Greenwalt was the right age, in the right place, and in the right occupation. It all fit.

Linda had also found his obituary. Although born in Russia, he was of German ancestry. Dick knew that many Germans had immigrated to Russia during the reign of Catherine the Great. Al had had nine siblings, all born in the United States. His parents had evidently immigrated to Colorado from Russia, and at some point Al had gone into business with his father.

Then Linda handed Dick another piece of the puzzle. "The obituary mentions a daughter," she said. "You have a half sister. I have her name, address, and phone number. Are you interested?"

Of course he was interested, but once again he thought carefully and prayed long before making the call, knowing that life could change both for him and for this sister he had never met. The address Linda had given him was Riverton, Utah, a suburb of Salt Lake City. *This person is either Mormon or surrounded by Mormons,* he thought. Either way, she would understand genealogy. That's where he would start.

Picking up the phone, he called.

On the fourth ring a sprightly voice said, "Hello, this is Barb Aebi."

"This is Dr. Dick Stenbakken," he began. "We've never met, but I'm doing family genealogy research, looking for the Greenwalt family. I understand that your father was Al Greenwalt. I think I'm related to the family."

"And how might you be related to the Greenwalts?" Her sprightly voice had slowed down just a little.

"Well, according to my research," he replied, "we share the same birth father."

"Hah! That sounds just like him!"

Dick and his sister chatted for quite a while. He told her how he'd traced her down. Then he told her about himself, and she told him about herself. They hung up, agreeing that they would get together in person soon.

Later he learned that after she had put the phone down, her husband, Chuck, came into the house and found her standing by the phone with tears streaming down her face.

"What's the matter, hon?" he asked, alarmed to find his normally cheerful wife so upset.

"Nothing is the matter," she said, smiling through her tears. "I have a brother. I've always wanted a brother. I have a brother."

Dick flew to Salt Lake City to meet Barb. At the top of the airport escalator, Kay Schwindeman, the official military endorser for the Church of Jesus Christ of Latter-day Saints, met him. An old friend, he had been involved in Dick's research to find his birth family. He gave him a big bear hug, welcoming him to Salt Lake City.

At the bottom of the escalator stood Barb Aebi, Dick's sister. She was short, barely reaching five feet tall, with wispy brown hair turning to gray. Her hazel eyes were dancing, and she couldn't stand still. A smile spread across her face; she was holding a red rose. She looked like a little kid about to go into an ice-cream shop.

Barb's story was pretty simple. Her mother had been briefly married to Al Greenwalt, but the marriage broke up before Barb was 2. Al had abandoned his wife and daughter and had had nothing further to do with Barb. Barb had never known her father, but she had been curious, always asking aunts and uncles about him. In her late teens she had cornered one aunt, who had told her how to find him, but had sworn her to secrecy.

Barb had married and had had two children, but it was an abusive relationship, and she was struggling to get out of it. Out of desperation she had contacted her birth father for help. He had told her to go to hell. "You're just like your mother," he had snarled.

Eventually she escaped from her abusive husband, running away in the middle of the night with her two small children. Her neighbors, who were Mormons, helped her flee. They gave her, among other things, a bagful of Mormon books. Much later she had read the books and had eventually become a member of the LDS Church.

She and Dick found much to talk about. They'd be talking on the phone, and Barb would make some wisecrack. "People tell me I have a weird sense of humor," she'd say.

"That lines up with me, too!" he would reply. "People have been telling me I have a quirky sense of humor all my life."

They both liked bittersweet chocolate—the darker the better. Both enjoyed fishing, and they both loved Johann Pachelbel's Canon. Barb had driven an Eddie Bauer Ford Bronco, and Dick had owned the same car in Alaska. You'd probably never pick them out as siblings in a crowd, and although they took a DNA test, they really didn't need it to convince them that they were brother and sister. Dick had found his third sister, and Barb Aebi had the brother she had always wanted.

"You Have Been With Me From the Beginning"

Dick sat in his study in the house on Frances Drive in Loveland, Colorado, reviewing his schedule for the next few months. He and Ardis had moved to the comfortable home after their "retirement," but he had to admit, looking at the many penciled-in dates in front of him, that the word didn't seem quite appropriate. His passion for ministry wasn't the least bit diminished just because he'd turned in his General Conference building pass.

Dick still traveled widely, doing first-person presentations at camp meetings and other church-related events. So far he had logged seven prayer breakfasts at the Pentagon and six Bible study groups at the United States Senate.

Currently he was working on a series of 24 television shows featuring his first-person Bible presentations. He had appeared on numerous TV channels and programs, including Trinity Broadcasting, 3ABN, *It is Written*, and the Hope Channel.

His life thus far had been guided by the verse in John 15:27—the text that first came to him in 1958 when he prayed for direction in making a decision about his life's work. "And ye shall also bear witness, because ye have been with me from the beginning." Dick believed with his whole heart that the text had been a direct message from God. It was the pillar of his calling—the force behind the passion for ministry that had been the theme of his life.

He thought back to the search for his birth heritage, and how "from the beginning" had taken on fresh meaning as each new piece of the puzzle revealed itself. At each stage of his life God had watched over him. From a tiny, premature, unwanted but not unloved baby, through his adoption, his loving parents, his relationship with his aunt Stella, which led to his conversion and baptism—God had led him forward, protecting him and guiding his every step.

Dick had never questioned his call to ministry. Not even when he had realized that as a minister, a silver Porsche—like the ones in the doctors' parking lot at Porter Adventist Hospital—was probably not going to be in his future. Never for an instant had he doubted his calling, but the unfolding of his birth story made God's call deeper and more meaningful, enriching and enhancing the joy he found in every day of life and in his sense of mission.

He continued to enjoy friendships with people all over the world and of many different faiths. Just that morning he had chatted by phone with Father Bob Imming, the Catholic priest who in 1961 had taken the time to talk to a young college kid who had been wide open about not wishing to become a Catholic—just wanting to understand what they believe. As the years had gone by, Dick had developed a deep appreciation for all people of faith, even when their faith was different from his. That openness, he believed, made him a stronger Seventh-day Adventist.

Dick looked at the photographs that ornamented his desk. He and Ardis enjoyed their family and especially their four beautiful and exceedingly bright (in their grandfather's unbiased opinion) grandchildren. Fervently he wished for them the same sense of self that his adoptive parents—with God's help—had instilled in him.

Somehow he had never felt personal insecurity or angst, never a core questioning of who he was or what he was capable of. That assurance had allowed him to take risks in life—and each risk had brought new rewards.

As he gazed out his study window at the glorious sunshine and the stunning view of more than 100 miles of the front range of the Rocky Mountains, he mused, *Who knows what's around the next corner?* What opportunities for ministry and enjoyment would appear just around the bend? Dick was sure that God wasn't through with him yet—and he eagerly looked forward to whatever lay ahead.

Then he shook his head. That was enough serious thinking for one day. Leaving his study, he walked out to the driveway, climbed into his convertible, and, grinning from ear to ear, roared off down the open Colorado road.

A personal note:

If you enjoyed this book and
want to keep the dialogue going, let's network!

Go to Dick's Web site at www.biblefaces.com,
or e-mail him at dickardis@comcast.net.

E-mail Susan at susanandrhea@msn.com.

Or join us on Facebook and Twitter. We'd love to hear from you!

—Susan Harvey and Dick Stenbakken